Richard Stanton was born in Scotland in 1982
and read English at Balliol College, Oxford. He
writes about video games for the *Guardian*,
Polygon and *RockPaperShotgun*, and is the
former features editor of *Edge* magazine. He
lives in Bath, UK, and has saved the universe
more times than you'll ever know.

S0-BFC-026

Recent titles in the series

A Brief Guide to James Bond
Nigel Cawthorne

A Brief Guide to Secret Religions
David V. Barrett

A Brief Guide to Jane Austen
Charles Jennings

A Brief Guide to Jeeves and Wooster
Nigel Cawthorne

A Brief Guide to The Sound of Music
Paul Simpson

A Brief Guide to The Hunger Games
Brian J. Robb

A Brief Guide to British Battlefields
David Clark

A Brief History of Walt Disney
Brian J. Robb

A Brief History of Magna Carta
Geoffrey Hindley

A Brief History of Angels and Demons
Sarah Bartlett

A Brief History of Bad Medicine
Ian Schott and Robert Youngston

A Brief History of France
Cecil Jenkins

A Brief History of Ireland
Richard Killeen

A Brief History of Sherlock Holmes
Nigel Cawthorne

A Brief History of King Arthur
Mike Ashley

A Brief History of the Universe
J. P. McEvoy

A Brief History of Roman Britain
Joan P. Alcock

A Brief History of the Private Life of Elizabeth II
Michael Paterson

A Brief History of Mathematical Thought
Dr Luke Heaton

A Brief History of Video Games

Richard Stanton

ROBINSON

RUNNING PRESS
PHILADELPHIA · LONDON

ROBINSON

First published in
Great Britain in 2015 by
Robinson
1 3 5 7 9 8 6 4 2

Copyright ©
Richard Stanton, 2015

The moral right of the author
has been asserted.

All rights reserved.
No part of this publication
may be reproduced, stored
in a retrieval system, or
transmitted, in any form, or
by any means, without the
prior permission in writing
of the publisher, nor be
otherwise circulated in any
form of binding or cover
other than that in which it
is published and without a
similar condition including
this condition being imposed
on the subsequent purchaser.

A CIP catalogue record for
this book is available from
the British Library.

ISBN 978-1-47211-880-6
(paperback)
ISBN: 978-1-47211-881-3
(ebook)

Typeset in Klavika by
Thextension
Printed and bound in China

Robinson
is an imprint of
Constable & Robinson Ltd
Carmelite House
50 Victoria Embankment
London EC4Y 0DZ

An Hachette UK Company
www.hachette.co.uk

www.constablerobinson.com

First published in the
United States in 2015
by Running Press Book
Publishers, A Member of the
Perseus Books Group

All rights reserved under
the Pan-American and
International Copyright
Conventions

*This book may not be
reproduced in whole or
in part, in any form or
by any means, electronic
or mechanical, including
photocopy, recording, or by
any information storage
and retrieval system now
known or hereafter invented,
without permission from the
publishers.*

Books published by Running
Press are available at special
discounts for bulk purchases
in the United States by
corporations, institutions
and other organizations.

For more information, please
contact the Special Markets
Department at the
Perseus Books Group,
2300 Chestnut Street,
Suite 200,
Philadelphia, PA 19103,
or call (800) 810-4145,
ext. 5000, or email
special.markets@
perseusbooks.com.

US ISBN: 978-0-7624-5615-4
US Library of Congress
Control Number: 2014954820

9 8 7 6 5 4 3 2 1
Digit on the right indicates
the number of this printing

Running Press Book
Publishers
2300 Chestnut Street
Philadelphia, PA 19103-4371

Visit us on the web!
www.runningpress.com

To my dad, for everything.
But especially for the Spectrum 48K.

Acknowledgements

Top of my thank-you list are Claire and Judith Lambourne who enabled and somehow tolerated my months of video-game monomania – *plus ça change*. Thanks to Keith Stuart for first suggesting the idea, and generally being a good egg. My thanks also to the old Edge crew – Martin Davies, Tony Mott, Alex Wiltshire, and the dynamic duo Craig Owens and David Valjalo – for teaching me all I know. Further debts are owed to the kind friendship and expertise of Tom Bramwell, Matthew Castle, Christian Donlan, Owen Hill, Keza MacDonald, Simon Parkin, Margaret Robertson, Martin Robinson and Oli Welsh. If I've missed anyone you know why – this was done a little too close to deadline. The fact it got done at all is down to the copyediting of Howard Watson and the gentle encouragement of Duncan Proudfoot and Emily Byron – thanks to them and everyone at Constable & Robinson. Huge thanks to Duncan Harris, the hero video games deserves, for letting me use some of his fantastic Dead End Thrills work throughout. Time to go home and be a family man.

Contents

Introduction 10

1 The Prehistory of Video Games 14

2 Baer's Brown Box 22

3 *Spacewar!* 32

4 Atari's Born 40

5 VES vs VCS 48

6 *Oregon Trail* 56

7 A Tale of Two Adventures 60

8 Uncle Clive and Big Jack 70

9 Atari Shock! 86

10 The Golden Age of the Arcades 94

11 The Rise of Nintendo 110

12 Simpatico 130

13 *Doom* 101 138

14 The Console War 158

15 The 'Nintendo' PlayStation 178

16 A Dream Dies 204

17 An Ugly Motherfucker 216

18 Pocket Monsters:
The History of Handhelds 242

19 Mobile Gaming 258

20 eSports 266

21 Metal . . . Gear? 276

22 Here Comes Everybody 290

23 Revolution 302

24 Steam and Valve 322

25 Go Anywhere, Do Anything:
Grand Theft Auto 332

26 Indie-pendence 340

27 Continue? 348

Notes 360

Bibliography 363

Index 364

Introduction

➔ It all begins with the atom bomb. One of the scientists that helped bring the Manhattan Project to fruition was William B. Higinbotham – who would spend the rest of his life preaching nuclear non-proliferation. In the 1950s Higinbotham worked at the Brookhaven National Laboratory and, to interest visitors in the Donner Model 30 Analogue Computer, created a program to demonstrate its capabilities.

➔ In the 1940s and early 1950s computers were already being programmed to play rudimentary games – Alexander Douglas's *OXO*, for example, was a form of noughts and crosses developed in 1952. But Higinbotham's first-of-a-kind creation was *Tennis for Two*, a game that could be controlled in realtime on a screen. The project never seemed especially inspired to Higinbotham, who preferred to focus on his later work, so it was put on show for two weeks and then packed away, never to be heard of again until decades later.

Nevertheless, this is the first video game that wasn't based on simulating a board game.

→ Video games are gradually overcoming all past stigmas as they become ever-more popular and more people grow up playing them, but the popular mechanics, styles and platforms are always changing – as, of course, a thousand niche communities and genres form, revolt against and reinvent themselves. The subject is protean and feels endless – no one knows how many video games have been made or how many have been lost.

→ A point to bear in mind is that interactive entertainment is a relatively new industry and, though the commercial side looms large within this technology-led medium, it is sometimes not best represented by the games that shift the most copies. *God Hand* may well be the greatest 3D beat-'em-up ever made but, given its complete commercial failure, its subsequent influence is limited. *Mortal Kombat*, on the other hand, is a terrible game with a much broader cultural impact and a series that continues to this day. The history of games is not a straight line of jewels but a twisted path with many beautiful failures and inexplicably popular dead ends.

→ It is also worth remembering that, while the evolution of games is led by technology, this does not necessarily mean that the most powerful technology wins out. Take, as an example of this, two of Nintendo's home systems: the Game Boy, a monochrome handheld console released in 1989, and the home console Wii released in 2006.

→ The Game Boy was considered woefully underpowered next to the prospective competition – full colour handhelds from Sega (the Game Gear) and Atari (the Lynx). But its lack of a colour screen meant that, where its competitors would chew through batteries in a couple of hours, the Game Boy would last much longer with less. It also had a far superior software lineup and so became the biggest-selling handheld of all time (until Nintendo's successor system, the DS) whereas the Game Gear and Lynx were commercial failures.

➡ Just under twenty years later, the Nintendo Wii was widely considered an underwhelming competitor to Sony's PlayStation 3 and the Microsoft Xbox 360 – the latter having high-definition visuals and far more comprehensive online features. But Wii's innovative control scheme, married to exceptional first-party software, saw it find a mainstream audience of 'non-gamers' of which Microsoft and Sony could only dream.

➡ It is no accident that both of these examples feature Nintendo. By some distance the oldest company in the video-game business, with forty-odd years in the industry, the Kyoto-based company has been a relentlessly original presence – and a video-game developer of the highest quality. As venerable as it is, Nintendo remains an oddity; its hardware relies overwhelmingly on Nintendo's own software, whereas other consoles largely depend on third-party products.

➡ Then there is the PC, the ultimate platform. Always a presence in the history of video games, the PC has the most diverse and rich selection of software. Publishing a game on almost any other platform requires licences, a lengthy accreditation period, upfront fees, even having to prove your business is viable – not to mention the specialist hardware 'development kits' required. Developing and releasing a game on PC requires nothing more than a PC; no wonder it is the natural home for independent developers.

➡ Over the following pages we will move from the emergence of a new entertainment medium through its successes and failures, seeing how the form has morphed to incorporate both sophisticated expression and idle distraction. A pleasing trend in the last decade has been the increasing accessibility of video games, and the growing audience they serve. New ways to create and play appear every year, from playing *Angry Birds* on the bus to (virtually) shooting shrill-voiced American teenagers in *Call of Duty*, and even friend-barging party games like *Johann Sebastian Joust*.

➡ A few notes on the text. This is a history of video games in the west and Japan – simply because consumer technology in nations like China and Russia has, until recently, tended to lag behind, resulting in home-grown histories beyond the scope of this book. There is also a greater emphasis on technology and personalities in the earlier chapters, simply because many of the first video games are triumphs of engineering but may not appear this way to the modern eye. As video games became a major commercial industry, by contrast, the technology becomes less restrictive and the number of individuals involved in creating games increases exponentially.

➡ Video games are already too numerous and diverse for the term to be anything but a catch-all equivalent to 'books' or 'movies', and this is just the beginning. Already you can enter virtual reality with headsets, haptic feedback rigs can let you 'feel' virtual items as if they're real, and it's possible to rule a space empire with thousands of people doing your bidding. The future of interactive entertainment is really a number of futures, and the term 'video games' signifies more ways of playing than can possibly be codified. Only one thing is certain: games will be everywhere, and everyone will be a player.

The Prehistory of Video Games

➲ United States Patent no. 2,455,992 is for a 'Cathode-Ray Tube Amusement Device' and reads: 'This invention relates to a device with which a game can be played.' In 1947 Thomas T. Goldsmith Jr, an early television pioneer, and Estle Ray Mann constructed a prototype video game from analogue circuits and a cathode ray tube (CRT). Although it would never be released, they applied for and were granted a patent in 1948.

➲ The machine did not, however, work in quite the way that the patent suggests. The intention was to recreate something akin to a World War II radar display (appropriate, as the cathode ray tube was developed for US missile defence systems), where the player used several control knobs to manoeuvre an on-screen dot that represented a missile's speed and trajectory. But the targets were painted onto the screen, with the device calculating 'good' shots and rewarding players with an explosion.

➲ The previous year, on 14 February 1946, the Electronic Numerical Integrator and Calculator (ENIAC) came to life. Funded by the US Army, ENIAC was designed to calculate artillery firing tables and the machine was a monster: over 30 US tons of switches, crystal diodes, resistors, capacitors, vacuum tubes and relays. ENIAC occupied around 1,800 square feet, and both input and output were handled by punchcards. But ENIAC's most revolutionary capability was simple, and a first: it could be programmed.

➲ The greatest minds of the day saw even further. The British mathematician and code-breaker Alan Turing believed that the focus of computer theory should be on artificial intelligence, based on his idea that any thought of the human brain must be a computable operation and therefore capable of simulation. Alongside his colleague David Champernowne, Turing posited that having a computer play chess to a level whereby it could defeat an average human player would be a milestone. To this end, in 1947, Turing began to construct a framework for writing the first-ever computer chess program. The only problem was that ENIAC wasn't powerful enough to run it. Then, in 1952, Turing was arrested and convicted of the then-crime of homosexuality, and two years later, isolated and ashamed, committed suicide.

➲ Turing never finished his chess program, though it would later be completed by others and known as 'Turochamp' – and played at a Turing conference in 2012 by chess grandmaster Garry Kasparov. 'I suppose you might call it primitive,' said Kasparov after winning easily. 'But I would compare it to an early car. You might laugh at them but it is still an incredible achievement.'[1]

➲ Turing's work inspired fellow computer scientist Christopher Strachey to begin work on a checkers program which, after he contacted Turing, was completed in 1951.

Although not generally included in video game history this program certainly should be, as it featured an opponent artificial intelligence (AI), a visual representation of the board and text output.

➲ By far the most interesting quality of *Checkers*, however, is that Strachey – a member of the highly distinguished British family of whom the best-known is writer and critic Lytton Strachey – imbued his creation with the illusion of personality.[2] He later presented a paper explaining this.

In addition to showing a picture of the board with the men on it in a cathode ray tube, and to printing out moves on a teleprinter, the machine makes a sort of running commentary on the game. For instance it starts by printing 'Shall we toss for the first move? Will you spin a coin?' It then calls, in a random manner, and asks 'Have I won?' There's no

cheating in this, at any rate as far as the machine is concerned. **The player has then to feed his moves into the machine according to certain rules. If he makes a mistake the machine will point it out and ask him to repeat the move. If he makes too many mistakes of this kind, the remarks printed by the machine will get increasingly uncomplimentary, and finally it will refuse to waste any more time with him.** [3]

➲ Strachey's game was completed in the summer of 1951 but, although the subject of much interest among the computer cognoscenti of his day, never achieved widespread recognition. Contemporaneously, a very different group of engineers was working towards a more public demonstration of computer capabilities. Often (erroneously) described as the first game that could be played on a computer, *Nim* was designed for the 1951 Festival of Britain. The celebration was a year-long attempt to bring some stardust to a nation still recovering from World War II, and British firms such as the computer company Ferranti were encouraged to come up with eye-catching exhibits.

➲ A Ferranti employee, Australian John Bennett, was tasked with creating the company's exhibit, and in his turn was inspired by something from the 1940s World Fair in New York: the Nimatron. This was a mechanical device that could play the parlour game *Nim*, which Bennett thought would suit the number-crunching abilities of a computer. *Nim* is a counting puzzle: a game played with various piles of matches, where players take turns to remove one or more matches from any single pile until the winner removes the last match.

➲ Bennett designed a computer version of *Nim* but the game was built by engineer Raymond Stuart-Williams, who constructed a custom machine nicknamed Nimrod. It enraptured audiences, who were much less interested in the genius of a responsive machine than the bank of flashing lights Nimrod used to represent matches. Nimrod proved so popular it went on tour to an industrial show in Berlin, where it defeated Germany's chancellor Ludwig Erhard, but after these showings was dismantled and simply forgotten about.

→ At the UK's University of Cambridge, meanwhile, PhD students and professors were getting to grips with a custom-built computer called the Electronic Delay Storage Automatic Calculator (EDSAC). Like ENIAC this was constructed from vacuum tubes and occupied a huge space, but it also had three CRT monitors that displayed dots in a 35 x 16 grid. EDSAC was the world's first 'stored-program' computer,[4] meaning that routines could be kept in memory and run when required (the ENIAC could be programmed,

but did not have the memory to store programs).

→ PhD student A. S. Douglas had an idea about this screen; it had just the right dimensions to display the board for noughts and crosses. For Douglas's dissertation on human–computer interaction, he programmed EDSAC to play noughts and crosses against a human opponent, and called the program *OXO*.

→ To play *OXO* you used an old-fashioned telephone (rotary) dial on the front of EDSAC to select a number corresponding to an on-screen square, and the design allowed for either human or computer to play first. Thanks to EDSAC's 35 x 16 cathode ray tube display, this is the first-ever game to display visuals.

→ Whether *Checkers*, *Nim* and *OXO* should be considered the first video games is arguable. These games were transpositions of existing real-world games into a computer

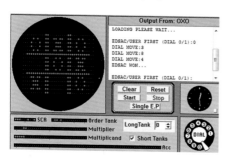

An emulation of EDSAC on a modern PC playing Douglas's OXO program. EDSAC's display is in the top-left corner, and the controls elsewhere represent the physical buttons and levers used to control the computer – note particularly the rotary dial in the bottom right.

William Higinbotham was a nuclear physicist and the first chair of the Federation of American Scientists – a position he used to preach nuclear non-proliferation. Also the head of Brookhaven Laboratory's Instrumentation Division, he thought that having a game to play might 'liven up the place' for visitors. (Courtesy of Brookhaven National Laboratory)

environment, intended to demonstrate the capabilities of their respective machines rather than represent the future of computers. With that said, the complexity of what these pioneers achieved cannot be overstated; if not the first video games, they are at least the very first steps towards the new medium.

⬤ Let's return to *Tennis for Two*. William Higinbotham was the head of the Brookhaven National Laboratory's Instrumentation Division, and he had a problem.

⬤ Brookhaven often played host to groups of visitors, curious about this new wave of 'electronic brains' but ultimately bored by the huge banks of switches and dry mathematical explanations that greeted them. Higinbotham, a chain-smoking pinball lover better known to his friends as Willy, wanted to demonstrate the capabilities of computers in an engaging and fun way, by creating a demonstration that could interest

the layman as much as any professional.

⬤ Brookhaven's annual open house was a few months away, in October 1958, and Higinbotham knew that one of the institute's computers was a custom-built analogue machine designed to plot missile trajectories. But the computer's instructions also included an example of how to calculate a bouncing ball's trajectory. So using its graph routines to simulate a game of tennis rather than a bouncing ball – to a man of such exceptional talents – was not a million miles away. Within a few weeks Higinbotham, with the help of his colleague Robert V. Dvorak, had developed *Tennis for Two*. Two players knocked a ball back and forth across a net using a controller with a button, which 'hit' the ball, and a knob that was twiddled to change the angle of return. The game's physics took account of gravity, with the ball bouncing at decreasing heights and rebounding from the net with decreased velocity.

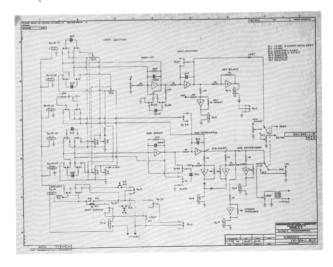

One of the original electrical schematics for *Tennis for Two*. The key to Higinbotham's design was that the ball, the net and the court were displayed at separate times – but the oscilloscope's refresh rate of 36 Hz means the eye sees them all at once. (Courtesy of Brookhaven National Laboratory)

→ The court looked like a squashed, upside-down 'T', there were no bats, and there was no way to keep score or 'win' the game. But this was all irrelevant: *Tennis for Two* was fun. 'The high-schoolers liked it best,' recalled Higinbotham's contemporary, Dave Potter. 'You couldn't pull them away from it.' 5

→ So many early video games are variants on the *Pong* model that it would be easy to mistake *Tennis for Two* as the start of this lineage. But in fact it's a more unusual beast, built on and taking advantage of oscilloscope technology for crisp visuals and smooth motion.[6] Even today the phosphor monochrome display is a thing of beauty. Higinbotham's achievement is remarkable in the context of what others were doing (though the visuals are down to the type of equipment he was using).

→ But the man himself never quite saw this. Higinbotham made *Tennis for Two* as a demonstration and considered it a simple

The black-and-white photograph shows a later version of *Tennis for Two* from 1961, which played on a larger screen and allowed players to select different gravity effects. The colour photograph is a reproduction of *Tennis for Two* made to celebrate the game's fiftieth anniversary – the ball is looping over the net. (Courtesy of Brookhaven National Laboratory)

diversion – despite its huge popularity among the visitors, which saw an upgraded version return to Brookhaven in 1959. He never thought to patent his invention (a good thing for consumers as any patent would have belonged to the US government) and in later years preferred to discuss his work

The 1958 exhibit for which Higinbotham created *Tennis for Two*. The oscilloscope display is the small circular screen towards the left edge. (Courtesy of Brookhaven National Laboratory)

against nuclear proliferation rather than his role at the dawn of video games. *Tennis for Two* remained largely unknown until a 1983 article in *Creative Computing*, in which David Ahl revealed the game's largely forgotten existence and dubbed Higinbotham 'the Grandfather of Videogames'.

➡ The first fully formed video games were about to be created. But the 1950s had one last surprise in store, thanks to MIT's 'Transistorized Experimental computer zero' – known as the TX-0, or more affectionately as the 'tixo'. The TX-0 is an incredibly important machine in the history of computing, but it also played host to some early attempts at interactive entertainment – a version of noughts and crosses, and much more intriguingly a program called *Mouse in the Maze*.

➡ The creator of *Mouse in the Maze* is unknown, but it is a pioneering piece of software – perhaps the first to understand the fun to be had with user-generated content (UGC). UGC has always been in the background of gaming history, and decades later would become a major buzzword and focus. It starts here.

➡ *Mouse in the Maze* allowed a player, using a light pen on the TX-0's CRT monitor, to create a maze and place various objects within the walls. One of these would be a piece of cheese and, when the player was satisfied with their creation, a mouse could be released into the maze – which would then try to find the cheese. Players could give the mouse certain characteristics, like following the left or right walls, add effects like glasses of martini, and then sit back and watch their creation play out.

➡ Less a game, perhaps, than a fore-shadowing of the game construction kit, *Mouse in the Maze* never made it outside the walls of MIT. But by this time, the video game was about to move to the next level.

A modern PC emulating a TX-0 and running *Mouse in the Maze*. The player begins the game by 'erasing' walls from a grid to create the maze, then placing the cheese, then releasing the mouse.

Baer's Brown Box

In 1948 Ralph Baer graduated with a B.S. in Television Engineering, the first degree of its kind awarded in the US. During college he had a part-time job working on television studio equipment and, while employed by the firm Loral, designed a commercial TV set. 'Ironically,' said Baer, 'I then spent the next sixteen years engineering or managing engineers in every area of electronics except television.' [7]

There was an itch in the back of Baer's mind about what televisions were being used for. When building Loral's TV set over 1950–1 he had used test equipment that displayed lines and checkerboards on-screen, which made him wonder whether he could incorporate some kind of simple game into the TV set as a feature. His boss told him to forget about it and, once the job was finished, Baer was moved over to defence electronics. Over the next fifteen years, his idea of using a TV to play games was on the backburner.

Baer ended up working for Sanders Associates, a large R&D (research and development) engineering company that worked almost exclusively on military projects. During a business trip to New York in 1966, he ended up waiting at a bus terminal for a colleague. 'I took advantage of my free time and jotted down some notes on the subject of using ordinary home TV sets for the purpose of playing games,' Baer recalls. 'I have a distinct image in my mind of sitting on a cement step outside the bus terminal, enjoying a nice, warm, sunny summer day, occasionally looking out at the passing traffic, waiting for my associate to show up and scribbling notes on a small pad. It was "Eureka" time . . . but of course I didn't know that then.'

After returning from the trip Baer wrote up his notes into a four-page document, dated 1 September 1966, which included his ideas for the kinds of games that might be possible:

Ralph Baer in the workshop. Before serving in the US Army during World War II, Baer ran three radio service stores in New York City, and after the war gained his Bachelor of Science in Television Engineering – the first degree of its kind.

action games, boardgames, card games, educational games, sports games, racing games and artistic (drawing) games.

'What I had in mind at the time was to develop a small "game box" that would do neat things and cost, perhaps, twenty-five dollars at retail.'

Sanders's business was the military, and Baer knew he stood no chance of convincing his superiors to back the idea without something exciting to show. On 6 September 1966 Baer designed an elementary schematic and managed to persuade a department manager to assign him a technician, Bob Tremblay. Tremblay started to build a proof-of-concept for Baer's idea and by early December had constructed a piece of hardware out of vacuum tubes, which allowed a user to manipulate a vertical line on a TV screen. It was labelled TV Game Unit #1 (TGU #1).

Baer had something to show and chose to go straight to Sanders's corporate director of R&D, Herbert Campman, as the most likely source of funding. Campman saw the potential and gave Baer $2,500 in funding to build a more impressive demonstration of the idea.

Baer brought technical engineer Bill Harrison on board, and on 12 February 1967 the pair moved into a small lab that had once been the company's library. Another engineer, Bill Rusch, had given Baer the idea of a quiz game controlled by a light pen pointed at the screen, and Harrison's first job was building a prototype. Progress was slow not because Harrison couldn't build the thing (he did), but because he was recalled to another Sanders project and wouldn't return until May, by which point Baer had produced a company memo outlining twenty-one different games.

Over May 1967 Baer and Harrison made enormous progress. On 15 May the pair was able to play what had been nicknamed 'The Pumping Game', where both participants had

A contemporary photograph of the unit used to control 'The Pumping Game'. Despite all the switches the game itself was played with one button per player and was won by whoever 'pumped' fastest.

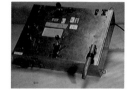

A BRIEF HISTORY OF VIDEO GAMES

to whack a button in order to move a line on the screen up or down. By 22 May they had two dots on screen that could be moved horizontally and vertically, independent of each other, and by 25 May the prototype TGU #2 could detect when the dots had collided.

❯ By early June, Harrison had constructed two 'light guns' that used photo sensors to hit on-screen targets (which could be moved randomly by the hardware or by another player). This use of the technology particularly impressed Herb Campman, the man holding the purse strings, such that by 14 June Baer was confident enough to give Campman and others a formal demonstration – which resulted in more funding and an agreement that the project was sufficiently advanced to be shown to senior management.

❯ On 15 June 1967 the TGU #2, and seven games that could be played on it, was demonstrated to Sanders's biggest cheeses: the president, executive vice-president,

various vice-presidents and several board members who happened to be in town. 'The demonstration was well-received, although there was more than one expression of doubt that we could make this into a business,' recalls Baer. 'Management's edict now became: "Build something we can sell or license."'

❯ The difference between a prototype and a commercial product is the difference between a skilled engineer building one item with no cost restrictions and a factory producing tens of thousands of items at minimal cost. Although Baer's initial idea was for a box that could retail at around $25, he soon realized that this was unrealistic. 'We had thrown out anything that wasn't absolutely necessary to play chase and gun games. That included colour, timers, and some of the other doodads like the random number generator and the "pumping" circuitry.'

❯ The other problem was the games. Baer

A photograph of the Brown Box and 'lightgun' prototype, which did more than anything else to persuade Baer's superiors that there was potential in his idea. The original intention was to bundle the gun with the console, but it was sold separately.

understood that what the team had produced so far was great for demonstrating potential, but a consumer product would need to offer a higher-quality experience. Bill Rusch, the creative engineer who had first suggested a quiz game, joined the project in August 1967, while Bill Harrison continued to experiment with and work on the hardware.

➔ 'Ping-pong, tennis, hockey, soccer, and handball games were conceived in rapid succession, at least on paper,' says Baer. 'Unlike the two manually controlled spots we had been using, the third spot's movement was to be machine-controlled. Bill Rusch came up with the idea of using that spot as a "ball" so that we could play some sort of ball game with it. We batted around ideas of how we could implement games such as ping-pong and other sports games.'

➔ Over the next few months the team refined both the hardware and software around this concept, and by November had a functional ping-pong game on the TVG #4. A further infusion of R&D cash meant that by early 1968 they had a machine playing *Ping-Pong*, *Hockey*, *Target Shooting* and various chase games – all of which were displayed with different background colours.

➔ Baer's ideas, by this stage, were in a marketable shape – and he began to think of how to make them even more appealing to potential partners. He tried to interest cable companies like TelePrompTer and Manhattan Cable because this would mean that the games could be played with backgrounds broadcast by the companies selling the device – that is, rather than playing ping-pong with a flat colour background, the cable companies could broadcast a top-down ping-pong table over which the game would be superimposed. TelePrompTer was interested but, despite repeated meetings, the company was in financial trouble and Baer's quite brilliant concept never came to pass. [8]

All seven of the main TVG units (the annotations are by Baer himself). The 'eighth' TVG was not a standalone unit, but plugged into the TVG #7 to allow another game to be played, making it arguably the first console hardware expansion.

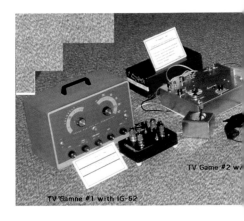

With the cable companies out of the game, Baer's team were by now onto TVG #6 and focusing on selling it to another company as either a standalone product or an in-built part of a TV set. Bill Harrison had managed to cut down on the circuitry involved, and Baer was particularly happy with *Ping-Pong*, which he believed would alone justify the projected $50 RRP.

Further engineering wizardry let the team add two more games, *Volleyball* and *Golf Game*, which meant that TVG #7, despite its design being drastically stripped back from the prototype that had been shown to Sanders's board, still featured seven games. It had two hand-controllers, a lightgun, a 'golf joystick' and switches on the machine's body to move between the available games. Harrison covered the machine's aluminium chassis with brown, self-adhesive vinyl in a wood-grain pattern. At this point TVG #7 became known as the Brown Box.

In January 1968 the Brown Box was in a finished state, the first functional home games console. Although further minor improvements would be made, the problem was selling it. Sanders tried to interest TV manufacturers but buyers, faced with this radical new concept, simply failed to see the potential. By spring 1969, over a year after the unit was complete, only RCA had enough interest to begin negotiating a licence – which came to nothing.

But Bill Enders, a member of the RCA team, had since left and joined Magnavox. Enders had been seriously impressed with the Brown Box, visited Sanders again personally, and pressed Magnavox's management to consider the product. Finally, after yet another presentation, Magnavox president Gerry Martin decided to take a chance in the summer of 1969.

What happened next is the kind of tragedy only big business can produce. It took another

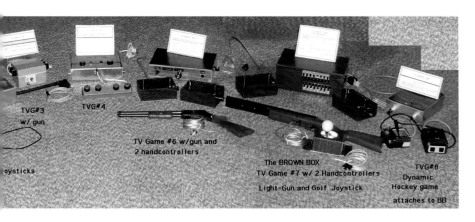

TVG#3 w/ gun

TVG#4

oysticks

TV Game #6 w/gun and 2 handcontrollers

The BROWN BOX
TV Game #7 w/ 2 Handcontrollers
Light-Gun and Golf Joystick

TVG#8
Dynamic
Hockey game
attaches to BB

THIS IS ODYSSEY™

The advertising for the Magnavox Odyssey went for a futuristic vibe and emphasized the physical machine over the visuals it produced. Many of the components in this picture were sold separately.

Ralph Baer with the Odyssey. It had been more than a decade since he first had the idea of moving things around on a TV set, but Baer's persistence saw him dubbed 'the father of home video games'.

nine months for Martin to persuade his board about the product, and a preliminary agreement between Sanders and Magnavox was signed only in January 1971 – three years after the Brown Box was finished. Sanders handed over the designs and documentation, and promptly set its own engineers onto working out to minimize component cost.

➲ Over the next months Magnavox's engineers, aided by Baer and his team, gradually converted the Brown Box design into what would become known as the Magnavox Odyssey (Magnavox's initial name for the console was the hilarious 'Skill-O-Vision'). The aim was to release the console in May 1972, and consumer testing indicated the machine had broad appeal – with 89 per cent of participants saying they 'liked it very much'. The long wait to get the product to market took a toll on Baer who, in the face of mounting financial problems and layoffs back at Sanders, found himself increasingly despondent about his work. The arrival of the first licence cheque from Magnavox for $100,000 made a difference. 'Miraculously, my depression evaporated instantly as if someone had flipped a switch.'

➲ On 22 May 1972 Magnavox officially launched the Odyssey TV Game System. It was advertised on TV by Frank Sinatra and reaction was initially enthusiastic. The system came with pack-in goodies, some of which made sense (transparent television overlays for certain games) and some of which were bizarre (playing cards and dice).

➲ Magnavox's cost-cutting, however, went hand-in-hand with greed. The system sold for a whopping $100 rather than Baer's projected $50, with a rifle sold separately at $25 and additional games held back to be sold on two plug-in cartridges. The most counter-productive saving had been made by removing the Odyssey's sound chip, meaning the games played in silence, which

An example of the Odyssey's lightgun game without the overlay – one player controls the white 'target' while the blue reticule shows where the gun is pointing.

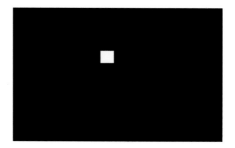

Baer recognized as a serious issue and tried to remedy with the addition of a sound accessory – this was released commercially but, incredibly, Magnavox's own retail stores didn't carry it. The A/C power adapter was also sold separately (although the Odyssey could be powered with batteries). This was bad enough, but Magnavox went out of its way to imply that the console would only work on Magnavox televisions (it would work with any television) and limited supplies to its own authorized dealerships.

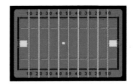

The Odyssey's American Football game with the overlay emulated on a modern PC. The distinctions between Odyssey games seem minor to modern eyes, but almost every early console would follow this pattern.

➜ Despite this, the Odyssey was original enough to sell over 100,000 units over Christmas, and would go on to shift around 300,000 total. And from this vantage point the sales are the least interesting thing about it: the Odyssey was the first home games console, and the beginning of an entertainment industry that has never looked back.

➜ Baer's instinct about the ping-pong game was right; it did justify the machine nearly single-handedly. Two variants, *Tennis* and *Table Tennis*, were included with the console, with the only substantial difference being the background colour. Whereas much of Odyssey's software is so basic it's hard to understand how it could have been fun even in 1972, the variants of the ping-pong game created at Sanders are still fun to mess around with today. This is largely thanks to the decision to add 'english', the ability to alter the ball's flight after it has left the bat, which in turn is a function of the Odyssey's

The advertising took some liberties with the Odyssey's capabilities, and emphasized the admittedly beautiful overlays included with the console. The games are much more rudimentary than the artwork suggests.

A BRIEF HISTORY OF VIDEO GAMES

odd controllers: upright cuboids with a knob on either side, with the left-hand knob featuring a 'serve' button.

⊙ *Tennis* moves surprisingly quickly, and the ball seems to sink into either player's paddle for a split-second before bouncing back. Where later games of this ilk depended on physics-based behaviour to determine shot angles, here it's all about faking out your opponent with the outrageous swerves that the 'english' controls allow. As a simulation of tennis it leaves something to be desired, but as a video game such flights of fancy work beautifully.

⊙ As part of Odyssey's promotion Magnavox toured the machine around trade shows, and the machine was displayed in California on 24–5 May 1972. Among the names in the guestbook was one Nolan Bushnell, a man thinking about how he could follow up a project called *Computer Space* with something that would appeal to a broader audience. He'd found it.

Tennis both with an (emulated) overlay, left, and without, right. The latter is what most Odyssey games resemble without the overlays to differentiate the interactions required.

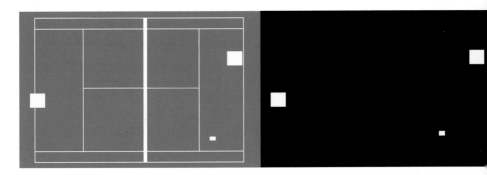

Spacewar!

One of the earliest video games, created on the PDP-1 super-computer, had the bombastic title of *Spacewar!* Conceived in 1961 by a group of students at the Massachusetts Institute of Technology, it was developed by Steve Russell, Martin Graetz and Wayne Wiitanen to show off what the machine could do. 'We decided that probably you could make a two-dimensional maneuvering sort of thing,' says Russell, 'and naturally the obvious thing to do was spaceships.' [9]

Spacewar! features two spaceships nicknamed 'the needle' and 'the wedge' that can be turned 360 degrees and moved forwards through a thrust button – with the centre of the screen being a gravity well that affects their motion. Each ship has a limited number of missiles and the goal of the game is to shoot the other player while avoiding being sucked into the centre. Although a fantastic achievement for its time, *Spacewar!* was limited in exposure because the PDP-1 was an enormously expensive machine only found in places like MIT.

But it would become the basis of the first arcade game. Ted Dabney hailed from San Mateo, a town south of San Francisco – a Silicon Valley native. After a four-year stint in the Marine Corps, where he studied at the Navy's electronics school, Dabney was discharged in 1959 and ended up working at a company called Ampex. It was here that his path crossed with fellow engineer Nolan Bushnell. Both were assigned to an Ampex product called Videofile, an early and groundbreaking method of document storage that could hold a quarter of a million document pages on one 14-inch disk. Dabney and Bushnell shared an office with a young engineer called Al Alcorn and a programmer called Larry Bryan.

Nolan Bushnell was a charismatic and clever guy who had developed an interest in the primitive entertainment machines of

Steve Russell at the opening of the Computer History Museum, 2011. (Extracted from an original, photo credit: Vonguard)

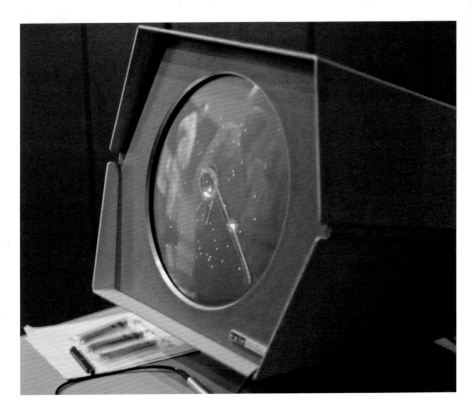

Spacewar! running on a PDP-1. Over time the game's features expanded enormously as the dedicated programmers who could access it made improvements.
(Photo credit: Joi Ito)

the time. While working his way through college, he became the game manager for an amusement park where he was responsible for the park's breakdown-prone electromechanical machines. These were things like shooting galleries and racing games constructed from film stock, relays and various mechanical components.

➡ Bushnell had no shortage of ideas about the next step in entertainment but, much more importantly, had the salesman's touch of being able to convince others to throw in with him. He and Dabney became firm friends and, over games of chess and the Chinese boardgame Go, Bushnell would talk about plans he had for businesses. One was a pizza joint filled with arcade games and animatronic characters that played music (a family-friendly alternative to amusement arcades with their links to organized crime). Another was using computers and TV sets – as both technologies became more common – to

somehow deliver arcade games into the home.

➡ 'Nolan came to me one time and he said, "On a TV set, when you turn the vertical hold on the TV, the picture will go up, and if you turn it the other way, it goes down. Why does it do that?"' said Dabney. 'I explained it to him. It was the difference between the sync and the picture timing. He said, "Could we do that with some control?" I said, "Yeah, we probably can, but we'd have to do it digitally, because analog would not be linear."' [10]

➡ Some of Bushnell's ideas may have seemed like pipe dreams, but Dabney was taken with this – so much so that he took over his daughter Terri's bedroom and turned it into a makeshift workshop. He worked on the idea for several months and eventually produced a TV set modified so that an on-screen white dot could be moved around. This was the proof-of-concept for which Bushnell had been waiting. Dabney and Bushnell agreed that to take the idea any further

Spacewar! running on an emulated PDP-1. The two ships are differentiated by shape, and often the gravity well in the screen's centre is more deadly than the other player.

The gravity well is key to one of *Spacewar!*'s most enjoyable tricks, which is learning to move in at an angle and then use the momentum to 'slingshot' back out.

would require a programmer, and interested Larry Bryan in the idea – who came up with the company name of Syzygy, meaning the alignment of three celestial bodies. But when it came to each of the three investing $100 in start-up costs, Bryan bowed out.

COMPUTER SPACE

NA-2010

➡ As Bushnell and Dabney thought on the idea further, they realized that computers in the late 1960s were far too expensive for the idea to be feasible as a consumer product. But the pair's imaginations were fired, and they began looking for other ways to create a new type of video game. Bushnell was convinced that a version of *Spacewar!*, which he had played while a student at Utah, would make a great arcade game. 'I loved the game and played it every chance I could get,' said Bushnell. 'I didn't get as many chances as I wanted.'[11] In 1970, and initially without Dabney's knowledge, Bushnell managed to interest Bill Nutting of Nutting Associates in his plan.

➡ Nutting was desperate for a new kind of product and so enamoured of Bushnell's idea that he offered the pair overly generous terms, including the ownership of the original concept. Bushnell quit Ampex to start work as Nutting's chief (and only) engineer. Over the next year Dabney continued to work at Ampex while moonlighting part-time for Nutting,

The rather saucy advertisement for *Computer Space* was an attempt to move away from the image of dingy bars, though the see-through dress makes the effect unintentionally seedy.

helping Bushnell test his work and designing a cabinet for the new machine.

➡ Soon enough Dabney left Ampex and the pair were reunited at Nutting. The game was now known as *Computer Space* and, as a new type of entertainment in bars and restaurants, Bushnell knew it had to make a big impression. Dabney's original casing was only big enough to house the prototype, so Bushnell threw it out and designed a huge fibreglass cabinet that came in four different colours; sweeping curves enveloped the TV screen, the machine leaned towards its player, and the four buttons were set in an aviation-inspired panel with individual labels.

➡ The game was released in November 1971, and advertised widely with a young lady posing next to the cabinet. Nutting's initial production run was 1,500 units and, though Bushnell disputes this, only between 500 to 1,000 were sold. Although *Computer Space* was popular with young people and tech-minded individuals, the fact it was a new kind of experience and fairly complex to control at the same time meant that it died a death in bars. The average punter simply couldn't get their head around it.

➡ Regardless of this modest reception, *Computer Space* is the first commercially sold video game of any kind and became the model for the future of arcade games – dedicated cabinets that were built to play one title. It also made Bushnell and Dabney around $150,000 each, thanks to Nutting's generous agreement.

➡ Bushnell's design added a great deal to the basics of *Spacewar!*, primarily a pair of flying saucers that acted as the game's antagonists. These would zigzag around the screen in tandem, firing shots at the player's ship, which was controlled by changing orientation and hitting the thruster button. The game kept score up to a maximum of fifteen, with each death being one point, and in another

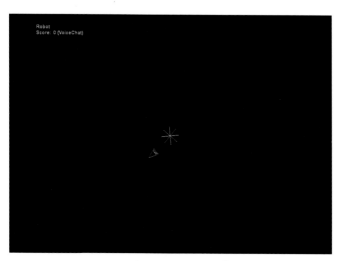

Making a version of *Spacewar!* is a rite of passage for many would-be game designers and even professionals. This non-public version was made by Valve to demonstrate Steam's networking features to developers.

influence on later arcade games each session lasted ninety seconds. There was a trick: if the player managed to score more points than the saucers, the screen would show a 'hyperspace' effect and grant another ninety seconds of playtime. Sounds easy, but of course *Computer Space* is a tough game for just this reason. Few players were good enough to get 'free' time extensions.

➲ *Computer Space* got there first – but only because, six miles away, the men who could have trumped it were more concerned about quality than commerce. Bill Pitts and Hugh Tuck were students at Stanford University and, unbeknownst to Dabney and Bushnell, had similar ideas about making a coin-operated version of *Spacewar!*

➲ The difference was that Pitts and Tuck, though focused on improving the game, wanted to make their version as faithful as possible – and only had plans to make one machine. *Spacewar!* had been programmed

on the PDP-1, but the Digital Equipment Corporation had recently released the PDP-11/20 minicomputer – a relative snip at $14,000 (not including display). After borrowing money from family and friends, Pitts and Tuck formed a company, Computer Recreations Inc., in June of 1971 to buy and reconfigure one of these machines as a coin-operated video game.

➲ Bill Pitts was a computer hacker, so programmed the game and dealt with the innards, while mechanical engineer Hugh Tuck constructed the enclosure that would attract customers. Within three months their work was complete. The Vietnam War was a hot topic on any American university campus, so they decided that a game with 'war' in the title wouldn't do – and settled for the ambiguous title of *Galaxy Game*.

➲ Pitts wrote about their machine over two decades later, when invited to restore it for Stanford:

Computer Space in action – the two saucers float around shooting at the player ship, which makes staying alive quite difficult at first. This steep learning curve turned off many contemporary players immediately.

The first version of *Galaxy Game*, packaged in a walnut veneered enclosure, incorporated a PDP-11/20 computer, a simple point plotting display interface, and a Hewlett Packard 1300A Electrostatic Display. The PDP-11/20 cost $14,000 and the display cost $3,000. Coin acceptors and packaging brought the total cost to approximately $20,000. Playing of the *Galaxy Game* was priced at 10 cents per game or 25 cents for 3 games. If at the end of the game your ship still survived and had some fuel left, you got a free game. Given the investment, perhaps [we] were not the most astute of businessmen. [12]

● *Galaxy Game* was released two months before *Computer Space*, installed in a coffee shop on the Stanford campus, and so is often cited as the first commercial video

game. While this may be literally true, it is also an extremely generous interpretation of 'commercial'. *Galaxy Game*, at a cost of around $20,000, simply wasn't scalable. Pitts and Tuck made an expensive one-off that had trouble paying for itself, and was only to be found in a single place. Bushnell's ambitions were on a different level. Pitts and Tuck 'were kind of funny guys that were technical,' said Bushnell. 'But not focused on world domination.'

● Despite *Computer Space* selling a 'mere' 500–1,000 units, Bushnell, having learned a great deal from the experience, wanted to aim higher. He needed a better game: a simpler game. Something anyone could play and understand in an instant, even if they'd had a few beers. At a trade show in May 1972 he saw Ralph Baer's Odyssey playing *Tennis* – and for the next three decades would pretend he hadn't.

Galaxy Game in emulated form; although this is black and white, the original's display was tinted green. The first machine was installed in the coffee shop at Stanford from 1972 until 1980, at which time it became less reliable and Bill Pitts removed it.

Atari's Born

➔ Shortly after the release of *Computer Space* in November 1971, Nolan Bushnell and Ted Dabney parted ways with Nutting Associates. Bushnell had considered revising his design with the lessons learned, but demanded 33 per cent of the company to do so – he was offered 5 per cent, not ungenerous considering the circumstances, but decided to go it alone. Nutting released his own two-player *Computer Space* cabinet a year later, designed by one Steve Bristow, but by that time *Pong* owned the market.

➔ Bushnell and Dabney had made enough money from Nutting to found their own company but, upon trying to trademark the name Syzygy, found it was already taken. Perhaps recalling their days at Ampex, they decided to use a term from Go that is roughly equivalent to 'check' in chess: Atari.

➔ On 27 June 1972 Bushnell and Dabney applied to have Atari incorporated, investing an initial $250 each. One of their first contracts was to design extra-wide pinball tables for manufacturer Bally, which led to the pair buying their own pinball machines on the cheap and installing them across local student haunts. This became a not-insignificant money-spinner for Atari's early years, so much so that when Dabney left years later he accepted it as part of the settlement.[13]

➔ Atari's first employee was Cynthia Villanueva, a seventeen-year-old who had babysat Bushnell's children and needed a summer job. Ever the salesman, Bushnell instructed her to make Atari seem bigger than it was by putting callers on hold until he was 'available'. The second employee, known to both founders from the Ampex days, was young engineer Al Alcorn.

➔ Alcorn's first job, though he didn't realize it, was more of a test. Bushnell described a simple ping-pong game with two bats, a ball and a score tracker. Alcorn started work on a prototype. Bushnell was inspired by the

Odyssey's *Tennis* but thought of this more as a training exercise, believing the future of Atari lay in either selling a new variant of *Computer Space* or possibly a racing game.

➤ Within three months Alcorn had completed the unnamed game. He had mounted a $75 black-and-white television in a four-foot-high cabinet, and hardwired everything inside. Alcorn hadn't been content to merely follow the basic outline provided and made a number of significant improvements to how the game played. As soon as Bushnell and Dabney played it, they knew the young engineer had produced something special.

➤ The key to Alcorn's design, and what set it apart from the Magnavox Odyssey *Tennis* game, is that the bat is invisibly divided into eight vertical segments. Depending on which one of these the ball hits, the angle of return will be different, creating an effective illusion of racquet physics and a replacement for 'english'. The middle segments would return in a straight line, the next ones would return at a shallow angle, and the outer edges hit the ball at a forty-five-degree angle (which created the tactic of bouncing the ball off the 'sides' of the court to confuse an opponent). He also made the ball accelerate after a certain number of returns, meaning that rallies between good players would quickly get intense.

➤ Alcorn had also jury-rigged a 'bloop' sound effect when the ball was returned, and the overall impression the machine creates – particularly with regard to what had come before – is minimalist sophistication. Bushnell christened the game *Pong* and added an instruction card that continued this theme. Where *Computer Space* had created confusion with its complex rules, *Pong* relied on one sentence that even the most inebriated player could understand: Avoid Missing Ball for High Score.

An original *Pong* cabinet signed by Al Alcorn, photographed at the 'Golden Age of Video Games' exhibit at Neville Public Museum in Wisconsin. Note the front panel's simplicity compared to *Computer Space*. (Photo credit: Chris Rand)

➡ Also, and so obvious it's easy to underestimate, *Pong* is a two-player game that was placed in social settings. Although the game could be played against a respectable 'AI' opponent, *Pong* was and is at its best with friends, the kind of thing that can break up an evening and spark minor rivalries among patrons. The resemblance to table hockey probably didn't hurt either.

➡ The story goes that, when the prototype unit was installed in Andy Capp's Tavern in Sunnydale, California, Atari shortly received an angry phone call complaining that the machine had broken down. Such malfunctions were commonplace and, worried about some unforeseen problem, Alcorn was dispatched to investigate. The machine was working just fine. But the bar's patrons had fed so many quarters into the coin slot that it simply couldn't take any more. (For years this story was regarded as half-myth until Dabney, not a man given to exaggeration, confirmed that it happened – so many times, in fact, it was considered something of a routine.)

➡ Bushnell and Dabney knew that Atari had a potential mega-hit on its hands: but it also had contracts with larger, established companies. 'Nolan decided he didn't really want Bally to take *Pong* because he knew it was too good,' recalls Alcorn. 'So he met with Bally and Midway and decided to tell Bally that the Midway guys didn't want it. And so the Bally guys decided that they didn't want it. Then he told the Midway guys that the Bally guys didn't want it. He got them convinced that it was no good. [Once they heard that] it didn't take much convincing.'

➡ Atari was still a tiny company, unable to fill the kind of volume orders that *Pong* would soon command, and traditional sources of finance (who elided video games with pinball and therefore organized crime) wouldn't touch it. Bushnell eventually secured funding from Wells Fargo, who extended a credit line of $50,000 – less than Bushnell wanted but it had to do. He hired workers direct from the unemployment office and, despite constant mishaps and problems along the way, *Pong* machines started rolling off the production lines.

⊙ Atari sold *Pong* for $1,200 upfront cash, the production cost being $300–$400. The orders began rolling in, a dribble that rapidly turned into a flood as distributors and bar owners caught on to the fact that here was a bona-fide phenomenon. *Pong* was and remains one of the most profitable coin-operated machines in history – where an average machine might be lucky to pull in $50 a week, *Pong* would take four times that. By the end of 1973 Atari had sold 2,500 *Pong* machines. A year later it was more than 8,000. *Pong* was so successful that it even today it is often mistakenly cited as the first

video game, by virtue of being the first to achieve mainstream prominence. The rise of video games, and Atari, had begun.

⊙ Bushnell had also, somewhat inadvertently, pioneered a business model that is still widespread in the industry today: copying another game. Over the next few years the situation would reverse as every amusement manufacturer scrambled to produce a *Pong* clone. A small Japanese company, Taito, started making video games with *Elepong*, the first Japanese arcade game, and even Atari themselves produced several variants like *Quadrapong*.

⊙ Faced with a flood of copycats, Bushnell, now in sole charge after Dabney's departure in 1973, felt that Atari could stay ahead of the pack by – ironically enough – focusing on original ideas. Over the next two years it produced games like *Gotcha*, a maze-chasing game about kissing where the controllers were joysticks set in a resemblance of rubber

The aim of *Pong* is to reach eleven points before the opponent, a perfectly pitched target that gives a few minutes' entertainment and encourages swift rematches. *Pong* would still do good business in any contemporary bar.

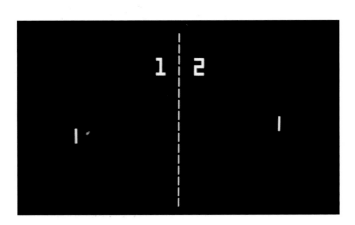

breasts; *Space Race*, where players had to dodge through asteroid fields; and *Qwak*, a lightgun game about hunting ducks.

➤ Perhaps the greatest game Atari produced in this period was loosely based on one of the few other original machines out there. Bushnell's former employers Nutting Associates had produced the innovative *Missile Radar*, in which players had to shoot down incoming missiles. It was a neat idea, but an average game. Atari's *Missile Command* vastly improved upon the basic mechanic, with three turrets at the bottom of the screen protecting cities from an incoming hail of missiles.

➤ *Missile Command* used a trackball to control an on-screen cursor and any of the three turrets could then fire at that spot – when the shot 'hit' the cursor's original placement, it would create an expanding circular explosion that destroyed any missile within the radius. The incoming fire started slowly, but soon numerous trails were criss-crossing the screen and the only way to survive was for each shot to catch multiple missiles – with those that got through either destroying the cities at the bottom of the screen (lose them all and it's Game Over) or even taking out one of the player's own turrets. In a society gripped by cold-war paranoia such a scenario seemed eerily topical, but what makes *Missile Command* great is the contrast between your natural panic at twenty incoming missiles and the superhuman coolness required to calculate the best angles and execute the shots.

➤ During this period Atari also made the first-ever driving video game, *Gran Trak 10*. Viewed from a top-down perspective, in truth the appeal was largely down to its novelty – the entire racetrack was squashed onto one screen. But Atari spared no expense in bringing the machine to life, and the cabinet

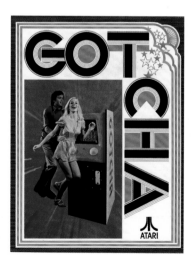

Atari's advertising flyer for *Gotcha* made no bones about what the game was attempting to simulate, though one has to question the distance between the control 'pads'.

featured a steering wheel, foot pedals and a gear stick. It was an enormous success and, because of this, nearly bankrupted the company. Thanks to the complex hardware involved Atari had underestimated the total cost of producing *Gran Trak 10*, underpriced it and lost money on every machine sold.

➤ Thanks to an ill-advised foray with Atari Japan, which ate through around half a million dollars and achieved little, Bushnell's dream of conquering the world looked like collapsing as soon as it had began. Things were saved by engineer Steve Bristow and, in a funny coincidence, his desire to revise *Computer Space*. Bristow had worked on updated versions of the original and, unlike many others, eventually saw past the 'complexity' of *Computer Space* to the great game that lay beneath. He felt that the core could be repurposed with something less intimidating to the average player.

➤ 'As a youth my uncle had put me to work clearing his orchard using a Caterpillar tractor, which drove like a tank,' recalled Bristow. 'I thought that could be turned into *Computer Space* done right.' [14]

➤ At the time Bristow was working for Kee Games, a bizarre enterprise owned by Atari that had been set up as a false competitor by Bushnell – a way of making deals with distributors that Atari couldn't agree for contractual reasons. The imaginatively named *Tank* transplanted the basics of *Computer Space*'s 1-vs-1 combat into slower-paced arenas where walls blocked off certain angles of fire. Scattered mines added another layer of challenge, and the game was a rapid success to the extent it allowed Bushnell to 'merge' the two companies.

➤ The money from this helped Bushnell turn a skunkworks project into the start of Atari's enormous home success. In 1974 work had begun on a home *Pong* console but – in contrast to the Magnavox Odyssey

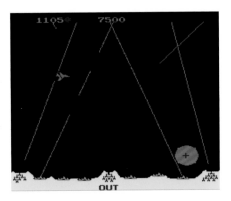

Atari created the *Missile Command* arcade game in 1980. It is one of the most enduring games from the 'Golden Age of Video Arcade Games' and has been widely cloned.

The Sears Tele-Games *Pong* console, opposite. Atari initially received a cool reception from toy and electronics buyers but, inspired by the Magnavox Odyssey's placement in Sears's sporting goods department, persuaded the giant retailer to take a chance – hence the name. (Photo credit: Evan Amos)

– the new technology of integrated circuits drastically reduced the cost of each unit. *Tank*'s profits meant Atari could seek further funding and, once venture capitalist Don Valentine invested $20 million, the company had a product and the money for a production line.

➤ Released as the Sears Tele-Games *Pong*, thanks to an exclusive distribution deal, the console shifted 150,000 units over Christmas 1975. Although it was only an incremental improvement over the Magnavox Odyssey, and featured less variety, the simple name-recognition factor of *Pong* saw greater success and – more importantly – awoke Bushnell to the potential of home gaming. (Ralph Baer graciously admitted that, although *Pong* was derived from the Odyssey's games, its success helped Magnavox shift more units than it might have done.)

➤ The success of Atari's home *Pong* machine

again saw a rush of imitators – this time, thanks to the fact that the integrated circuit's design could be easily copied. Two years later there would be more than 60 'home *Pong*' consoles on the market, and well over ten million machines sold in the US.

➤ But Atari was already thinking about what was next. The company's key players knew that the future wasn't in the integrated circuit, but in the new technology of the microprocessor. Where an integrated circuit could perform the single function for which it was programmed, a microprocessor was flexible – at the time, it was referred to as 'a computer on a chip'.

➤ The importance of this for video games was obvious: you could sell a machine and then sell individual game cartridges that contained memory chips.[15] Plug and play. The only problem was that, as Atari desperately sought the funding to bring the concept to market, someone else had got there first.

The original *Tank* was released under the Kee Games label, an Atari front, but the success was such that later versions (such as this eight-player variant) trumpeted the true creators to the skies.

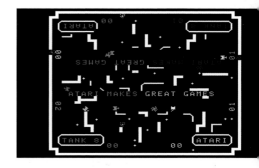

VES vs VCS

Gerald 'Jerry' Lawson and Ron Jones were members of the Homebrew Computer Club, a group of hobbyists that included the likes of then-Atari employees Steve Jobs and Steve Wozniak. Lawson was an engineer at Fairchild Semiconductor who knew his video games[16] – and in 1975 he had one hell of a job on.

In 1974 Fairchild had announced the impending release of the Fairchild F8, an 8-bit microprocessor that was at the bleeding edge of CPU (central processing unit) technology and would soon become the bestselling computer chip in the world. Although Fairchild was a manufacturer first and foremost, the recent popularity of home video games led the company to try its hand at designing a console that could use this technology and take over the marketplace.

But this was a secret project from the very top – even Lawson's own line manager wasn't allowed to know what he was doing. Along with designer Nick Talesfore and mechanical engineer Ron Smith, Lawson created a revolutionary product – the first ROM cartridge-based games console and the first to use a microprocessor.

'What was paramount to our system was to have cartridges,' recalled Lawson. 'There was a mechanism that allowed you to put the cartridges in without destroying the semiconductors.' The 'Video Entertainment System' also had 64 bytes of RAM, an audio chip that fed to an internal speaker, a hardwired RF (radio frequency) cord, and could output a possible eight colours with a resolution of 128 x 64 pixels.

The most unusual part of the design was the two controllers: the main bulk was a large vertical hand grip, with a triangular eight-way joystick on top that could also be pushed down or pulled up as a fire button. The most visionary was a 'hold' button that allowed players, for the first time, to 'pause' the game (as well as change the speed).

Jerry Lawson, creator of the Fairchild Video Entertainment System. Later in the 1980s he would found and run Videosoft, a video-game developer that made games for the VES's one-time competition, the Atari VCS. Lawson died in March 2011, but not before being honoured by the International Games Developers Association as an industry pioneer.

The Video Entertainment System (VES) was launched in November 1976, and by the end of the year had six 'videocarts' available for purchase. Over the next year the console would sell a quarter of a million units, and a total of twenty-seven videocarts would be released over its lifetime.

➔ Despite initial success the VES was ultimately a failure for two reasons. The first was that the games, even by the standards of the day, were nothing special. Lawson personally had the chops to design great games, as his coin-op *Demolition Derby* showed, but Fairchild simply didn't have enough experience in the field to take advantage of the VES's main selling point of interchangeable cartridges. The second reason was that the VES had scared Atari and, if Atari knew anything, it knew video games.

➔ The prototype known as 'Stella', named after an engineer's bicycle, had been in development at Atari for years before the VES shocked the company out of its slumber. Bushnell instantly realized that the console would have to hit the market soon before a flood of competitors ruined Atari's chances. The need for instant cash to start production, which Atari simply didn't have, meant that Bushnell sold the company to Warner Communications in 1976 for $28 million, on the condition that Stella became a commercial product as soon as possible.

➔ The Atari Video Computer System (VCS), named specifically to invite comparisons to the VES, was launched on 11 September 1977 at $199. The VCS came with two joysticks, two paddle controllers and a single cartridge: *Combat*. A multiplayer-only game, *Combat* was a top-down 2D shooter that offered twenty-seven different arenas and three different vehicles for players to blast each other with. Successful hits scored a point and sent your opponent into a momentary spin, while certain modes changed up the rules

The Atari VCS had switches to alter the display and select different game 'modes' – the latter an extremely common feature used by smarter designers to alter basic rules and increase the lifespan of what were relatively simple games.

The Fairchild VES (later renamed the Channel F). The 'hold' button, unique to this console, can be seen on the front panel. Note also the unusual controller design – players held the long grip in one hand and the joystick with the other. (Photo credit: Evan Amos)

A BRIEF HISTORY OF VIDEO GAMES

slightly, such as 'Tank Pong' where shots had to be bounced off the wall before hitting.

➡ The VCS quickly sold more than any other console in history, 250,000 by the end of 1977. Fairchild's VES simply couldn't compete at this level and quickly withdrew from the market, leaving it entirely to Atari. But thanks to yet more inefficient production methods Atari was still losing money on the VCS, producing hundreds of thousands more than it sold, and after Warner was forced to bail it out in 1978 Bushnell left the company.

➡ Over the next few years, however, the VCS started to sell in ever-greater numbers, thanks to its increasing software library (which included licensed versions of arcade hits) and a series of price cuts and revisions. By 1982 the console had sold ten million units, and by the time it was discontinued in 1992 (fifteen years after launch!) had altogether sold thirty million.

➡ The VCS had legs because Atari had great developers and was able to convert its hit arcade games (and those of others) to run on the home machine. *Pong* had been cloned mercilessly over the years, but the best 'sequel' was concepted by Bushnell and Steve Bristow – and this time, it was an original idea. The game that would become known as *Breakout* (1976) had a bat that moved horizontally across the bottom of the screen and a ball that was bounced up towards a wall made of layered lines of bricks; every one it bounced off would be destroyed.

➡ *Breakout*'s elegance lies in how the goal of destroying all bricks gradually increases the skill required to do so. As bricks disappear there are fewer to aim at and the ball's speed increases, meaning that the focus switches from simply hitting the ball back to hitting it precisely, banking shots off walls and trying to get the ball trapped in a pocket where multiple bricks can be taken out at once. There's also a dastardly twist of the

The success of the Atari 2600 led to some hilariously bad attempts to made 'adult' video games. Developer Mystique's 1982 game *Beat 'Em & Eat 'Em* has the player control what is allegedly a pair of naked women trying to catch the sperm of a man masturbating above them.

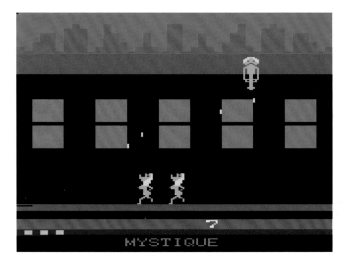

knife when the topmost layer of bricks is pierced – the first time the ball hits the top of the screen, the size of the player's paddle is halved.

→ *Breakout* is one of the few Atari games that can be called timeless. Where others are influential or historically important, this exact design is mimicked to the present day by countless developers: it remains a favourite among both casual players and the more dedicated.

→ *River Raid* (1982), designed by Carol Shaw, was a top-down shooter that gradually narrowed the player's options, in one sense literally: forcing them to fly down ever-smaller corridors where a wall collision was fatal. It is perhaps most notable for being one of the first games to randomly generate the placement of enemies and items within its levels, meaning that players could not memorize routes and 'master' the game in a conventional sense.

→ There are many more VCS titles that could be mentioned like *Pitfall* or *Rainbow Walker*. 1982's *Yars' Revenge* (Yars is an anagram poking fun at Atari's fearsome then-boss, Ray Kassar, making the game's true title 'Ray's Revenge') was a side-scrolling shooter where the player controlled a flying bug facing off against an alien called Qotile that is protected by shields. The most unusual aspect of its design is a 'neutral' zone in the middle of the screen where the player can avoid taking damage from the enemy's missiles but can't shoot back.

→ Alongside the VCS, Atari continued to produce excellent arcade games (see Chapter 10: The Golden Age of the Arcades) and eventually a series of 8-bit computers. These were inspired by the growing home-computer industry and, though they were never as successful as the VCS, did result in one of Atari's most important games.

→ *Star Raiders* (1979) remains something

Early Atari employee Steve Jobs was assigned to develop *Breakout*'s prototype and was offered $750 plus a reward for every transistor-transistor logic chip (under a baseline of fifty) he could remove from the design. Jobs convinced Steve Wozniak to do it in exchange for splitting the profits. Wozniak's brilliant design resulted in a bonus of $5,000, of which Jobs gave him $350.

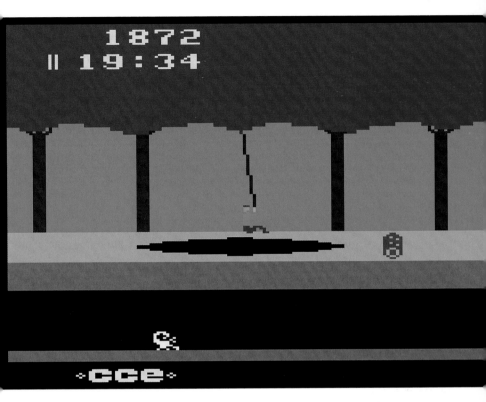

Pitfall! was created by Activision programmer David Crane, who had worked out how to display a realistic-looking running animation on the Atari 2600 and made a game that would showcase it. Pitfall! was a real technical achievement of its time, also boasting non-flickering multicoloured sprites and animated vines.

River Raid is an early example of procedurally generated content, using an algorithm to make the layout of terrain and other objects different every time. Its violent theme, despite being no more exceptional than many other games, also saw it banned in West Germany.

of an unknown classic – created by Doug Neubauer, an Atari engineer, it is regarded by fellow designers as perhaps the greatest programming accomplishment of its time. Casting the player as basically a space pirate, it was the first free-roaming first-person perspective game, and mixed both strategy and shooting as you moved around a galaxy and got into dogfights.

➡ The later BBC Micro game *Elite* (1984) was heavily inspired by *Star Raiders*, lifting many elements directly, and is oft-cited as one of the most important titles ever released. It presented a cold-hearted universe where the only rules were get rich and don't get caught (which probably says something about the atmosphere in 1980s Britain, where it was created). *Elite* had dogfighting similar to *Star Raiders* but, when co-developers David Braben and Ian Bell found this a little dull, a layer of amoral capitalism was added on top – the player can trade everything from food to weapons to slaves. What makes it resonate even now is the vast scale of its eight galaxies; the feeling that there's always something new to find. What makes *Elite* a classic is that there always is.

➡ In the early 1980s Atari was the king of an industry it had created. There was no arguing with the sales of its VCS, and it seemed like the gravy train wasn't slowing down. But the company's business practices were increasingly questionable and counter-productive – for example, its refusal to credit designers led to disgruntled employees leaving to form their own companies (including Activision, now the world's largest third-party publisher). Atari also had several internal divisions that were competing with one another, and the gradual loss of much of its talent was leading to a lack of quality-control over software. This hadn't affected sales – yet. But the company, and the industry, would soon be scrambling to survive.

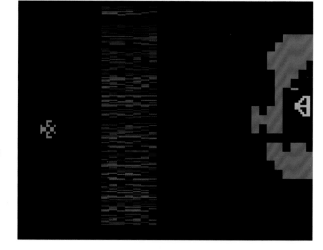

The brilliant *Yars' Revenge* would become the bestselling original title on the Atari 2600, though it was outsold by the awful licensed version of *Pac-Man*. Designer Howard Scott Warshaw would later make the infamous 2600 version of *E.T.: The Extra-Terrestrial*

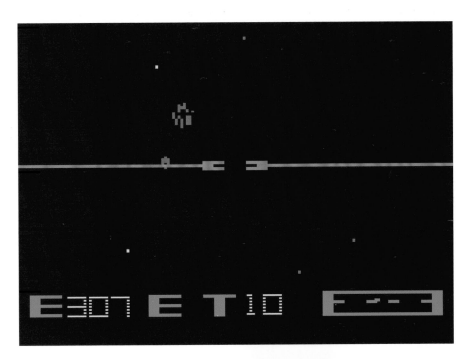

Star Raiders designer Doug Neubauer was inspired by text-based *Star Trek* games from the 1970s, where players would navigate their ship across a 2D grid – which became the Galactic Map that divides and gives form to this universe.

Although heavily inspired by *Star Raiders*, *Elite* was also a true step forward for video games and was ported to almost every platform going in the 1980s. It has a narrative to follow, but what blew players away was the freedom to ignore it and simply explore this expansive universe.

⊙ Let us briefly step back from the white-hot frontline of the commercial video-game business, where everything was about quarters and retail sales. In 1971 Don Rawitsch was in his final year at Carleton College, Minnesota, and, as part of his course, he was teaching American history to young teenagers. He lived with fellow students Bill Heinemann and Paul Dillenberger in an apartment where they would swap teaching (and cooking) strategies over dinner.

⊙ Rawitsch was no ordinary teacher. He wanted kids to see beyond the dates and names of history to the people who had lived it, going as far as teaching his classes dressed as historical figures. One of the topics he had to teach was the 2,000-mile journey that pioneers in the nineteenth century had made from Missouri to Oregon in the hope of a better life.

⊙ Rawitsch thought a board game might illuminate this period of history, and began drawing a route on an 1800s frontier map while writing things like 'dysentery' and 'broken arm' on cards. Players rolled a die to advance forward and would encounter random misfortunes along the way: this was the *Oregon Trail*.

⊙ When the game was complete Rawitsch showed it to his roommates, both of whom taught maths and had taken computer-programming classes. Dillenberger and Heinemann instantly saw that the game would work beautifully on a computer, and started throwing ideas back and forth about how best to program it. Over the next two weeks they did just that, spending every night in a tiny room tapping code into a teletype machine – which was basically a typewriter connected via phone line to a computer.

⊙ There was no monitor, so the teletype printed out the game's descriptions and asked for the player's instructions by return. On

'The three of us who made the game never earned a cent of royalties,' says Don Rawitsch. 'That's because in the 1970s, before personal computers, nobody knew there would be an actual school/consumer software market. So I donated the program to MECC and have the satisfaction of knowing it had such a big impact. So – fame but no fortune.'

3 December 1971 Rawitsch rolled the teletype into his classroom and divided his students into teams, handing out copies of the 1800s frontier map for them to follow along.

➡ 'They loved it,' Rawitsch recalled. 'The person who was good at the map kept track of where they were, the person who was good at math kept track of the money. They formed a little collaborative.'[17]

➡ The game was loaded onto the Minneapolis district's 'timesharing' system, which meant any school's teletype could access it, and proved enormously popular among the region's children. But when that term ended, Rawitsch figured that *Oregon Trail* was done with. After printing out the source code, he deleted the program.

➡ *Oregon Trail* may never have been seen again except for Rawitsch stumbling into a job with the Minnesota Education Computing Consortium (MECC) three years later. The group wanted more programs and, over a

long weekend with a teletype, Rawitsch painstakingly typed out the original code while making historical improvements.

➡ Over the next decade *Oregon Trail* would become a video game found in almost every school in America, the ultimate Trojan Horse. This was thanks in part to the MECC's forward-thinking licensing approach and to the rise of the Apple II version, which would become best-known due to being both widespread and featuring basic visuals to illustrate the journey's progress.

➡ But more than anything this popularity was down to *Oregon Trail* being a brilliant and unusual kind of game. It is often considered the pioneer of 'edutainment' (there is stiff competition, but this is probably gaming's most hideous portmanteau) software but really it was the first strategy game, built around careful planning, resource-management and calculated risk. Features like the ability to name your five settlers

The original *Oregon Trail* was text-only, though the evocative visuals created for the Apple II version are what have subsequently lodged in the popular imagination. Its cultural impact in the USA is enormous thanks to its ubiquitous presence – even today – in school lessons.

Countless versions of the *Oregon Trail* have been made and it would be a surprise to find a platform that hadn't played host to it at some point. It is estimated that, in total, over sixty-five million copies of the game have been sold.

A BRIEF HISTORY OF VIDEO GAMES

added a touch of pathos to the simple narrative (especially when a settler died) and the random chance in the journey's afflictions made each playthrough feel different.

◉ Or maybe you should cut down the rations to stretch them out, save those dollars for something else and try your luck hunting along the way? The core of *Oregon Trail* is a risk/reward flip that, for all its moments of randomness, forms a consistent arc of lessons learned. Experienced pioneers will never skimp on spare parts, or ford a river, or trade their oxen away. You learn to hoard not for the sake of it, but because you've been down this road before and know that you'll eventually need every scrap you can get.

◉ Whether this is educational really depends on what one expects from education; as a facts-and-figures primer *Oregon Trail* is pretty hopeless, but as an imaginative exercise in the trials and tribulations of nineteenth-century pioneers it is exceptional. Over multiple playthroughs you learn the importance of husbanding supplies, minimizing risk and keeping everyone well fed.

◉ Over the next decades *Oregon Trail* would be remade countless times and continue to find new audiences. It also inspired a 2010 tribute, *The Organ Trail*, which transplanted the basic mechanics into a zombie apocalypse (the theme *du jour* for contemporary gaming). *The Organ Trail* is worth pausing over because it shows that these simple mechanics can still work for modern audiences with a bare minimum of tweaking, albeit dressed up in a modern theme and vibrant aesthetic.

◉ *Oregon Trail* can be played on almost any modern device, free emulated versions are easily found online, and it will reward your time even now – not something you can say about many games in their fourth decade. If all goes well, it doesn't take more than an hour to reach Oregon. But you'll remember the journey for a lot longer.

The excellent tongue-in-cheek tribute *Organ Trail* was released in 2010 by developers The Men Who Wear Many Hats. Despite its irreverent humour *Organ Trail* sticks closely to the mechanics of its inspiration, and in doing so proves their durability.

Organ Trail was popular enough to warrant a Director's Cut soon after release, which speaks not just to the quality work of its developers but also to the power of nostalgia among gaming fans – video games that remind people of childhood are always a sure-fire route to success.

A Tale of Two Adventures

I know of places, actions and things. Most of my vocabulary describes places and is used to move you there . . . You are in a maze of twisty little passages, all alike.

William Crowther's *Adventure*

➤ William Crowther is a programmer's programmer. As a member of the consulting firm Bolt, Beranek and Newman (BBN), he was a key part of the team behind the creation of ARPANET, the first step towards what is now known as the internet. Crowther was a member of a team working on the project, but he was perhaps the most important. 'Most of the rest of us,' one teammate later recalled, 'made our livings handling the details resulting from Will's use of his brain'.[18]

➤ When he wasn't working Crowther liked to spend time outdoors, rock-climbing and later caving. 'There are groups in every big city in the country that go caving and I picked up with one of those groups and started caving in New York,' says Crowther.[19] He enjoyed poking around in caves, finding new routes and surprising formations, and when a friend bought some land with a mysterious hole in it he and Crowther decided to explore.

So I got a flashlight and crawled into the hole and we went a couple hundred yards, but it was beautiful because it was water cascading down a series of falls that were cut in the marble. So it was really - it was white polished rock with black bands in it. Sculptured into very unusual shapes. So I enjoyed that enough that I went around and found some people who were doing it and did some more of it. Eventually, I wound up going down to Kentucky for Mammoth Cave, which is the longest cave in the world.

⊙ Crowther met his wife on these caving trips, and along with the group they helped map out a part of the Mammoth Cave system. He began constructing a cave map on a computer, which seemed a sensible thing for a programmer, and was happily married with two young daughters. Inspiration was yet to strike and, sadly, it would take the form of heartbreak: Crowther and his wife divorced. Not only was this a painful experience, but it meant Crowther spent less time with his children and missed them terribly.

⊙ Crowther wanted to make a game that his children, Sandy and Laura, could play with him. Having met his wife while caving, he no longer hung out with the same group and other interests had taken over. In particular Crowther was a fan of *Dungeons and Dragons* (*D&D*), and had recently been playing in a campaign that lasted months (the participants included, among others, future Infocom co-founder Dave Lebling). *D&D* is a pen-and-paper role-playing game (RPG) that was enormously popular in the 1970s and adored by players for the freedom it allows in the construction of a world.

⊙ 'Related to the divorce . . . I was feeling kind of lonely and I wanted to write a game for my kids,' says Crowther.

Meanwhile, we had been playing Dragons & Dungeons games. You know, these role model, role playing games at the Dave Walden's house, and so I thought 'Gee, I'll make a computer version of the Dragons & Dungeon game,' and that turned out to be *Adventure*. I happened to write it in Fortran which was quite portable. And I wrote the silly thing and I left it in a directory on a machine here at BBN and then left.

What Crowther created was based on southwestern Kentucky's Mammoth Cave but, shot through with high fantasy and a dash of travel writing, it was far more than a reconstruction: this was *Colossal Cave Adventure*.

Although it would become known as *Adventure*, this original title is worth bearing in mind because the spine of Crowther's design is in realism both shallow and deep. Caver slang like Y2 (map notation for a survey point) rubs up against rooms named after specific formations like 'Bedquilt', of which he was especially fond.[20] Many players complain that leaving a room by the north exit doesn't mean that you'll head south on the return – which can quite easily be the case inside a cave.

The game is entirely text-based and begins by describing a location next to a stream. From then on it is up to the player to type in appropriate commands: 'follow stream' would work, as would simply 'south' or 's'. Upon moving, the player is given a description of their new surroundings and can then either interact (picking up items or solving basic puzzles) or move on.

The importance of *Adventure* is in what it asks of the player. Until this point games had been mainly about action and reaction – hitting balls, shooting ships, driving cars and jumping pits. But *Adventure* required logic to progress, an internal sense of geography and resource management (the player character could only carry so many objects).

Beyond even this the game had well-written descriptions that drew the player into this weird world of 'Walls [That] Are Frozen Rivers of Orange Stone'. More than anything the prose is brilliant at scenery; many locations have one- or two-line descriptions, but certain ones are outlined in highly suggestive detail. Although Crowther created *Adventure*, the game as it became

Adventure has been shaped by many players over time to the extent that there is no 'definitive' version. This emulated example is as close to the original as it's possible to get and comes complete with the lightly teasing pleasure of trying to work out what verbs to use.

```
Colossal Cave Adventure • Score: 36 • Turns: 8

At your feet all the water of the stream splashes into a
2-inch slit in the rock.  Downstream the streambed is bare rock.

> rock

You are in a 20-foot depression floored with bare dirt.  Set
into the dirt is a strong steel grate mounted in concrete.
A dry streambed leads into the depression.
The grate is locked.

> use keys

I don't know that word.

> unlock

The grate is now unlocked.

> down

You are in a small chamber beneath a 3x3 steel grate to the
surface.  A low crawl over cobbles leads inward to the West.
The grate is open.
What's next?
```

known was a much-improved version by Don Woods. Crowther's original was completed in 1975 or 1976 and lived a furtive existence on university networks, where it was hidden from zealous administrators (who loved deleting 'frivolous' programs) under the ambiguous and hopefully boring-sounding filename VAD.[21]

● Woods was working at the Stanford Artificial Intelligence Lab when he found a copy of *Adventure* on one of the facility's computers. This was not uncommon – PC gaming then was hidden on expensive government and corporate equipment (the only institutions that could afford powerful computers). But *Adventure* was different to everything else, and it consumed Woods.

● Crowther, at this time, was on a month's vacation in Alaska. Woods managed to get in touch through the simple strategy of emailing 'crowther' at every domain name then in existence, banking (correctly) on the name being unusual enough that he would find his intended recipient. With Crowther's blessing secured, Woods then took the source program and began adding to it. '[He] doubled its size and spread it all over the country,'[22] recalls crowther, 'so that when I came back from Alaska, people were playing it everywhere'.

● Woods's improvements were many. His version allowed players to 'save' their progress, take stock of their inventory, and check their score (out of a possible 250) for some primordial bragging rights. Saving was simply a practical measure: the game was likely to be played out-of-hours and under some kind of time pressure, an insight doubtless based on experience.

● This new *Adventure* expanded greatly upon Crowther's work, adding a new maze, a troll and a beanstalk, more magic words, a wandering pirate that would filch the player's treasures and numerous minor details like a bridge that can collapse. Woods made the existing maze more complex and gave objects new properties: in the original the player can acquire a bottle of water, used on a dying plant, but in Woods's version the container can then be refilled with oil at another location for use in a new puzzle.

➲ *Adventure* is the original inspiration to those who would go on to create the defining games in the genre. Don Woods, quoted in 'The History of Zork' in the Infocom 1985 newsletter: 'In early 1977 . . . [w]hen *Adventure* arrived at MIT, the reaction was typical: after everybody spent a lot of time doing nothing but solving the game (it's estimated that *Adventure* set the entire computer industry back two weeks), the true lunatics began to think about how they could do it better.'

➲ In particular, Woods's version was played in May 1977 at MIT by a group of players who, by June, had made serious progress on their own game called *ZORK*. Tim Anderson,

Marc Blank, Dave Lebling and Bruce Daniels designed and programmed a game about 'the ruins of an ancient empire lying far underground'. By 1979 they would form a company known as Infocom, which would be responsible for some of the greatest text games ever made.

➲ Scott Adams created a stripped-down version of *Adventure*, intended for a wider audience, known as *Adventureland*. Roberta Williams, who would found Sierra On-Line with her husband Ken, got hooked on *Adventure* and in 1980 the pair released *Mystery House*, the first text adventure game with visuals.

➲ But perhaps the biggest influence *Adventure* had was on a designer who was in a position to really do something about it. Warren Robinett was one of Atari's stars, in an environment where originality was prized above all, and realized that the premise and themes of *Adventure* could translate

Although the design of *Adventure* is pioneering, the quality of the writing is a big part of the appeal – and the game ebbs and flows with this, moving from terse 'exploratory' passages to long and languid explications of beautiful sights.

```
Colossal Cave Adventure ▸ Score: 65 ▸ Turns: 52
> LOOK
You are on the edge of a breath-taking view.  Far below you is an active
volcano, from which great gouts of molten lava come surging out, cascading
back down into the depths.  The glowing rock fills the farthest reaches
of the cavern with a blood-red glare, giving everything an eerie, macabre
appearance.  The air is filled with flickering sparks of ash and a heavy
smell of brimstone.  The walls are hot to the touch, and the thundering
of the volcano drowns out all other sounds.  Embedded in the jagged roof
far overhead are myriad formations composed of pure white alabaster,
which scatter their murky light into sinister apparitions upon the walls.
To one side is a deep gorge, filled with a bizarre chaos of tortured rock
which seems to have been crafted by the Devil Himself.  An immense river
of fire crashes out from the depths of the volcano, burns its way through
the gorge, and plummets into a bottomless pit far off to your left.
To the right, an immense geyser of blistering steam erupts continuously
from a barren island in the center of a sulfurous lake, which bubbles
ominously.  The far right wall is aflame with an incandescence of its own,
which lends an additional infernal splendor to the already hellish scene.
A dark, foreboding passage exits to the south.

> gorge

What?
What's next?
```

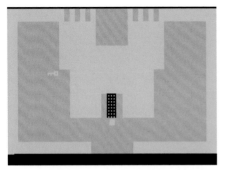

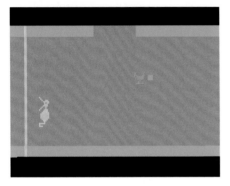

The opening screen of *Adventure* follows basic design principles, top, by giving the player a very simple puzzle to solve (take key to door), which will later occur in more complex configurations – in this case that means carrying keys across the map.

The dragons that haunt *Adventure*'s map, bottom, could hardly be described as visually terrifying, but the fact they instantly see and home in on your avatar – and will follow across multiple screens – raises the tension.

beautifully into a top-down 2D world.

➜ Robinett intuited that Atari's more mainstream audience could be drawn into *Adventure* as he had been, but only with a more direct and less frustrating interface – because the original was a confusing game, easily understood by the initiated but baffling to outsiders. It's not much fun cycling through different word combinations, and being told that the computer doesn't know what you mean when you don't know what it's looking for. (One could persuasively argue that Crowther's *Adventure* was popular among computer specialists precisely because it was obtuse, and did not give up secrets easily.).

➜ 'My boss told me not to work on it, because it was impossible to do on the Atari 2600 console, which had only 1/8 K of RAM and 4K of ROM,' said Robinett. 'But I worked on the idea anyway.'[23]

➜ Robinett had many problems to solve, not least because his take on *Adventure* would be a first in its own right – a 2D exploration game with many different rooms, items, and interactions. 'I just jumped in and started programming,' said Robinett. 'It evolved by trying things and seeing what worked . . . One of the first things I implemented was a dragon that chased you around. But there were no mazes at that point, and no bat, no way to kill the dragon, so it wasn't a playable game at that point, just an experiment with some promising elements.'

❯ The finished game has thirty rooms in all and the player controls a brave yellow square that explores this environment to find a sword, keys to unlock each of the world's castles, an item-attracting magnet and a magic bridge. The goal is to find the Enchanted Chalice, stolen by an evil magician, and save the kingdom.

❯ The game's most exciting feature is the three dragons that roam across this world, guarding various locations and items. If they find the player they give chase and will swallow their avatar in one bite. If this happens, the player can hit 'reset' on the Atari console to reincarnate at the starting yellow castle – but all objects will return to where they were and, as punishment, any dead dragons are also reincarnated. The 'continue' option is now an industry standard, but this was one of its first appearances.

❯ Killing the dragons was accomplished by finding a sword that the character could poke into them, and Robinett's *Adventure* innovated even further with a 'bat' that would fly around the game world randomly, picking up items and dropping them off. This humble bat is the first video-game sprite to have different behaviours: an 'alert' state where it will pick up and drop off items, and an 'ignore' state where it will be temporarily content with what it has.

❯ Robinett added a final flourish. One of

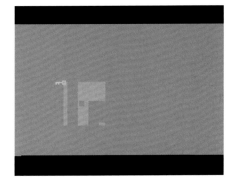

This may not look like much, but it's an example of Warren Robinett's genius at squeezing what he could from limited hardware – this *Adventure* maze is 'lit' only around the player's avatar, which makes navigating and remembering the route that much harder.

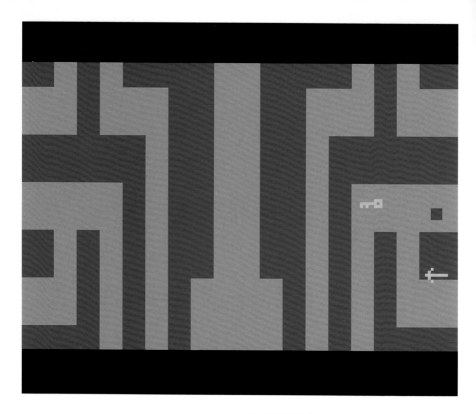

If you missed the player avatar in Atari's *Adventure*, no wonder – it's the same colour as the walls on the right edge of the screen. Such compromises are par for the course with the 2600. The 'arrow' is the game's sword, the point of which will subdue the dragons.

A BRIEF HISTORY OF VIDEO GAMES

Atari's most infamous and counter-productive policies was a refusal to give its designers credit. Robinett added a room, nearly impossible to find, that contained the text 'Created by Warren Robinett'. Years later it was discovered, by which time he had left the company, and Atari decided to christen the room an 'Easter Egg' and leave it intact.

⊙ Adventure would go on to sell over one million units and in turn was arguably a key influence on the design of later games like The Legend of Zelda, Shigeru Miyamoto's classic Nintendo series. Miyamoto has never gone on the record about Adventure or, indeed, ever been very forthcoming about direct influences from competitors, but Nintendo was well aware of Atari's work and it is inconceivable that a copy of such a popular game didn't end up in Kyoto.

⊙ As text adventures enjoyed their new commercial appeal, the only odd thing was that the original Adventure still hadn't been released to the public. Although the game was in a final form it took another protagonist – Jim Gillogly who worked at the Rand Corporation – to port the game from the original FORTRAN source code into C for UNIX. This version was released in 1981 with the blessing of both Crowther and Woods, and under the name of The Original Adventure was finally known to the public.

⊙ Perhaps the true measure of Adventure's greatness is that, even now, people can't agree on how to categorize it. Interactive fiction, hypertext, cybertext or text adventure; none captures it whole. Adventure is the first game to make exploration a focus of the player's experience, and in doing so crafted a linear structure that allowed for branching experimentation. In sparking the imaginations of millions of players and creators, then and now, it was the first virtual world to actually feel like one.

Uncle Clive and Big Jack

➔ Video games had so far found their biggest markets in Japan and the USA, but this didn't mean Europe had been sleeping. It just hadn't been well served. Similarly to the States, it had been flooded with own-brand *Pong* machines after the release of the Magnavox Odyssey, and home-grown consoles like the German-made Interton VC-4000 console didn't live up to their fantastical names.

➔ The biggest market for video games in Europe, to this day, is the United Kingdom – Eastern European states and Russia may be larger overall, but have the reputation of being somewhat black markets (this is an increasingly historical viewpoint, but remains true). And what cracked the UK market was like nothing else: the Sinclair ZX80 home computer.

➔ Known to his fans as Uncle Clive, Clive Sinclair was in the island's great tradition of tinkering inventors and had achieved fame through low-cost electronics products – anything from digital watches to portable TVs and calculators. Sometimes, as with the watch, the product was a dud and nearly bankrupted Sinclair, but he played a big role in bringing electronics to the mass market.

➔ The ZX80 was very much in this tradition. While America had the jaw-dropping but pricey Apple II, Sinclair produced a computer kit that sold at an unbelievably low price – £79.95 for the kit (with soldering required) or £99.95 assembled. The aesthetics probably had Steve Jobs choking on his cornflakes and the 1KB of memory certainly did, but this price point made the ZX80 truly accessible to a generation of young children and adults.

➔ It quickly became Britain's fastest-selling home computer and, over the next few years, would see the improved ZX81 (March 1981) and ZX Spectrum (April 1982). The last model, in its 48k and 128k incarnations, saw the greatest video games – though sadly Uncle

The ZX80 used a Z80 central processing unit, and the 'X' in the name was added to give it a sense of magic. Designer Rick Dickinson was responsible for the iconic look and one-piece membrane keyboard, though unfortunately such style came at the price of reliability. (Photo credit: Daniel Ryde)

The ZX Spectrum, top, was
the machine that really
took off for Clive Sinclair,
eventually selling over five
million units. Games were
loaded using a separate tape
deck, which later Sinclair
systems would incorporate
into the hardware.
(Photo credit: Bill Bertram)

The ZX Spectrum 128,
bottom, was launched in
1985 and added a huge
amount of functionality, but
more importantly fixed the
heatsink issues that had
plagued Sinclair machines
since the ZX80. It was also
the first to output sound
through the TV rather than
a tinny internal speaker.
(Photo credit: Bill Bertram)

Clive himself had no interest in the emerging medium. Sinclair's ambitions in creating a mass-market computer had been rather grander than a de facto games machine, but sadly 'de fact' of the mass market was that one type of software sold: games. Almost every Spectrum owner used it to play video games to the exclusion of all other possible activities. Sinclair never liked this.

➔ Luckily many others did, from the start, and so Sinclair's machines resulted in an outpouring of hobbyist creativity. It was relatively easy to program for the machines, and games were sold on audio tapes that could be easily copied – an entrepreneur's dream setup. The era of the bedroom coder had begun.

➔ Many of the names that made it 'big' are now forgotten: particularly early hits like *Miner 2049er*, developed by Big Five Software, which popularized platforming games on the Sinclair machines before the release of *Super*

Mario Bros. soon afterwards made it look like a fossil.

➔ Those that retain some vitality are the more experimental and freeform equivalents. *Chuckie Egg* was released in 1983, programmed by Nigel Alderton, and tasked you with nicking eggs while dodging the understandably angry hens. *Chuckie Egg* had fluid movement and a graceful jumping arc, but was endlessly replayable thanks to randomized enemy patterns and your inability to jump over hens to escape a corner. It even had a brilliant, surreal twist: throughout the game you're watched by an expressionless duck, caged in the top corner. Beat the game and things start up again. But this time the duck is free and flies around the level before homing in on you with pant-wetting precision.

➔ Similarly experimental, but even nuttier, was 1983's *Manic Miner*. Here you play Willy, trapped in a mine with a dwindling air supply, over a series of twenty themed rooms

Chuckie Egg was released simultaneously on the Spectrum and BBC Micro, the latter of which arguably had more to do with its subsequent cult appeal – the BBC Micro was widely adopted in UK schools and so became a focal point for illicit gaming sessions.

filled with deadly toilet seats, psychopathic penguins and poisonous pansies. Backed by out-of-copyright classical compositions, Willy has to nab a key and escape each screen as his air bar ticks ever-further down.

➔ *Manic Miner* was the first game from developer Matthew Smith, but *Jet Set Willy* is his lasting achievement – a complex twitch platformer full of tricks, where Willy has to clean the mansion he bought after escaping the first game with armfuls of lucre. The surrealist strain in British games like this probably owe as much to Monty Python as Salvador Dalí, and *Jet Set Willy* remains fondly remembered for set-pieces like 'The Nightmare Room' filled with ghostly housekeepers; Willy suddenly turns into a flying mouse and has to dodge giant feet.

➔ There are many more great games in a catalogue estimated at over 2,400 titles, but it's worth ending by considering what was particular about the commercial environment the Sinclair machines created. They were only really a success in the UK and of modest capabilities, but awakened a huge games-buying appetite that was capable of supporting a large development community. The Sinclair machine was also relatively easy to code for, dirt cheap and upgraded several times.

➔ This meant it could support a wide range of both authors and developers. Julian Gollop's Spectrum strategy titles are classic designs like *Rebelstar* (1986), where you control a group of raiders who have to infiltrate a moon base and destroy the core computer – before being hunted down by the AI defence squad. *Rebelstar* only had a single map but made it endlessly replayable by mixing deep strategic elements with a dash of the unpredictable – such as a raider panicking if morale gets low.

➔ *Rebelstar* also introduced 'opportunity fire', an incredibly important mechanic for strategy games whereby units 'covering' a patch of

Manic Miner was the first Spectrum title to feature in-game music and certainly went to town with it. The title screen plays an arrangement of 'The Blue Danube' while the in-game tune is a version of Edvard Grieg's 'In the Hall of the Mountain King'.

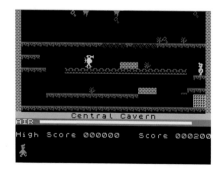

A BRIEF HISTORY OF VIDEO GAMES

ground can fire as opposing units move across them. The basic design of *Rebelstar* and its sequel *Laser Squad* underpins the brilliant XCOM series of games to the present day, while other Gollop titles are still admired for the elegance of their interlocking tactical options. *Chaos*, for example, casts players against each other as wizards summoning creatures to do battle – but you can also create illusions that, if they fool an oponent, might swing a battle.

➡ These video games have a great purity beyond their standard scenarios. Whether it's the simple inclusion of mind games as a key gameplay element in *Chaos*, or the way Gollop adds a 'realtime' element to turn-based strategy with 'opportunity fire', they are games with the clarity to understand what players might want to do in a given situation – and systems elegant enough to let them.

➡ The opposite extreme to such refined takes on established genre is designers

experimenting with the form itself. Designer Mel Croucher, who by 1984 was a veteran of the system's software landscape, teamed up with coder Andrew Stagg for *Deus Ex Machina*. The phrase 'god into the machine' originated in the irreconcilable entanglements Greek plays would often reach, which were solved by a god appearing onstage to sort out the problems with a bit of commandment. Here the phrase resonates through a game built around raising a living being from foetal stage to old age, via a machine.

➡ The creature is a 'mutant', some kind of unwanted side-effect from genetics trials, and exists in a nightmare dystopia that owes more than a little to *1984*. *Deus Ex Machina* was also more ambitious than a mere video game: this was a multimedia project that came bundled with essential atmosphere in the form of an ambient soundtrack, interspersed with dialogue (read by musician Ian Dury, comedian Frankie Howerd and

The gameplay sections of *Deus Ex Machina* loosely focused on body horror, with the clash of organic and inorganic matter the central theme. These visuals were, on the Spectrum, outstanding for their time.

The packaging and marketing campaign for *Deus Ex Machina* were as much part of the experience as the Spectrum game itself, and perhaps intended to deflect somewhat from what was actually possible on the machine.

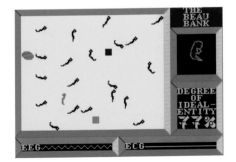

The trick to *Skool Daze* was in timing your pranks in such a way that another kid, preferably the bully Angelface, was in view when the teacher was looking for a culprit. Accumulate 10,000 lines and it's game over.

A BRIEF HISTORY OF VIDEO GAMES

actor John Pertwee), designed to be played alongside the game. The action takes the form of abstract minigames, with everything themed around nurturing and caring for the creature.

● It's even more of an abstract and weird experience now, because in 1984 *Deus Ex Machina* was presenting a cutting-edge society through reasonably impressive technology. The current era makes even the Spectrum's best software look horribly dated, but oddly enough this retains a hypnotic charm even now – the huge sprites, gentle style of play and unsettling background chatter still create an original headspace.

● With such big ideas and sculpted execution, *Deus Ex Machina* was released to a great critical reception, mainstream interest and almost complete commercial failure. It was probably always a hard sell but the project's nature and high cost to the consumer, in a market built on budget compilations, meant many traditional retailers simply wouldn't stock it.

● Finally, the oddballs. Pure excellence and lofty artistic ambitions are one side of history, but it wouldn't be complete without the likes of *Skool Daze*. Created by a husband and wife team, *Skool Daze* is a genuine charmer that takes the mundane and makes something memorable. You play schoolboy Eric, and on-screen can see the whole school and other characters – the headmaster, teachers, the bully, the swot and so on. Your goal is to get Eric's report card out of the headmaster's safe, but there were countless ways of doing this. And the pleasure of *Skool Daze* wasn't in beating the game anyway, but in playing around with it – causing mischief for others to take the blame, setting traps or just watching the little people tick over.

● The Spectrum was the original computer for the masses. It just so happened that this mass was on one island. Clive Sinclair holds an odd place in British society, a genuine superstar long since dropped from the limelight, regarded as an amusing boffin by some and as a failure by others (Sinclair's post-Spectrum V-5 electric bike is a famous disaster). But for anyone who grew up gaming in 1980s Britain, there's a reason for Sir Clive Sinclair's nickname, used with genuine affection: he will always be Uncle Clive.

➡ 'Computers for the masses, not the classes' was a favourite saying of Jack Tramiel, who realised his own business could take some inspiration from the ZX80. Tramiel was the founder of Commodore International and one of the most exceptional men in gaming history. He was one of the Polish Jews rounded up by the Nazis during the Second World War and sent to a concentration camp – in his case the most infamous of all, Auschwitz.

➡ Almost everyone Tramiel knew would die over the next six years, but he survived.

At an early stage the Nazis had asked for volunteers to work on building the Autobahn road network: constant hard labour, watched over by soldiers that would beat the prisoners for punishment and amusement. But Tramiel knew it was in the Germans' interests to keep their labourers productive and well fed, and so he made it through to the end of the war.

➡ After being liberated by the United States, Tramiel, with little to go back to in Poland, decided to join the US Army. He was stationed in New Jersey and, among other things, learned how to repair typewriters. He saved his money, opened a typewriter repair store in New York and shortly afterwards founded the Commodore Portable Typewriter Company in Toronto in 1954.

➡ The story of how this grew into Commodore International is its own book, but much of it depends on Tramiel's absolutely ruthless business practices and a sharp eye for upcoming trends. Perhaps because he had seen the real thing, Tramiel had no difficulty declaring (often) that 'business is war' and referring to his hard-nosed philosophies as 'the religion' of Commodore. Payment from dealers was demanded immediately. Suppliers were paid late. Some companies were driven to bankruptcy by unpaid bills, then 'saved' by a Commodore takeover (at a knock-down price). Employees that didn't practise what Tramiel preached were soon looking for work elsewhere.

● Commodore had entered the calculator market in the 1960s, and the big moment for Tramiel came when the company was on its knees in the midst of a price war. In 1975 Texas Instruments, the main supplier of calculator parts, had decided to take over the industry by putting out its own range of cheap machines and then raising component prices for the competition. Only a fresh injection of capital from Commodore's chairman and main investor, Irving Gould,

kept the company alive and allowed Tramiel to start reinforcing his supply chain.

● Tramiel bought several small chip manufacturers in 1976, including MOS Technologies for $800,000. The company was bought because it had been making computer chips since 1969 and was in financial trouble (which always suited Tramiel), but there was one condition: chip designer Chuck Peddle had to join Commodore as head of engineering. The reason? MOS's new killer product: the 6502 microprocessor (which would become a key component of the Apple II and Atari 400/800 computers). Peddle had designed a small computer based around the 6502, the KIM-1, and had soon convinced Tramiel that calculators were a dead end.

● Tramiel knew the value of owning your production facilities, and aimed to move into home computers by creating low-priced computers. Steve Jobs gave Peddle a demonstration of the Apple II, hoping to sell it to Commodore, but Tramiel thought the price too high. Instead, he ordered three engineers to create a computer in six months, announcing the PET 2001 in January 1977, and produced the first all-in-one home computer and the first to retail at under $1,000.

● The Commodore PET series, however, was about Serious Computing – they were designed for schools and offices, with robust cases and monochrome visuals. And were a big success in the educational sector. But Tramiel saw a future beyond this: one where Commodore could become the Ford Motors of the silicon age.

● By 1980 competition had become fierce, and Tramiel wanted a cheap colour computer ready to go. Commodore almost stumbled into releasing the VIC-20. The first computer ever to sell a million units, the VIC-20 was cheap-and-cheerful but thanks to this popularity and the ability to program the machine's (tiny though expandable) memory

it became a classroom for many future programmers. Unfortunately the VIC-20 was too underpowered to do more than play host to bad arcade conversions and so-so ports of Spectrum games. The big exception was the work of Jeff Minter, who as Llamatron produced great versions of *Gridrunner* and its sequel *Matrix*, and continued supporting the machine after its peak with excellent shooters like *Laser Zone*.

● Commodore's programmers and engineers, bored with the company's PET line, proposed to Tramiel a true sequel to the VIC-20. An affordable machine for the masses, sure, but one that could actually go toe-to-toe with the competition on performance. The project was given the subtle codename 'VIC-40', and designed over three months by Bob Russell, Bob Yannes and David Ziembicki.

● At the January 1982 Consumer Electronics Show the machine was presented and rebranded as the Commodore 64 (referencing

![Gridrunner screenshot]

Jeff Minter's *Gridrunner* design has gone through several iterations over the decades – and was most recently seen as an ios

version. Minter's trademark as a designer was reworking and updating classic shooter designs, and keeping them relevant.

The Commodore 64 faced more competition than preceding systems but showed incredible longevity thanks to a virtuous cycle of high software sales and continued third-party support. (Photo credit: Evan Amos)

A BRIEF HISTORY OF VIDEO GAMES

the memory size in Kbytes, in-line with Commodore's other products). The machine blew the minds of journalists and industry alike, but the killer fact was the price tag: $595. The Atari 800 sold at $899; the Apple II at over $1,200. The Commodore 64 was released in August 1982 with the unforgettable advertising line 'You won't get a better computer for double the price'. (It seems churlish to point out that part of the reason for this was that the C64 was sold as a standalone computer, while the Apple II came with its own monitor and disk drive.)

➜ The C64 sold rapidly and excited developers, who were enthused by the size of such a user base and pleasantly surprised at the detailed documentation provided by Commodore (Atari, for example, kept its technical information secret). It is estimated that for the first few years of its life Commodore sold around two million units a year, and by the time the C64 was

discontinued in April 1994 the total sold was, depending on whom you believe, as low as 12.5 or as high as 30 million.

➜ The sales and open architecture of the Commodore 64 meant it quickly saw high-quality developers making software – and, just as importantly, publishing cross-platform. One of the classics was originally designed for the Atari 400/800, Danielle Bunten's *M.U.L.E.* (1983), a four-player trading game (opponents could be either human or AI) about colonizing a planet through effective resource management. The core mechanic was the M.U.L.E.s themselves, which were purchased and upgraded before being assigned to mine resources – but had a nasty habit of running off.

➜ The reason *M.U.L.E.* is so good comes down to its sophisticated economic system, which is built around supply and demand of the planet's minerals and a few other resources. Players end up competing against

M.U.L.E. stands for Multi-Use Labor Element, the four-legged workers that the player uses to develop and harvest resources from the land acquired. Many later games pay tribute to this, with a particularly nice reference in *Starcraft II* where the Terran race calls down M.U.L.E.s to harvest minerals.

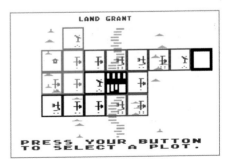

each other through a realtime auction system that can be both manipulated and predicted – where essentially success comes down to out-thinking your opponents. Smart design balanced out the struggle so, for example, the losing player would win an auction in the event of a tied bid and be less likely to suffer from one of *M.U.L.E.*'s random catastrophes.

⬤ More straightforward, but an equally tight design, was Andrew Braybook's *Paradroid* (1985). Braybook was something of a C64 wizard, producing the absolutely gorgeous shooter *Uridium*, but *Paradroid*'s genius was in the interlocking mechanics. You play an 'Influence Device', basically a floating robotic head, trapped aboard a ship infested with much more powerful droids. But you can sneak up on these opponents and 'link' to them, initiating a hacking minigame where success lets you take them over – and failure means your current host is destroyed (fail a hack as the Influence Device and it's game over).

⬤ The twist is that droids can only be occupied for so long before you need a new host, and so *Paradroid* can become an extraordinarily tense experience. The ship's layout mixes wide-open spaces with twisting corridors, forcing changes of strategy, and the need for new hosts means you have to 'sneak' around as fast and aggressively as possible. The switch between controlling the Influence Device and the killer droids is as sweet a central twist as could be had: like *Pac-Man*, that regular flip between hunter and hunted really gets the adrenalin pumping.

⬤ A brilliant oddity is Ocean Software's *Wizball* (1987), a game about bringing colour to a monochrome planet, which begins with your controlling a bouncing ball. It seems unpromising, particularly given the lack of guidance, but soon you realize that picking up pearls unlocks the *Wizball*'s latent abilities: seven in total ranging from shooting to thrust control to antigrav and even summoning

Paradroid was one of the first games to reward players for achievements beyond the core goals, for example, clearing ships entirely of enemy robots. It also features an early example of 'New Game+', whereby completing the game simply makes it restart with higher difficulty.

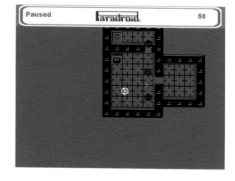

a cat to hoover up goodies on the floor. There's been nothing else quite like *Wizball* because it's such a singular mix of genres and capabilities, in essence a game about working out a strange system, mastering it and bringing a world back to life.

➜ Perhaps the most influential game ever released on the Commodore 64, however, was regarded as more of a curiosity at the time. Designers David Crane and Rich Gold worked at Activision and had an idea for a 'life simulation game', but where the likes of *Deus Ex Machina* and *Alter Ego* were all portentous text and dark visions, this would be a much more cheery affair.

➜ *Little Computer People* (1985) came with a manual that emphasized these little people were real and you were simply the caretaker. At the start of the game is a side-on view of a house, and soon a little man walks in. And starts going about his business – cooking dinner, reading the paper, making a fire, going to bed, watching the telly and so on. You can interact with him by offering gifts, entering simple commands or playing a game of poker.

➜ This may sound a little passive but, especially at the time, no one had experienced anything like *Little Computer People*. The character wasn't just funny to watch, but its 'personality' was randomly generated by each copy of the game (so no two were exactly alike) and it would retain a basic memory of its interactions with the player. Sometimes he'd seem to sulk, at others he'd rap the screen for your attention. The bewitching effect is not quite so strong these days, but you feel an unmistakeable interest in what happens next. Sadly *Little Computer People* never saw its mooted sequel, though it inspired LucasArts's ambitious *Habitat* and later Will Wright's outstanding *Sims* series.

➜ *Alter Ego* started from a similar place but went in a completely different direction. Essentially a text adventure written by a

Expansions were apparently planned for *Little Computer People*, which would have added more objects and interactions to the original, but the muted commercial reception meant they never came to pass.

psychologist (one Peter J. Favaro PhD) *Alter Ego* – which has male and female versions – asks you to guide a person from birth to death through seven stages of life. This involves directing the character's behaviour and watching the consequences (if any) play out, either immediately or far down the line. Although the background statistics being tracked sound meagre ('Physical', 'Confidence', 'Intellectual'), the outcomes are a funny and often slightly disturbing read – a feeling encouraged by the psychological explanations offered up alongside the main text. The quality of writing helps enormously in pulling you into even the most apparently boring stages of life: 'You reach your destination, grasp the rattle confidently and drool on it in victory!' Later the death of a pet goldfish may bring you up short, as the game gently chides you on refusing to show emotion: 'little children and adults often hide their feelings by remaining aloof and unaffected

on the outside'. *Alter Ego* could be a little sanctimonious, but when did a game last speak to you like that?

➔ Among such innovators were great but more straightforward titles like *Impossible Mission* (1984), which casts you as a James Bond type infiltrating a secret lair under a strict time limit, and *The Last Ninja* (1987), which mixed arcade combat and puzzle solving with beautiful isometric visuals.

➔ *Project Firestart* (1989) was an early example of what would become known as the survival-horror genre, crafting a brilliant atmosphere through environmental narrative and let down only by invisible enemies. Then there's *Lode Runner* (1984), an excellent puzzle-platformer that achieved classic status through the simple idea of letting players construct their own levels (even today there are huge databases of levels online, though sadly an Xbox 360 remake proved far too over-fussy to recapture the original's magic).

Alter Ego shows a branching tree of your choices as you play. Although there's a distinct whiff of 'scienciness' about the psychology, there's no denying the intrigue its logic manages to create – and the general sense of humour makes the few dark moments all the more shocking.

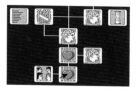

This is the barest sampling of what the Commodore 64 had to offer, and up until the early 1990s it continued to play host to original titles and conversions. The machine had enormous longevity and is still alive today thanks to its popularity in the demoscene subculture – which it kick-started. Although it may seem off the beaten track for video games, the demoscene is where many brilliant programmers and designers start out, learning to maximize a machine's capabilities by creating beautiful audiovisual 'demos'.

Over its lifetime the machine would see many hardware revisions (including the C64GS, which gave it the form function of a games console), the most important being the direct upgrade of the Commodore 128 – released in 1985. Although the C128 would sell around seven million units in total it was backwards-compatible with the C64, so sensible developers aimed their games at the larger joint market rather than taking advantage of the more powerful machine's capabilities.

Counter-intuitively, the Commodore 64's enormously successful strategy caused the end of Jack Tramiel. His goal with the C64 was market share and, with the low production price, the cost of the C64 was slashed repeatedly during 1983 to destroy rivals. Although this proved a sound decision in hindsight, the Commodore board of directors got cold feet. After an internal struggle and intense disagreement with Irving Gould, chairman of the board, Tramiel resigned in January 1984. He left Commodore International, the company he had founded in 1954, at the top of the video-games industry. A decade later it would declare bankruptcy. But that's another story, and Tramiel wasn't quite done yet.

Atari Shock!

→ If you were looking to buy a dedicated games console in 1982 you could take your pick from an abundance: the still-strong Atari VCS, the Atari 5200, the Bally Astrocade, the ColecoVision, the Coleco Gemini, the Emerson Arcadia 2001, the Fairchild Channel F II, the Intellivision and Intellivision II, the Magnavox Odyssey 2, various own-brand Sears systems, the Tandyvision, the VIC-20 and the Vectrex. Not a complete list, but this book is only so long.

→ The games available across these platforms varied wildly in quality, but an enormous amount of them were poor. This was mainly thanks to the 'gold rush' effect of Atari's boom years, which meant that quality developers were ever more outnumbered by a boggy mix of amateurs, opportunists and optimists producing software. There were too many video games, and too many of them sucked.

→ Consoles were also facing competition from their geekier older brother, the home computer, which had transformed during the 1970s from a hobbyist niche into widely available (through mail order at least) hardware. In 1977 the Apple II was followed to market by Commodore's PET and Tandy's TRS-80, by 1979 Atari was trying to shoehorn itself in with the Atari 400 and 800 computers, and in 1981 IBM's PC 5150 set a new industry standard (the omnipresent phrase 'IBM compatible' was born with this machine) and popularized the term 'personal computer' (*Adventure* was one of the IBM 5150's launch titles and by its very presence astonished industry-watchers, who had expected IBM's approach to be entirely business-focused). The release of the Commodore 64 in late 1982 also appealed to console owners – an affordable PC with internal chips specifically designed for use in games. By this point PCs were making existing consoles look like fossils and, as a bonus, PC games were easy to duplicate and much less expensive.

→ Atari was being unsteadily piloted by Ray Kassar who, in a moment of madness that must have seemed like genius at the time, had licensed *Pac-Man* for the VCS. The game's development time was extremely short, in order to hit Christmas 1981, and the resulting product is appalling.

→ The VCS system was never up to replicating *Pac-Man*'s array of sounds and colours, never mind the smooth motion, and it has to be acknowledged that designer Tod Frye was working under incredible restrictions. Nevertheless the Atari 2600 *Pac-Man* takes a vibrant and colourful original and strips almost everything that's fun away – the most egregious change being how the maze designs are reconfigured.

→ Despite the game being rushed to hit Christmas it wasn't released until March 1982, with Atari so confident of success it

manufactured an astonishing twelve million cartridges. At this stage the company hadn't sold twelve million 2600s to play them on. A similarly huge marketing spend saw the game race off shelves – at first. By the end of 1982 Atari had managed to ship seven million copies of *Pac-Man*, but still had five million, by which point the game had stopped selling completely and retail buyers started asking for refunds.

→ Amazingly, Atari would repeat this behaviour at the end of the year. Steve Ross, CEO of Atari's parent company Warner Communications, had taken it upon himself to negotiate the rights to Steven Spielberg's upcoming blockbuster *E.T. the Extra-Terrestrial* for a reported $20–$25 million. Ray Kassar, to his credit, called it 'a dumb idea'. But the deal was done by the end of July 1982 and the game needed to be ready by September to be manufactured for Christmas. Kassar asked Howard Scott Warshaw, a young

Although only one *Pac-Man* ghost can be seen in this screen, there are four in the game – but in order to display them the Atari 2600 has to flicker between the sprites, creating an extremely ugly and disorienting effect. It is the least of this game's crimes.

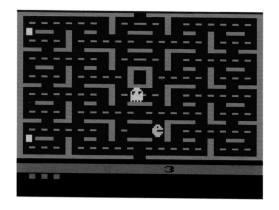

A BRIEF HISTORY OF VIDEO GAMES

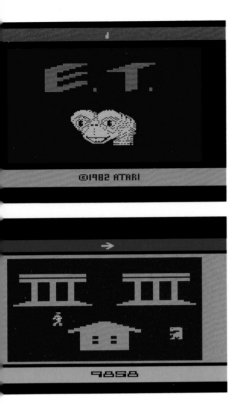

Atari designer, whether he could manage a previously unthinkable six-week turnaround. The prospect of meeting Spielberg, a holiday in Hawaii once work was complete and $200,000 persuaded him that he could.

➲ The game Warshaw produced is often described as 'the worst video game ever'. This is perhaps unfair, though it is certainly one of the worst high-profile video games ever made. The goal of the game is to phone home by finding phone parts scattered across a top-down 2D landscape, which is populated by adults that 'kidnap' E.T. and steal phone parts. The world is also full of pits which E.T. can fall into, and has a strict time limit.

➲ *E.T.* is infuriating to play even on a basic level, with E.T.'s movements sluggish and the pixel-perfect collision detection on pits utterly bizarre (you'll fall in when nowhere near because a part of E.T.'s head touches it). Finally the visuals, intended to ape a movie high in the cultural consciousness of the time, can't

Clearly all the effort involved in creating *E.T.* went into the title screen. What makes the game such a colossal indictment of Atari under Kassar isn't so much that it's a bad game, but that the company bet so heavily on it. Developer Howard Scott Warshaw, given the time he had to make the game, did well just to create something that worked.

help but make the venerable VCS look rather foolish. As a standalone surrealist experiment *E.T.* may have worked, but as a licensed video game it stains the genre to this day.

➔ Needless to say, Atari manufactured around five million cartridges and got ready to ride the gravy train. Initially *E.T.* sold about 1.5 million units, which officially makes it one of the best-selling VCS titles ever. But then sales flatlined, enraged customers started returning the game and retailers in turn began demanding refunds.

➔ Two points about these games. The first is that with *Pac-Man* Ray Kassar destroyed any remaining vestige of Atari's hard-won reputation for producing quality software – not just by developing the game in such a half-cocked manner, but by then marketing it so thoroughly. The second is that both games badly damaged relationships with retailers, who had spent a year with *Pac-Man* cartridges piling up after being persuaded to place gigantic orders, and now had a ton of *E.T.* cartridges to boot. Atari would never again enjoy its former position or influence.

➔ These games shouldn't be taken as the sole authors of the crash, but rather illustrations of the general state of the market at the time: consoles relied overly on arcade conversions which weren't very good, variants of successful games that had been around forever, and in technological terms simply weren't moving with the times. There were plenty of other high-profile software failures like *Skeet Shoot*, alongside poor hardware options and a flood of me-too clones. But it is undeniable that one company's unsold inventory and bottom line started the panic: Atari was in serious debt.

➔ On 7 December 1982 Ray Kassar announced a hefty cut in Atari's revenue forecast to the stock market and, immediately afterwards, parent company Warner saw its shares dive 35 per cent (losing

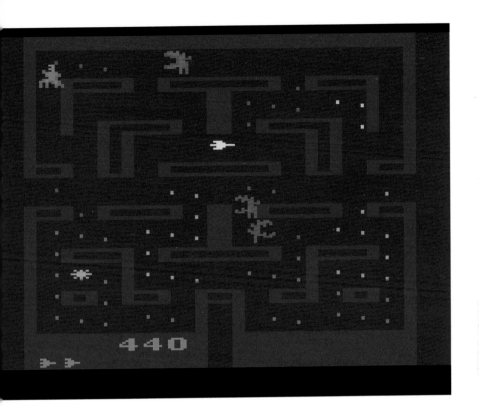

Although hardly as famous as the Atari *Pac-Man* and *E.T.*, turning Ridley Scott's *Alien* into a *Pac-Man* clone takes some beating for chutzpah. It also features three aliens, which is an early example of how little respect games sometimes show for grade-A source material.

$1.3 billion in value). Over 1983 Atari would cut a third of its workforce and haemorrhage around $400 million as it tried to recover. Ray Kassar was ousted, the problems grew, and in 1984 Warner finally sold Atari to former Commodore CEO Jack Tramiel.

➔ On shop floors it was a bloodbath. The marketplace was over-saturated with poor-quality titles that weren't selling and ended up filling bargain bins for $5 (previous RRP $35). Shops tried to return unsold stock only to find many developers already bust (which meant more games in the bargain bin), and in turn the only developers left were adapting by producing low-quality games they could sell for $5.

➔ This was the end for Magnavox, which brought Ralph Baer's dream to life as the Odyssey in 1971. So too Coleco, which abandoned the ColecoVision in favour of trying the PC market with the Coleco Adam (1985), but soon abandoned electronics

altogether. Countless minor developers and publishers either went bankrupt or limped on, irreparably damaged.

➔ The crash was perceived at the time as heralding the end of US consumers' appetite for video games; certainly by toy retailers, who regarded video games as a fad and wouldn't stock them again for years. With hindsight this may have been a misreading: the crash shows that the audience was becoming increasing discerning about the quality of its entertainment, while simultaneously the industry was trying to serve swill.

➔ The dedicated games machines available at the time of the crash were in some cases six years old, their libraries stuffed with pale conversions of arcade hits and shovelware from a whole host of poor developers out to strike gold. In contrast to this were the more expensive but more powerful home computers, which offered unquestionably better gaming experiences. The market had segmented between these two options and nothing sat in the middle.

➡ It is telling that, first of all, the Commodore 64 sold well – the capabilities, price point and software were impossible to resist. But equal weight should be given to the machine that later showed the crash was over, the Nintendo Entertainment System (NES). Launched in the USA in 1986, in the face of enormous apathy from retailers, the NES was a dedicated games console but became a phenomenon because of software quality.

➡ The most emblematic story from 1983's video-game crash comes from that September. It involves ten to twenty trucks pulling up to a New Mexico landfill at night and burying millions of dollars worth of unsold Atari inventory, including countless *E.T.* cartridges. It was reported at the time, but Atari claimed to the *New York Times* that it had only dumped broken items and returns.

A few days later, for reasons unknown, the site was covered in concrete.

➡ Over the years this became something of an urban legend until production company Fuel Industries was granted permission to excavate the site in 2014. Former Atari manager James Heller admitted he had been responsible for the original burial, and the concrete, but that 'only' 728,000 cartridges had been buried.

➡ Almost immediately the excavators started finding cartridges in the landfill: some crushed beyond recognition, others flattened like trading cards. Among them were copies of *Yars' Revenge*, Howard Scott Warshaw's great first game, next to all those *E.T.* cartridges he had a hand in, as well as *Star Raiders*, *Warlords*, *Defender*, *Centipede* – the list goes on with almost any game you care to name. The idea was always that the landfill contained just *E.T.* cartridges. Now we can see it was, in reality, Atari's grave too.

The Golden Age of the Arcades

Amusement arcades existed even before *Pong*, filled with electro-mechanical games like Sega's *Periscope* (1966), *Missile* (1969) and *Grand Prix* (1969). These machines used a mixture of lights, projected film scenes, plastic objects and bespoke controllers to create one-off entertainments that certainly earned their quarters but were not video games.

The success of *Pong* changed everything, with the industry shifting steadily towards fully electronic cabinets – not least because they were easier to mass-produce and had fewer moving parts, so less maintenance was required. Arcade games began to be seen in bars, bowling alleys and restaurants, while slowly but surely dedicated venues became more common.

In the 1970s and throughout the 1980s arcade machines had a key advantage over home video games: these dedicated and expensive cabinets offered visuals, sound effects and processing power far outstripping anything that could be bought in retail stores. The pay-to-play nature of arcade games also resulted in particular design focus, that of giving the customer value for money while somehow also getting them off the machine as quickly as possible, resulting in many of the best and most innovative games of the time – often housed in custom cabinets to even further enhance the experience.

Opinions differ as to when the golden age of arcades began but it is difficult to see why: the first bona-fide arcade phenomenon was Taito's *Space Invaders* (1978), which was so popular that following its Japanese release arcades dedicated to the game were opened. Designed by Tomohiro Nishikado, with enemy designs inspired by H. G. Wells's *The War of the Worlds*, the *Space Invaders* cabinet used custom hardware and plastic overlays to colour its black and white visuals. From June 1978 to the end of the year Taito sold 100,000

Space Invaders machines and grossed $600 million, and by 1980 300,000 machines were installed around the globe.

➔ *Space Invaders* is in some respects the first modern video game – using the tools available to not only give feedback to the player but to act upon the player as well. You control a small ship, Earth's last line of defence, which can be moved horizontally across the bottom of the screen. Four barriers sit just above your firing position, which will stop incoming shots. Then there are the massed ranks of the invaders.

➔ The invaders are in five even horizontal lines that move from left to right, accompanied by rhythmic bleeps, and, when they reach the right side, drop down one line vertically. The goal is to stop the invaders reaching Earth, and as invaders are destroyed the remaining enemies move faster. Previously, the audio in games had mainly been part of the title screen or an isolated sound effect. *Space Invaders* enveloped not just the player's fingers and eyes but their ears, too, the beat's tempo paralleling the increasing speed of the ever-closing invaders.

➔ The player's ship shoots straight upwards, and there can be three shots on the screen at one time. This is crucial because any missed shot will stop you firing until it has passed off the top of the screen, making wild firing the worst kind of tactic – and the surest route to defeat. Shots also take their time to travel, meaning that a player has to compensate as the invaders get closer and closer.

➔ The best *Space Invaders* players seem almost superhuman in their precision, whittling down the massed enemies one-by-one in a relentless pattern of predictive bullets. This mindset is the key to *Space Invaders*'s enduring appeal, even now. It hits a primal part of the mind and causes the player to feel some kind of panic, when the only way to play is with cold-minded efficiency.

The first *Space Invaders* cabinet had black and white visuals, which were soon jazzed up by the addition of coloured strips across the screen and eventually superseded by a colour version of the game.

A BRIEF HISTORY OF VIDEO GAMES

From simple elements *Space Invaders* crafts a complex and enduring masterpiece.

◉ *Space Invaders'* popularity was such that it inspired many games that were either outright clones or used similar mechanics. But it also made arcades popular enough to support more unusual titles. One of Atari's most interesting arcade games was *Lunar Lander* (1979), a physics-based simulation that had you trying to delicately set down a craft on the moon's surface. Although it lacked the lurid sensationalism of other titles, *Lunar Lander's* abstract visuals and simply gorgeous controls – which see you balance fuel and momentum by thrusting the craft's jets and taking advantage of gravity – created a unique world. And one that, in the midst of the invaders and brightly coloured bullets elsewhere, actually felt a little bit more like an accurate illusion of space.

◉ Atari at this point were on something of a hot streak, and there's no better example than *Battlezone* (1980). This used vector graphics, which allow visuals to be created from simple and clean lines, rather than amassing blocky pixels. Like all techniques it has advantages and disadvantages but it was perfect for *Battlezone*, which wowed players by creating a wireframe 3D landscape populated by marauding enemy tanks. It is difficult now to imagine just how much impact this visual style had: in a world of 2D top-down experiences, *Battlezone* felt and looked like a 'world' to be explored, filled with rich details like a background volcano, mountains and even the odd UFO.

◉ Playing the game is an equally revolutionary moment. Where earlier attempts at 3D are rudimentary, *Battlezone's* smooth motion led to an amalgam of styles: strategically manoeuvring your tank into the right position on an enemy, then firing the shell at just the right moment to catch them flush. The experience was so impressive that

Although nearly everything in *Battlezone's* world is hostile, only one enemy will ever engage the player at a time. It is also something of an early cover shooter, as 'solid' objects in the world will block enemy fire (and yours).

the US military requested Atari produce a more 'realistic' version for their use, which the game's creator Ed Rotberg agreed to only under duress and with the promise of a guarantee he would never have to do such work again. The crossover of video games and military training would become something of a minor theme in the future, and it began here.

→ 1980 also saw the release of *Defender*, the first notable game from one Eugene Jarvis – one of the great figures of the golden age of the arcades. Jarvis was the master of creating extremely difficult but scrupulously 'fair' systems that tapped into a subsection of the gaming audience increasingly comfortable with the challenges they met in arcades. *Defender*, a 2D side-scrolling shooter, was more complex than almost anything else available, and faster, but combined this with a looping landscape and highly unpredictable enemies. The title also hinted at its unusual

objective: the player's goal was to save little spacemen on the planet's surface from enemy craft that would swoop down and try to kidnap them (if they succeed, an even tougher enemy spawns).

Dave Theurer's *Tempest* was a 1981 'tube shooter', where the levels are viewed from a fixed perspective while enemies move towards the screen and rapidly swirl around the level's skeleton. A brilliant game in its own right, it has an unusually strong legacy thanks to Jeff Minter's various direct sequels.

Defender was the first original video game from Williams, a highly-regarded maker of pinball machines, and Eugene Jarvis was made head of development for his track record with same. The high difficulty and skill ceiling of *Defender* seems more understandable in this context.

A BRIEF HISTORY OF VIDEO GAMES

Defender is a hellishly difficult game, with your early hours guaranteed to be spent in failure. But the design underpinning it has such precision and potential it's near impossible to resist: the player's craft may be fragile, but it's also capable of withering firepower that blasts the alien hordes into beautiful pixel showers, a hyperspace mode that can escape certain death, and such sheer speed it's thrilling to play as a dodge-'em-up. *Defender* asks a simple question: are you really as good as you think?

➡ Many early arcade games were shooters, but among these are creepy originals. The most inspired is Atari's 1980 *Centipede*, designed by Ed Logg and Dona Bailey. *Centipede* is differentiated first and foremost by favouring a trackball for controls – which gives the player finer degrees of precision when aiming. *Centipede* is all about planning your shots. Set in a surreal garden landscape, a giant centipede starts at the top of the screen and moves across horizontally before descending one row closer to the player. The key mechanic is that each shot to the centipede's body turns that section into a solid 'brick' and divides the creature's body in two. These bricks also send the backmost segment downwards, so that your first shot usually makes two centipedes out of one and splits the incoming threat.

➡ The key to *Centipede* is that careless firing costs lives. The beast can be cleverly managed by experienced players, lining up fire on the screen's edges to take out multiple segments at once or even – an advanced tactic – creating little gulleys out of bricks left behind to shuttle centipede segments into upward fire. Strange as it is to say, *Centipede* is a management game – it's not how quick your trigger-finger is, but when you use it.

➡ The rise of the arcade business meant that all sorts of companies were trying to break in. A former manufacturer of fairground

The colour scheme and organic theme of *Centipede* were intended to make the game more attractive to female players. Author Steven Kent believes this was borne out in the arcades, though at this distance there's a lack of hard evidence – and the game remains a classic because of its design rather than its intentions.

rides in Japan, Namco, made its debut in 1979 with the impressive *Galaxian*. In contrast to the rigid alien ranks of *Space Invaders*, *Galaxian*'s enemies are brightly coloured craft that divebomb the player. *Galaxian* was something of a pioneer, its visuals regarded as groundbreakingly detailed, but it was Namco's next game that would put the company on the map.

➡ *Pac-Man* (1980) arrived on a scene dominated by shoot-'em-ups, and gobbled them up. Designer Toru Iwatani wanted to make a game that would appeal to women as much as men, and settled on the concept of eating as equally appealing to both. The moment-to-moment gameplay is eating dots spread around a maze, occasionally a piece of fruit, and the enemies were cute ghosts with bobbly eyes. The game was originally called *Puck-Man* thanks to the main character resembling a hockey puck but, fearing that the machines would be vandalized to say

something else, American distributor Midway changed the name.

➡ The beating heart of *Pac-Man* is a simple twist: one minute you are the hunted, and the next you are the hunter. Eating the dots is a satisfying reward in itself, mainly thanks to the accompanying wakka-wakka sound effect, but the true pleasure comes from the table-flipping moment when *Pac-Man* consumes one of each level's four 'power pills'. These are larger dots that, for a few seconds, allow *Pac-Man* to chomp ghosts and simultaneously cause the ghosts to turn blue in fear and run away.

➡ The configuration of the game's levels is designed to confuse the player into locking themselves in ever-smaller circles as the ghosts – all of whom have different behavioural AI – tighten the noose. Being boxed into a corner, swallowing the power pill and then gobbling up all four ghosts in quick succession feels like some kind of karmic

Galaxian's visuals pulled players in, but the surprise twist it had over other shooters at the time (most of which were content to copy *Space Invaders* to the letter) was the kamikaze dives of the alien craft, guaranteed to catch any new player off-guard.

A BRIEF HISTORY OF VIDEO GAMES

justice, a brief respite from the constant running and a sweet revenge that rewards you with a huge score bonus. In terms of feedback loops it is one of the most potent that video games has produced, effective to this day, and it saw *Pac-Man* become an instant smash-hit.

➤ In the two years following its release Namco sold 400,000 *Pac-Man* cabinets worldwide and, according to a very rough estimate by arcade specialists Twin Galaxies, its total gross in quarters approached $2.5 billion – making it the highest-grossing arcade game in history. The most successful American-made arcade game in history was *Pac-Man*'s sequel, *Ms. Pac-Man*, a particularly impressive feat given it began life as an unauthorized modification.

➤ In 1981 students Doug Macrae, John Tylko and Kevin Curran set up a company called the General Computer Corporation with the intent of making circuit boards that could be installed in pre-existing cabinets. *Pac-Man*'s success made it an obvious target for modification, and the team came up with a game called *Crazy Otto*. Things could have gone wrong for the General Computer Corporation but Midway, *Pac-Man*'s American distributor, saw the potential in an idea that allowed arcade owners to 'upgrade' their expensive pre-existing machines, and of course allowed it to revitalize stock yet to be sold.

➤ So *Crazy Otto* became *Ms. Pac-Man*, distinguished from her predecessor by a big red bow and lipstick. The biggest change over the original was that *Ms. Pac-Man* had four mazes, which introduced a degree of variety, and the new semi-random ghost behaviour which could catch out even the most experienced players. More of a remix than a true sequel, *Ms. Pac-Man* was nevertheless a high-quality game that happened to hit in 1981, when *Pac-mania* guaranteed success.

Although the movement of *Pac-Man*'s ghosts seems random, their behaviour is deterministic – something that Iwatani says was down to his wanting to give each one a personality. Enormous effort has been put into analysing how each one's behaviour can be predicted in order to play the 'perfect' game of *Pac-Man* – by reaching the maximum possible score of 3,333,360 points. Over six hours on 3 July 1999, Billy Mitchell became the first player to do this.

⮞ Namco's next game was the sequel to *Galaxian* and a cast-iron classic: *Galaga* (1981). Where the former was sometimes straitjacketed by the simplicity of its mechanics (one shot at a time, a single enemy diving pattern), *Galaga* takes off the shackles and lets the simple joy of blasting wave after wave of aliens dominate.

⮞ The killer touch is in just how good *Galaga* makes this constant destruction look. The insectoid aliens mass up in their ranks before looping downwards towards the player's ship at various angles, spiralling off the screen's bottom only to reappear at the top ready for another run. As your bullets hit, they explode into brightly coloured pixels with a satisfying boom, and the trick is to catch a line diving in at just the right angle: quick shots blast away each one in sequence, obliterating whole packs in a frantic second or two or jamming the fire button. Neat quirks in the enemy patterns keep their movements surprising,

and the addition of a horrible tractor beam enemy that periodically tries to suck up your spaceship adds a final flourish to this diabolical menagerie.

⮞ Konami's *Frogger* (1981) was altogether more unusual, presenting a scenario where the enemies weren't out to get the player at all. You control a charming yellow-and-green frog that has to first cross a busy intersection, dodging the oncoming traffic, and then make it over a rushing river by hopping on logs.

⮞ There's something of a Zen quality to playing *Frogger*, as you watch the traffic flow and wait for the right moment to jump across. It's a beautiful preparation for the much more difficult river crossing that follows, too, where the goal might be similar but the problem is inverted – now you have to time your leaps onto the moving logs, and be careful lest they float off the sides of the screen with your little frog still onboard.

⮞ *Frogger* squeezes everything from its basic

Galaga was a huge hit for Namco and would later become a sort of trademark flourish – it can be played as the company's PlayStation title *Tekken* is loading and is included as a bonus in several of the company's other games. Movie buffs should also keep an eye out for the cabinet's cameo appearances in *WarGames*.

The biggest gameplay addition of *Ms. Pac-Man* are the 'warp tunnels' on either side of the playing area, which have been a fixture in *Pac-Man* games since. It also added a basic between-rounds narrative where *Pac-Man* and *Ms. Pac-Man* eventually have a baby – who would soon star in the unauthorized Bally Midway game *Jr. Pac-Man*.

A BRIEF HISTORY OF VIDEO GAMES

idea: as the game progresses, traffic becomes faster, with trucks suddenly zooming forwards and trapping unwary players in the middle of the road. As well as logs, turtles float in the river and can be hopped onto – but will often sink underwater at just the wrong moment (you would think an amphibian could survive a quick dunk, but no dice). *Frogger* was an enormous hit for Konami, and its success over subsequent years bankrolled many of the Japanese company's more well-known hits.

● These early arcade games, though far advanced when compared to home consoles, were still presenting players with relatively abstract visual language: *Pac-Man*, after all, is a yellow circle missing a segment. So *Dragon's Lair* (1983) was a jaw-dropper.

● Don Bluth was a former Disney animator who had left the house of mouse to go it alone: his company's first animated feature, *The Secret of NIMH*, was a beautiful film that had little impact. In 1982 Rick Dyer visited Sullivan Bluth studios to talk about a new storage format: laserdisc.

● Laserdisc could be used to create a 'game' with high-quality video graphics – as good as a Disney movie. Although Bluth and his team knew little about video games, let alone making them, they were intrigued by Dyer's passionate pitch and agreed to work with him.

● Bluth's team produced a branching cartoon starring the cowardly knight Dirk the Daring, which was then chopped up and, at certain moments, required a player to react quickly and correctly to an on-screen prompt to proceed. Get it right and the movie played on, get it wrong and Dirk died one of many beautifully animated deaths. The problem with laserdisc was that you couldn't really make a decent game out of it – but in the context of other arcade machines of the time it looked like the future.

● *Dragon's Lair* was a total dog of a video

It is easy to see why *Dragon's Lair* was an enormous hit despite the limited interactivity it offered – just look at the visuals next to every other screenshot in this chapter. There were certainly bragging rights to be had for mastering it because everyone simply wanted to see the next brilliant animation for the buffoonish-yet-charming Dirk.

game, but the visuals were enough to see it become a huge worldwide success – despite the high cost to play, arcade-goers simply couldn't resist the alluring visuals. For a short time it seemed like laserdisc games might be the next arcade craze but as a series of problems surfaced, primarily the machines' tendency to break down, it became clear they were a fad. Nevertheless *Dragon's Lair* was enough of a hit to spawn a sequel, *Space Ace*, and has been re-released on countless formats over the years; a testament to Bluth's artistry if nothing else.

● The popularity of *Dragon's Lair* led to many copycat games, some of which were finished and then mothballed. The most interesting of these are *Sewer Shark* and *Night Trap*, which were resurrected years later as the 'killer apps' for the Sega Mega CD. These titles were, like every other laserdisc-based video game, appalling. What laserdisc did demonstrate, however, was the marketability

of 'interactive drama' in the form of multiple-choice video sequences – a theme to which we will (unfortunately) return when discussing the 2000s.

● Capcom's *Ghosts 'n Goblins* (1985) was the most extreme example of difficult-but-fair, to the extent that most players haven't seen past the first stage. Casting you as King Arthur in a 2D platformer, off to rescue Guinevere, Tokuro Fujiwara's masterpiece was built on precision and mastering the trajectories of the unusual throwing weapons. Not that you have much time to think about it because, where other games were content to bring on enemies at stage right, *Ghosts 'n Goblins* made them swarm from everywhere – ghouls from left and right, birds swooping from above and coffins rising from the ground to spew out even more. The game's difficulty was belied by a cute cartoony style, and in a humorous touch one hit reduces Arthur to his heart-patterned boxer shorts while a

1982's *Robotron 2084* was a Eugene Jarvis joint and may be his finest. It's a twinstick shooter that sees you trying to protect the last human family alive from ever-growing waves of sentient machines – an effort that is, thanks to Jarvis's unique idea of a difficulty curve, always futile.

second leaves him a pile of bones. The visually incredible but beastly bosses were just gravy. *Ghosts'n Goblins* is a masterpiece of a particular kind: precise, brutal and impossible to resist.

➡ The drive towards multiplayer resulted in many classics, including the four-player *Gauntlet* (1985). Created by genius Atari designer Ed Logg, *Gauntlet* was a top-down dungeon battler where the four characters had different abilities and working together was always at risk from the spectre of greed. Save the cornered Wizard or let him fight alone for a bit while you hoover up some treasure and then help?

➡ *Gauntlet*'s relentless enemies filled the simple layouts and swarmed players, gradually chipping away those precious 600 health units and putting food at a premium – which could be destroyed by careless shooting or snaffled away from desperate players by their greedy companions (at the price of a

friendship). The levels were short but packed, and with four players this is about as intense as arcade gaming gets.

➡ Among shooters *Gradius* (1985) stands tall, not merely for its detailed and colourful pixel art but for granting the player the ability to cycle through offensive tools by collecting glowing orbs. The greatest was called simply 'option', which manifests as a yellow support craft flying behind your Vic Viper and mimicking its fire – not just that, but collect more orbs and you can have multiple options snaking out behind the craft. *Gradius* has the chops to go toe-to-toe with any more straightforward shooter, but this introduction of tactics is what gives it a special pull.

➡ Taito's *Bubble Bobble* (1986) was a unique cooperative platformer: two dinosaur buddies, Bub and Bob, have to clear each screen by spitting bubbles at enemies and then 'popping' those trapped by touching them. Capture an enemy but fail to pop them and

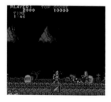

Ghosts 'n Goblins is a hard enough game but it had one touch that defies belief. If a player reaches the final battle without the right weapon, a cross, they are sent back two levels. If they have the cross and win, it's revealed the battle was a trap devised by Satan and the whole game needs to be replayed on a higher difficulty setting.

Ed Logg had the idea for *Gauntlet* after noting his son's interest in *Dungeons and Dragons*, hence the fantasy theme, emphasis on multiple players and inclusion of Atari's first-ever synthesizer chip for a 'dungeon master' to give tips. For most of its development, in fact, the game was called 'Dungeons'.

A BRIEF HISTORY OF VIDEO GAMES

they'll soon escape in a rage. The chase-now-be-chased rhythm this gives the game has a trace of *Pac-Man*, but the surreal world and, most importantly, that other player give it a magic all of its own. *Bubble Bobble* is so unusual it's something of a dead end – you couldn't call it an 'influential' game – but within itself it is simply perfect. The sequel, *Rainbow Islands* (1987), was just as wonderful.

● The highpoints of the golden age of arcades came from Sega's Yu Suzuki. *Outrun* (1986) was a technical showcase that, almost three decades later, remains a triumph of artistry. The technique it relies upon, sprite-scaling, involves making individual sprites larger to create the sensation of movement. It wasn't the first game to do this. But it was the first game to do it brilliantly at speed.

● *Outrun* is a fantasy game. The player drives a Ferrari Testarossa, while sitting in a replica if you're playing the deluxe

cabinet, and speeds through a vibrant hyper-picturesque vision of global landmarks and Americana. There are fifteen possible routes to take through the game, organized brilliantly into a pyramid that flows out from the starting point: at the end of each section the player chooses whether to go left or right, with left always being an easier option, and so dynamically adapting the difficulty as the ride goes on. The needy speedometer can be topped out and maintained by 'drifting' around corners, throwing the car into a slide and torquing it left and right to maintain the angle before shooting out onto the straight.

● *Space Harrier* (1985) is the ultimate arcade game in the golden age of the arcades. This is a blisteringly fast game that hurls the player's avatar forwards through crazy Chinese-style dragons, giant heads, alien octopuses, psychedelic flies, jet-helicopters and random bits of geometry. Although it's ostensibly a

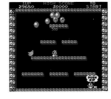

Bubble Bobble has multiple endings. If completed in single-player mode you're admonished to 'try again with a friend'. If completed in co-op, the ending shows Bub and Bob turning back into human brothers, and gives a code that unlocks a more difficult Super mode. Completing the game in co-op on Super mode reveals, rather disturbingly, that the final boss 'Super Drunk' was in fact the brothers' parents under a spell.

CREDIT   0   1986 ©SEG

One of *Outrun*'s most
defining touches was
allowing the player to select
their soundtrack of choice
at the start. All are in-house
Sega tunes that range from
manically upbeat to jazzy
rhythms, letting players tailor
the game to their mood. That
said, Splash Wave is best.

shooter, the game is really about dodging, staying alive to see as much as possible, and has a delicious kink in the controls to this end – the Harrier pulls back to a central position when you're not moving him. This acts as an essential fulcrum and factors into how you move all the time; the slow reset of position becomes a piece of momentum used between wild dashes, a slight adjustment already accounted for in the next swing.

● Breathtaking enough – but great systems don't always get the cash. The other side of Suzuki's genius for arcade games was, as *Outrun* also showed, their flashiness. The Space Harrier has a blonde mop, the reddest red jacket, blue jeans, and of course he can fly. The opening levels are crazy enough but soon the whole thing swings into psychedelia, giant purple mushrooms dotting the landscape as the scarlet sights of robots flash by, while the one-eyed mammoths simply wonder what that red blur was.

● The premium *Space Harrier* cabinet was a cockpit, complete with flightstick and surround sound. Even in the golden age of arcades Yu Suzuki was a special kind of designer: he exemplified the all-encompassing talent required to not only design a game, but do it alongside the development of the cutting-edge tech it would run on, and then at the end give the whole production physical form.

● Wonderful as it is, this kind of creation was always a doomed artform. But *Space Harrier* is one hell of a way to go. This monster of a machine's title screen shows a robot with gun barrel gleaming, a mammoth's eye swivelling back and forth, and brief cutaways into attract mode. The genius touch is that the *Space Harrier* is smiling and waving at you. A human face in the phantasmagoria, an invitation always waiting, the joy of the arcades encapsulated. A welcome to the fantasy zone. Get Ready!

The *Space Harrier* cabinet had an analogue flight stick, a first, and the deluxe version was also one of the first-ever sit-down cabinets that moved in response to the player's control inputs. The cabinet as well as the game were designed by Yu Suzuki and his team, pursuing an artform that is now somewhat lost to time.

The Rise of Nintendo

The most venerable company in video gaming was founded in Kyoto, Japan, in 1889 by craftsman Fusajiro Yamauchi. Nintendo Koppai's business was a particular type of playing card – *hanafuda*, 'flower cards' – illustrated with symbolic representations of the seasons and divided into twelve suits to correspond with the months of the year.

By the time Yamauchi retired Nintendo was the biggest playing-card company in America, and his successor Sekiryo Yamauchi consolidated this position with ruthless efficiency. Sekiryo and his wife Tei also raised their grandson, Hiroshi Yamauchi, after the boy's father had abandoned the family. In 1947, with Sekiryo's health rapidly declining after a stroke, Hiroshi was called back from Waseda University.

In 1949 Hiroshi Yamauchi was appointed the third president of Nintendo at twenty-two years old, and moved fast. Sekiryo had reluctantly agreed to fire Yamauchi's cousin; so there was no doubt over who was heir to the company, and once in power the young man was soon tested. Nintendo factory employees, suspicious of his lack of experience, called a strike and expected the new boss to cave. Instead, he fired the ringleaders and followed this up with an almost complete purge of Nintendo's senior management. Yamauchi wanted no one at the company who could threaten his authority or was too wedded to the old way of doing things.

Yamauchi modernized Nintendo's processes and then in 1956 came a turning point. Yamauchi visited the United States Playing Card Company in Cincinnati, which had become the biggest manufacturer of playing cards in the world, and was stunned to find an office and factory little bigger than Nintendo. Suddenly he understood that the playing-card business, which had brought the Yamauchi family great wealth, was severely limited.

Over the 1950s and early 1960s Nintendo

diversified into areas like instant rice, a taxi company called Daiya and 'love hotels', which rented rooms by the hour (rumour has it that Yamauchi had a significant personal interest in the latter). All failed in various ways and the company was near bankruptcy. Things changed when Yamauchi went to inspect the *hanafuda* manufacturing lines one day in 1966 and, by chance, spotted a retractable claw designed by maintenance engineer Gunpei Yokoi.

➔ Yamauchi called Yokoi into his office and, after establishing the young man had designed the toy himself, told him to develop it as a real product in time for Christmas. Yokoi developed the Ultra Hand, which sold over a million units. Yamauchi immediately established a toy division with Yokoi at the head, who over the next years designed a series of toys, often incorporating basic electronics, which would bring Nintendo back from the brink: the Ten Billion Barrel puzzle, the Ultra Machine (a baseball pitcher), a 'Love Tester', even a tiny remote-controlled vacuum cleaner called Chiritory.

➔ Despite this success Nintendo remained a minnow in the toy industry, and tried other ventures based on Yokoi's ingenuity – a recent fad had left bowling alleys across Japan deserted, which Nintendo converted into Laser Clay Shooting System entertainment venues. Its first involvement with video games was to license the Magnavox Odyssey for the Japanese market in 1974, before its own series of Color TV Game consoles. These were typical of the time: the machines played one game such as *Tennis*, but would claim to include more thanks to variations in the rule set (e.g. the Color TV Game 15).

➔ By 1975 Nintendo had begun producing arcade games, making its debut with Genyo Takeda's *EVR Race* (an unremarkable top-down driving game). But what really sold Yamauchi on the potential of the business was another Yokoi invention: the Game & Watch.

● Yokoi's personal philosophy about electronics design was the phrase 'lateral thinking with withered technology'. That is, Nintendo did not try to be at the cutting edge of the industry, but looked for 'withered' technology that was familiar and could be mass-produced cheaply. In 1979 Yokoi was riding the bullet train when he noticed a bored commuter passing the time by fiddling with a calculator.

● At the time Sharp and Casio were battling each other in the calculator market, which had led to a glut of cheap LCD displays and semiconductors. The bored commuter inspired Yokoi to create a pocket-sized watch that would double up as a game system with this technology. The first Game & Watch, *Ball*, was released in April 1980. Although it was not the first handheld games console (this honour goes to 1976's Mattel Auto Race) the

Game & Watch series popularized the idea through their phenomenal success. Sixty Game & Watch games were made in total, selling just under forty-four million units before the series was discontinued in 1991.

● Although the games themselves are amusements, it is worth pausing on one particular aspect of the Game & Watch series. After the success of *Donkey Kong* in arcades Nintendo made a Game & Watch version that required four-way directional control. Yokoi designed a simple cross overlay under which were four buttons at the extremity of each direction: the D-pad. Known as the 'cross' design, it would feature on every subsequent game controller made by Nintendo, and imitations abound across the industry.

● What Game & Watch really did was make Yamauchi pay attention to video games. Nintendo had enjoyed success before, but this time the scale was different and increased resources were poured into the

Ball was the first Game & Watch title, swiftly followed by many more. The initial designs had a single LCD screen but Nintendo would later introduce a two-screen 'clam-shell' design influential on the company's later and enormously successful DS consoles. (Photo credit: ThePViana)

arcade division. *Sheriff, Space Fever* and *Space Firebird* were decent games and saw modest success in Japan, and then in 1979 came *Radar Scope*.

➡ *Radar Scope* owed much to the popularity of *Space Invaders* and *Galaxian*, but nevertheless felt original thanks to its 3D third-person perspective. It was a huge success in Japan, second only to *Pac-Man*, which encouraged the newly founded Nintendo of America (NoA) to order a large number of cabinets.

➡ The cabinets arrived in late 1980 and there was a problem. *Radar Scope*'s visuals may have pulled punters in, but the repetitive gameplay quickly turned them off – the positive buzz that had caused NoA president Minoru Arakawa to place such a large order had all but dissipated, and he was faced with a warehouse of around 3,000 unsold machines. This was enough to bankrupt the company before it had even started. In desperation Arakawa called his father-in-law Yamauchi for advice, who came up with the idea of simply converting the machines into a new game. Yamauchi's main designers were busy with other projects, but he asked Nintendo's apprentice designer Shigeru Miyamoto (who had worked on *Radar Scope*) if he could think up something.

➡ Shigeru Miyamoto had ended up at Nintendo after his father, an associate of Yamauchi, wangled his son an interview. Miyamoto turned up to meet Yamauchi clutching a handful of designs for things like a seesaw with a swing in the middle, so three children could play at once, and wooden coat hangers with safe, rounded edges shaped like animals. None of these suited Nintendo but Yamauchi saw something in the shaggy-haired youngster, and gave him a job as the company artist. Miyamoto's first video-game-related job was the illustrations on the company's *Sheriff* arcade cabinet.

● The moment when Yamauchi assigned Miyamoto to redesign *Radar Scope* is the most important in Nintendo's history. It was soon clear that Shigeru Miyamoto was a genius at designing video games, and he would become the most important figure in the medium's history to date.

● Miyamoto was limited by the existing cabinet but, mentored by Gunpei Yokoi and full of questions for his more experienced colleagues, quickly worked out what was possible. Nintendo was close to securing the *Popeye* licence, and so Miyamoto designed a game built around three characters – but the deal fell through. Luckily Miyamoto had a talent for original characters. The lead was given a moustache to make his nose more identifiable, a cap in lieu of a non-animated haircut and a pair of dungarees that helped the motion of his arms stand out. His main action in the game was hopping over barrels and gaps, so he was christened Jumpman.

● The antagonist of the piece became a giant, surly gorilla – but he was not, as Miyamoto went to great pains to point out, an evil villain. In fact, he had been Jumpman's captive and, upon breaking free, had kidnapped Jumpman's girlfriend Pauline as some kind of revenge. Miyamoto thought the defining aspect of the gorilla's character was his stubbornness, and while looking through a Japanese/English dictionary hit upon the word 'Donkey' as capturing this. And everyone knew what King Kong was – so Donkey Kong was born.

● *Donkey Kong* is far from the first game with a story, but it is arguably the first non-text game to bother with details like giving its characters a motivation – the little interstitials that run at the start and end of levels. As impressive as this is for a first-time designer, however, *Donkey Kong*'s importance is much more about the game Miyamoto designed – an experience so singular that,

Shigeru Miyamoto is arguably the most influential video-game designer in history. He has created or had a key influence on games and series as diverse as *Donkey Kong*, *Super Mario Bros.*, *The Legend of Zelda*, *Starfox*, *Pilotwings*, *Nintendogs*, *Wii Sports*, *Wii Music* and many more. (Photo: courtesy of Nintendo)

where other successful arcade games were mercilessly copied, other companies looked at *Donkey Kong* and didn't even know where to start.

⊙ The game has three different levels, which it loops around when all are completed, and in essence *Donkey Kong* is a predictable system that has just enough randomness to mess up any player that gets too comfortable. In the first level, barrels thrown by *Donkey Kong* will roll down the girders and never seem to touch the long middle ladders, until you

risk a shortcut and Jumpman takes a barrel to the face. The second changes thing up so Jumpman has to run over 'bolts' in the level while avoiding wandering flames, and the third is a complex network of elevators, bouncing springs and ladders.

⊙ *Donkey Kong*'s mechanics play on how much we enjoy chance: there are very safe ways to play each level, which take time and don't feel quite so cool to execute, or there are super-fast techniques that feel great and usually result in an avoidable death.

⊙ 'With *Donkey Kong* I demonstrated how the game would basically work and [Mr Yamauchi] liked it,' says Miyamoto. 'He immediately demanded that I should stop all other work right now and concentrate upon finishing this *Donkey Kong* project.'

⊙ 'Honkey Dong?' Nintendo's American distributors weren't convinced, but Arakawa noticed that the employees who played the machine couldn't get enough of it.

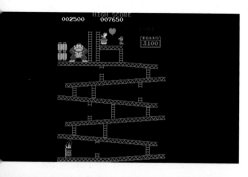

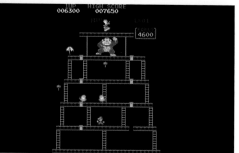

Rather than an artificial timer, *Donkey Kong*, above, spawns fireballs from the barrel in the bottom left of the screen after a short period of time – forcing Jumpman to move upwards rather than hopping over barrels indefinitely. There is also a hammer pickup that lets Jumpman destroy barrels and flames for points, but stops him climbing ladders.

The second level of *Donkey Kong*, below, changes the playstyle required, with Jumpman having to run across the yellow rivets to bring the giant ape crashing to earth. Most arcade games repeated the same mechanics, simply getting harder and faster, so the variety of *Donkey Kong*'s three levels was part of the appeal.

Donkey Kong would become Nintendo's first videogame mega-smash (not bad for a first try: Nintendo couldn't make the machines fast enough) and Jumpman, re-named to Mario, would become the company mascot. Legend has it that Jumpman was re-named Mario during the localization for the American market when NoA's landlord, Mario Segale, had a blazing row with president Minoru Arakawa over back rent – but ultimately left and gave him extra time to pay. No-one knows whether this is urban legend or fact, but the future icon had a new name.

➤ The success of *Donkey Kong* and Game & Watch convinced Yamauchi that Nintendo's future was exclusively in video games, and he gave the go-ahead for work to start on creating a cartridge-based console. Designed by Masayuki Uemura, the Famicom ('Family Computer') was originally concepted as a 16-bit powerhouse that could function as a home computer with a floppy drive and keyboard.

But this was not the Nintendo philosophy and Yamauchi demanded a much cheaper system without the trimmings, designed exclusively for playing games – although he also wanted an expansion port for future peripherals, just in case.

➤ The Famicom was released on 15 July 1983 for ¥14,800 (around £85) with versions of three arcade hits: *Donkey Kong*, *Donkey Kong Jr.* and *Popeye*. The price was right and a huge marketing campaign saw Nintendo sell around half a million units in the first six months. Just before Christmas the company started getting calls about defective units: a trickle that quickly turned into a flood. Certain games caused the Famicom to freeze.

➤ Masayaki Uemura and Gunpei Yokoi were assigned to work out the problem. After much testing with the affected titles they realized the problem was with the circuitry on one of the machine's chips – which meant the chips would have to be replaced. Fearing the

The Japanese Famicom: the controllers are hard-wired into the console's body, hence the design including side berths for storage. Initially joysticks were considered but, in what would become a theme of Nintendo's hardware design, it was decided that flat controllers posed less of a hazard when left lying on the living-room floor. (Photo credit: Evan Amos)

worst they reported this disastrous news to Yamauchi, known for his explosive temper. Yokoi suggested Nintendo replace defective machines as and when required. The reply was simple. 'Recall them all.'

→ The Famicom missed out on the biggest sales period of the year, but Yamauchi's instincts were once again proven sound. By the end of 1984 it was the most popular console in Japan, with around 2.5 million sold, and plans were underway to release in the USA. At one point Nintendo almost signed a deal with Atari to distribute the console as the Nintendo Advanced Video Gaming System, but the American company had other problems and eventually the deal went nowhere. Nintendo would go it alone.

→ Nintendo of America launched the Nintendo Entertainment System (NES) gradually, starting in October 1985, in the face of outright scepticism from many who remembered the recent crash all too well.

Everywhere Minoru Arakawa had gone he had heard the word 'Atari' from retailers so badly burned they never wanted to see a games console again. Nintendo did everything it could to differentiate itself, going so far as to rename common elements: the console was now a 'control deck' that didn't play cartridges but 'Game Paks' and the whole thing wasn't a console but an 'Entertainment System'.

→ These tactics and many, many more were employed, and eventually worked. Nintendo had gambled that the crash didn't happen because the North American market was bored with playing video games – on the contrary, it was sick of playing bad ones. The Famicom/NES became a smash in both Japan and the USA, the first console to do so, and would eventually sell 61.91 million units worldwide. One survey indicated that, by 1990, 30 per cent of American homes had an NES. This signalled a wider shift in the video-games industry. Until the NES games, consoles had

The redesign of the Famicom for the US market saw the console renamed as the Nintendo Entertainment System (NES), and thanks to its dimensions and front-loading slot for giant cartridges it became affectionately known as 'the toaster'. (Photo credit: Evan Amos)

A BRIEF HISTORY OF VIDEO GAMES

been largely designed and manufactured in the USA. In bedrooms across the globe, an era of Japanese dominance had begun.

➤ Although effective marketing undoubtedly played a big part in such success, this was a triumph of software and of software licensing. Nintendo was acutely aware of Atari's fate and to that end had designed the machine with a 'lock-out' chip to prevent unauthorized cartridges, then went on to insist on draconian terms from any would-be Nintendo developer. It was enough to put most developers off, until they saw the sales figures, at which point Nintendo had to beat them off with a stick.

➤ The single most important factor in Nintendo's success was the games of Shigeru Miyamoto. For the NES he was tasked with selling the hardware and returned to the Mario character with a technical innovation: side-scrolling. In previous platform games a character would reach the edge of the screen

and then the next would be loaded with a short delay, although particularly grand titles implemented a 'panning' effect. *Super Mario Bros.* was the first platformer where the levels smoothly scrolled from left-to-right as Mario moved through them. Miyamoto had already made one great game. But now he could build a universe.

➤ Mario ran and bounced through eight imaginative and increasingly difficult worlds, jumping on enemies and turning into Super Mario by catching an *Alice in Wonderland*-style mushroom. Someone had told Miyamoto that Jumpman looked more like a plumber than a carpenter, and so the world was punctuated by big green pipes (some of which led to subterranean lairs). The background was a pastel blue sky, the stages were constructed from chunky bricks that burst apart and some levels were even underwater. No one had seen anything like this before, least of all Yamauchi.

In stark contrast to the strategy pursued by Atari and its ilk, whereby game packaging featured lavish art that bore little relation to what was seen on-screen, Nintendo, left, chose to focus on bold sprites and colours that were illustrative of the game's contents.

One reason for the long-term appeal of the *Mario* games were the secrets, right, both intentional and otherwise, that their mechanics allowed. For example, Mario can gain 99 extra lives by jumping on a shell in a certain position near stairs, making it bounce off the stairs and back to be landed on again, resulting in an exponential points bonus.

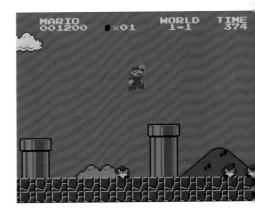

'When I first showed the demo of *Super Mario Bros.* [Mr Yamauchi] really liked it,' says Miyamoto. 'I still recall him saying "This is great, you can travel on the land, in the sky and even in the water. This is going to be amazing."'

The world's visual language was surrealism: suspended blocks, bridges to nowhere and even sections where Mario had to run out of the screen. There are warp pipes that let Mario skip worlds, found by riding a lift upwards and then jumping on top of the 'roof' to dash towards this great secret, a playfulness with form that is one of the hallmarks of Miyamoto's work.

Even now it is a delight to experiment in *Super Mario Bros.* and see what is possible, before finding the proof that someone thought of it first. A block might break apart to reveal nothing or it may hide a beanstalk leading who-knows-where, or it may have been a stepping-stone to somewhere that is now unreachable. Sometimes an unexpected jump may find a block that didn't seem to be there – an invisible surprise!

All of these factors are important but it is also worth emphasizing the brilliance of the 'practical' design of *Super Mario Bros.* An example from the first level: first Mario comes across a few piled blocks to jump up, with a gap in the middle and then a pile on the other side. The player jumps across but, if they fail, the 'hole' in the middle has solid ground at the bottom so Mario can hop out and try again. A few seconds afterwards Mario encounters the exact same obstacle, except this time the gap is a bottomless pit that means certain death. This kind of design, teaching the player the world's rules through allowing them to practise in safety, underpins every subsequent platformer and many other genres besides.

Video games had never seen such visual panache and, married to the brilliant levels

The iconic 'super mushroom' power-up in *Super Mario Bros.* was a happy accident. Initially the game was designed around a smaller sprite, with the intention being to scale it up for the final game, but Nintendo's designers decided that becoming bigger while actually playing was a fun addition.

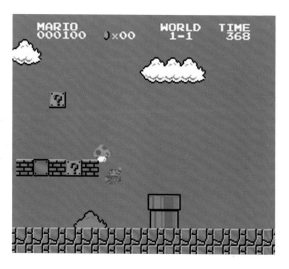

A BRIEF HISTORY OF VIDEO GAMES

and inch-perfect controls, *Super Mario Bros.* was a sensation. Excluding later remakes and re-releases it sold just over forty million copies and made the character Mario into an icon – the first of many brilliant transformations he would undergo. It is no accident that video-game history is littered with Mario clones, but only Nintendo has managed to both exploit and reinvent its mascot so successfully.

→ *Super Mario Bros.* swiftly received two sequels: the game made for the Japanese market was basically a harder version of the original (with nasty inversions like poison mushrooms) and NoA considered it unsuitable for America. Nintendo of Japan had a game called *Doki Doki Panic*, built around distinct mechanics like vegetable pulling. With a substantial visual overhaul and some extra polish, *Doki Doki Panic* became *Super Mario Bros. 2* (1988). Although lacking the verve and speed of *Super Mario Bros.*, it's a clever and inventive game that, in mixing up the successful formula, showed a company willing to take risks with its prize property. Nevertheless, it was *Super Mario Bros. 3* (1990) that would see Miyamoto take the plumber into the stratosphere.

→ *Super Mario Bros. 3* was, and is, a bona-fide cultural phenomenon. The game had originally been released in Japan in 1988 but western anticipation was red-hot, stoked by Nintendo's crafty marketing: the game was the climax to 1989 movie *The Wizard*, with a sneak peek months before release showing Mario's new ability to fly (pre-internet, this was a genius ploy). *Super Mario Bros. 3* not only lived up to this hype but exceeded expectations as one of Miyamoto's greatest creations – though equal credit goes to the oft-unsung Takashi Tezuka, who would go on to be the main driving force behind *Super Mario World*.

→ One of the reasons *Super Mario Bros. 3*

Although not strictly a 'true' *Mario* game, *Super Mario Bros. 2* was of a high enough quality that some fans to this day prefer its unique and slower-paced style over the main 2D *Mario* series entries.

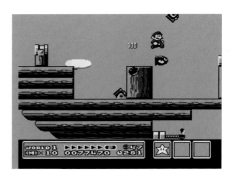

Among *Super Mario Bros. 3*'s many innovations were flying fortresses at the end of worlds, which housed antagonist Bowser's children. If you failed one attempt the fortress would fly to another part of the map and have to be chased down for a retry.

is a masterpiece is its conscious artifice: the first thing you see is a curtain rising, as in a theatre, to show the title screen. The levels are constructed from blocks visibly bolted onto the background, platforms are suspended by jerry-rigged ropes that attach to an unseen ceiling, and each level ends with a serrated vertical line dividing the course from a black background – end of the set. How does Mario power-up? He puts on costumes.

➡ And what a performance. *Super Mario Bros. 3* was one of the first platformers to have both an X and Y axis, levels asking the player to explore up and down as well as left and right, its locations crammed with cubbyholes and secret routes that reward a curious mind. The difficulty curve is also perfectly judged, not least because the player mediates it: progress results in a cornucopia of power-ups that can be stored and used when desired, hoarded for a challenge you suspect is coming.

➡ The inventiveness never lets up. Where *Super Mario Bros.* let players run along the top of the screen to find a warp zone, *Super Mario Bros. 3* has Mario escape the game: disappearing into unseen zones outside of the screen, and pressing up to enter invisible doors. To obtain the first warp whistle, Mario drops behind the scenery – an incredible discovery that not only reinforces the theatrical metaphor but was the whisper in every playground.

➡ The surreal setting almost seems normal by now: the cacti that bop along to the beat, the anthropomorphic clouds and hills that silently watch the spectacle unfold, and a rogues gallery with such sheer verve each one is impossible to forget. Chain Chomps bark and strain at their leash to get you; an Angry Sun gees itself up before swooping down in a burning crescent; Boss Bass and Big Bertha, blimp-like fish, leap out of the water to try and swallow Mario whole or wait below the surface. During development Takashi Tezuka worked one late night too many, and his normally placid wife flew into a rage when he got home. The next day he told Miyamoto, and Boo was born – a shy ghost that hides its eyes when Mario faces it but homes in when his back is turned.

⮞ *Super Mario Bros. 3* is a magical creation. It's a game that starts off gently and soon ramps up into not just a test of skill, but a challenge to the player's curiosity and imagination. It's a game that holds so much, can be played in so many ways and yet is still at bottom Mario with a princess to rescue. With Bowser vanquished and Princess Peach saved – what then? The last sight in the NES's finest game is simple. The curtain falls. What a show.

⮞ While still working on *Super Mario Bros.*, Miyamoto and Tezuka had sketched out a design for a new kind of game: where Mario was linear and all-action, in this new project you could explore and chew over puzzles. Miyamoto and Tezuka worked together, often on the same pieces of graph paper, drawing an overworld, dungeons and a fearsome menagerie of enemies, all bound up in a folder labelled 'Adventure Mario'.

⮞ *The Legend of Zelda* is inextricably bound to Shigeru Miyamoto, and more specifically to the experiences of his childhood. Miyamoto was born and raised in the small town of Sonobe, in Kyoto – also the home of Nintendo – and by all accounts was a curious child: poking into cupboards in the family home, rambling over fields and, very occasionally, finding something he never expected.

⮞ One of the most notable absences in *The Legend of Zelda* is an overworld map: in dungeons, the player can find a map to help navigate, but above ground they have to rely on memory. Exploration is key to *Zelda* but, more than this, what infuses every pixel is Miyamoto's curiosity.

➔ 'When I was a child, I went hiking and found a lake,' Miyamoto says. 'It was quite a surprise for me to stumble upon it. When I travelled around the country without a map, trying to find my way, stumbling on amazing things as I went, I realized how it felt to go on an adventure like this.'[24]

➔ He remembers especially an unfamiliar cave, dark and forbidding. The child couldn't pluck up the courage to plunge in immediately, but returned the next day with a lantern. 'The spirit, the state of mind of a kid when he enters a cave alone must be realized in the game,' Miyamoto says. 'Going in, he must feel the cold air around him. He must discover a branch off to one side and decide whether to explore it or not. Sometimes he loses his way. If you go to the cave now, as an adult, it might be silly, trivial, a small cave. But as a child, in spite of being banned to go, you could not resist the temptation. It was not a small moment then.'

➔ Takashi Tezuka's influence on *Zelda* was more straightforward: he joined Nintendo in 1984, just before development began, and to Miyamoto's childhood fantasies wedded a love of traditional fantasy – specifically, J. R. R. Tolkien's *The Lord of the Rings*. *Zelda*'s universe is a kind of patchwork with elements of *Peter Pan* and King Arthur, among others, and the game's arc is in this sense elemental. 'Link is a normal boy, but he has a destiny to fight great evil,' says Miyamoto. 'Many people dream about becoming heroes.'

➔ *The Legend of Zelda* was soon known internally as 'Adventure', the 'Mario' long since dropped. This game would have no high scores or discrete levels. Miyamoto and Tezuka's drawings were of a giant open world, a land full of caves and lakes and forests that the player could explore from the get-go. It was filled with monsters and treasures and, most of all, secrets.

➔ *The Legend of Zelda* was released

alongside Nintendo's new add-on, the Famicom Disk System, in Japan on 21 February 1986. The Disk System allowed several tantalizing features, but perhaps the most important was the ability to save progress. Sadly the hardware proved something of a flop and so by the time *Zelda* reached the USA the game was in cartridge format, the first with built-in battery-powered RAM for saving progress. Saving wasn't merely innovative: it also differentiated *Zelda* from the transience of arcade games and video games in general, which were largely designed for short play sessions. Home consoles like the NES couldn't approach arcade-level visuals, but here was something an arcade game couldn't offer: progress and persistence.

➔ Miyamoto wanted to give players 'a miniature garden they can put inside their drawers' and, to that end, *Zelda*'s open world was huge – 128 screens and 8 dungeons

that could be completed in any order. Players ended up exploring because they were unsure where to go next, a new kind of freedom. '*The Legend of Zelda* was our first game that forced the players to think about what they should do next,' says Miyamoto. 'We were afraid that gamers would become bored and stressed by the new concept. Luckily, they reacted the total opposite.' *The Legend of Zelda* was the first million-selling console game that Nintendo made and, to date, the series has sold over sixty million copies.

➔ What is most remarkable now, after almost three decades of sequels and refinements, is how fully formed *Zelda* was: it created a template the series has followed since with spectacular results – the overworld, the dungeons, the progression structure of acquiring items, the gradual growth of Link from a weak squirt waving a wooden sword to a gadget-flinging superhero. Even the enemies are all there: rock-spitting Octoroks,

The Legend of Zelda's design combined an overworld with many 'caves' of the type seen here, both visible and hidden, as well as the dungeons Link would need to conquer to beat the game. This overarching structure ties everything together, and relates Link's increasing abilities to the sense of exploring a universe.

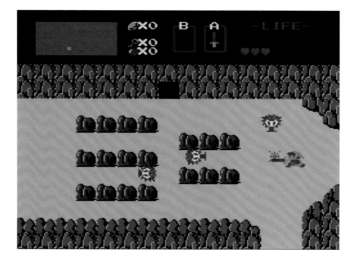

burrowing Leevers that burst from the sand, boomerang-tossing Goriyas, Peahats with weird propeller heads, Tektites skittering and hopping around, grotesque Moblins – the list goes on.

➡ Then Link himself: the greatest name in gaming. The word indicates that the character is somehow joined to the player, a mute adventurer defined by your actions – a presence and door into the gameworld. Miyamoto wanted players to see some part of themselves in Link, whether wide-eyed child or hardened adult. *The Legend of Zelda* is, in digital form, what everyone really wants from the world. It's an awfully big adventure.

➡ The main competitor to the NES in this era came from the Sega Corporation. Sega was one of the finest and most successful makers of arcade games in the world, but in 1982 a downturn in profits had led to a severe corporate restructuring of the company – and a new strategy. Sega of Japan's president Hayao

Nakayama recommended that the company use its arcade expertise to enter the nascent Japanese home-console market, and the company began development of the SG-1000.

➡ Although an important console in the history of Sega, the SG-1000 was doomed by circumstances. Nakayama had correctly identified a gap in the market but the console was launched on 15 July 1983 – the very same day as Nintendo's Famicom. The SG-1000 was underpowered by comparison and, where the Famicom launched with great conversions of arcade sensations *Donkey Kong* and *Donkey Kong Jr.*, Sega's software was underwhelming at best. The console would last barely a year in the market before being replaced by a slight upgrade, the SG-1000 II, and neither saw much success.

➡ During this period Sega of Japan was the subject of corporate manoeuvring that saw co-founder David Rosen resign before returning at the head of an investment group.

The same overworld principle of the original underlies *Zelda II: The Adventure of Link* but a major distinction is that, during combat, town and dungeon sequences, the game switches from an overhead 2D view to the side-on perspective seen here. Stylistic switches such as this can work but here it feels like the world loses some coherence.

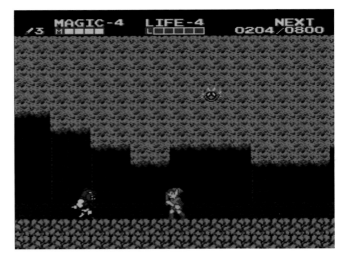

A BRIEF HISTORY OF VIDEO GAMES

Sega was owned by the giant conglomerate Gulf+Western, which didn't really have any idea what to do with it, and Rosen saw that the games market depended on being much more nimble and decisive – not unlike Nintendo.

➡ And Nintendo was always on Sega's mind. The third version of the SG-1000 was a reboot, aimed at carving a slice out of the giant market the Famicom had created in just two years. Released in 1985 as the SG-1000 Mark III, this machine had a faster CPU than the Famicom, could display more and brighter colours and had more than double the amount of memory. The hardware was objectively superior.

➡ But the software still wasn't quite there. Sega had learned its lessons and focused on releasing games more than ever, but a failure to plan ahead meant tight development times and often underwhelming games. This alone was bad enough, but Nintendo's draconian licence terms with third-party developers explicitly stopped their games from appearing on rival systems.

➡ Nevertheless Sega had a good console and the turning point came with the American release. This was the company's first console release overseas and, noting how the Famicom had become the NES, Sega completely redesigned the hardware to look more futuristic. The greatest lineage of home console names begins here, with the Sega Master System.

Nintendo's licensing terms meant that popular arcade titles such as Konami's *Gradius* had NES ports but no presence on the Master System. *Gradius* is interesting, however, thanks to Konami making a thinly disguised version called *Nemesis* for the MSX home computer – which then saw an (apparently unauthorized) Master System port released in South Korea only.

The Master System launched in North America in 1986 for $200, including one of Sega's better arcade conversions, *Hang-On*. The story was similar to Japan, with the NES enjoying a stranglehold on distribution and third-party developers, but the Master

System's superior hardware and range of well-designed peripherals carved it a niche.

➔ One notable success was Europe, where Nintendo's dominance wasn't so pronounced – and a series of distributors did a better job than Sega of America ever had, with the

The North American design of the Sega Master System. Note the slot in the front right corner, which was used to play 'Sega Cards'. These were intended to retail for less than cartridges but, thanks to their lower storage capacity, proved unpopular and the card slot was removed in a later redesign. (Photo credit: Evan Amos)

The SegaScope 3D Glasses used a shutter system to rapidly close the right and left lenses and create a 3D effect – and for the time a very impressive one, with the only downside being a noticeable drop in frame rate. They were designed by a young Mark Cerny, who would later design the Sony PlayStation 4. (Photo credit: Evan Amos)

A BRIEF HISTORY OF VIDEO GAMES

system eventually outselling the NES. But the Master System never had the games or the marketing clout to seriously trouble Nintendo's global business. The arcade conversions got better but in the meantime Nintendo (and its captive third parties) had started churning out home-console classics with which Sega, try as it might, simply couldn't compete in either quantity or quality.

→ There are exceptions. *Phantasy Star* (1988) took and built upon the new Japanese role-playing games (JRPG) genre, easily surpassing the visuals of the popular *Dragon Quest* with pseudo-3D dungeons and spectacular attack animations. Its characters were not the blank avatars of most RPGs but distinct and well-written personalities, while the science-fiction setting was a welcome break from high fantasy. *Wonder Boy III: The Dragon's Trap* (1989) combined side-scrolling platforming mechanics with an RPG-lite structure, allowing the player to explore a large world with some freedom and upgrade their character (it shares a great deal with *Metroid*). And some of Sega's arcade hits translated well, like *Fantasy Zone* and *Golden Axe*, though the less said about its transfer of *Space Harrier* the better.

→ Over its lifetime the Master System would sell thirteen million units worldwide, compared to sixty-two million NES consoles. Although the bare numbers indicate a hammering, it's worth considering that from the SG-1000's launch Sega was behind in a game where the deck was stacked against it. The Master System came too late for its minor hardware superiority to make much of a difference to perceptions of the NES, and it never offered a comparable software library. But what it did do was give Sega a foothold, and some blunt lessons about selling video-game consoles. The next round wouldn't be so one-sided.

Wonder Boy III: The Dragon's Trap received much praise for its nonlinear structure, solid colours and large sprites, though unfortunately during play the sprites flicker and there is noticeable screen tear. Nevertheless this was one of the few Master System exclusives that Sega fans could genuinely crow over.

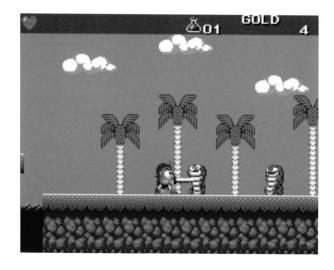

Simpatico

In 1987 Will Wright and Jeff Braun co-founded Maxis for one reason: no publisher was interested in selling their games. Braun's title, a wireframe fighter pilot simulator, was at least comprehensible. But Wright had made a game like nothing anyone had seen before: *Micropolis*, later to become better known as *SimCity*.

➔ Wright had got the idea while designing his first game, *Raid on Bungeling Bay*, a top-down 2D shooter most notable for the way that its islands 'evolved' over time. While working on the title Wright realized he gained more enjoyment from the map editor than the game itself and so began developing it further as a personal project. This inspired a deep interest in urban planning and particularly the theory of system dynamics: that is, how system behaviour depends on internal feedback loops and the way resources flow from one part to another.

➔ *SimCity* was first developed for the Commodore 64 in 1985, but it would be four years before it saw general release (hence Maxis). Wright's great innovation was, essentially, understanding that the goals and rigid rule sets of previous games simply didn't have to be there. Why does a game need to be won or lost – can't it simply be played?

➔ The only objective in *SimCity* is to build a city and it's up to the mayor/player how to do it. Land can be designated as commercial, industrial or residential, specific buildings can be constructed, and roads or railways

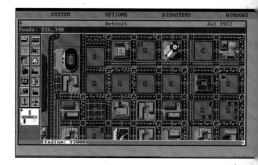

The original Mac release of *SimCity* was in black and white, though almost all subsequent releases have been in colour. Both Will Wright and Maxis president Jeff Braun believed that the game's mechanics, however subtly, pushed a political agenda – which of course it did.

Will Wright speaking at the 2010 Game Developers Conference. Wright's final game to date is *Spore*, released in 2008, an attempt to build a game around evolutionary and scientific mechanics. Following this he left EA Maxis and currently pursues various non-game projects. (Photo credit: Official GDC)

connect everything together. Beyond this the player has to decide the city's tax rate, choose the type of power to rely on (then build the infrastructure), and deal with the occasional natural disaster.

➡ This is an open-ended style of design, one where the objectives are almost entirely self-chosen. It's an enormously creative and freeing type of play that, in one sense, is circumscribed only by Wright's personal bias for or against certain aspects of urban living: nuclear power plants, for example, are unrealistically dangerous while a city linked entirely by rail will have a 'happier' population than one criss-crossed by highways.

➡ Some players like to plan far ahead, laying out a future utopia one segment at a time and fine-tuning the various little feedback loops as 'Sims' (the invisible inhabitants of your masterwork) move in and begin responding. I prefer a more sprawling approach to urban construction, building

SimCity 4 introduced a 3D engine to the series, albeit with the viewing angle fixed, and looks stunning even now. It also had a day and night cycle, although this had no impact on the experience beyond aesthetically pleasing make-believe.

A BRIEF HISTORY OF VIDEO GAMES

great limbs outwards and joining up the dots afterwards, leading to huge ghettos, long commutes and usually a pretty pissed-off population. But then, I enjoy 'fixing' things. The brilliance of SimCity's design is that (almost) every problem the city will face is a consequence of your earlier decisions.

➡ The greatest testament to *SimCity* is not the sheer number of sequels and spinoffs, nor the enormous sales figures, but that even the most recent version in 2013 (confusingly also titled *SimCity* as a 'reboot') is unmistakeably built on those 1985 foundations. The series highlight is arguably the superb *SimCity 4* (2003), the first to build in a 3D engine, meaning the camera can be rotated around your awesome creations while onlookers gasp in awe. *SimCity 4* also stripped back some of the over-fussy aspects previous sequels had added while retaining the deep complexity of underlying systems. This is Maxis at its best: approachable and fun to

toy with, but devilish beneath the surface.

➡ Maxis is far from a one-trick pony, however, even if its naming policy can suggest the opposite. After the success of *SimCity* the developer moved on to a succession of different *Sim-* titles, including *SimFarm*, *SimEarth*, *SimLife*, *SimTower*, *SimIsle* and *SimHealth* – all of which are fun games. The most interesting offshoot is also the oddest: *SimAnt*.

➡ Subtitled *The Electronic Ant Colony*, *SimAnt* was inspired by Wright's reading E. O. Wilson and Bert Hölldobler's encyclopaedic work *The Ants*, a detailed examination of how ant colonies operate. This may sound a little dry but, probably conscious of how hard a sell it was going to be, *SimAnt* is more traditionally gamey than Maxis's other titles: the player controls a black ant colony in a backyard that has to gradually expand, fight off red ants, and eventually drive away both the scarlet devils and the occupants of the house.

The yellow ant is the player's avatar in *SimAnt*. The original release had a chunky instruction manual that explained the simplified workings of an ant colony – principles that players would need to understand in order for the game to make sense.

SimAnt remains fascinating to play because it is an accurate (though simplified) representation of how an ant colony works, which a player can then mess about with by controlling individual ants and laying 'pheromone trails' to guide operations. The simulation can be observed on the micro or macro scale through three different modes and, once other insects turn up, plays almost like a strategy game – spiders, antlions, red ants, inadvertent human activity and even too much rain can quickly ruin your day. It's entirely possible to play SimAnt for hours and be hypnotized into dumb awe, like staring at a fish tank.

The culmination of Maxis's work is The Sims (2000). This title began as a kind of architectural simulator where players would construct individual houses and then visiting 'Sims', little computer people, would pass judgement on the result. This changed when the developers realized the Sims themselves were the real stars, but not everyone was on board with the concept. 'It was a battle, the first few years inside Maxis,' says Wright. 'It was referred to as "The Toilet Game". It was the game where you clean the toilet. We had a product review meeting at Maxis where we had to decide whether we'd publish this thing or not . . . and the executive said no.'[25]

Despite the game testing badly, and little faith from the higher-ups, Wright defiantly kept 'The Toilet Game' alive as a secret project, with one or two staff working in secret. The core of The Sims is the AI of its titular characters, who have to be able to react to any layout a player can conceivably produce, but the real magic of this is that they are quirky – fun to watch, fun to prod and oh-so-easy to get attached to.

The game begins with your purchasing a vacant lot and constructing a house in Build mode (or simply buying a pre-built dwelling), after which your Sim or Sims move in. From

An enduring fascination for players of The Sims is how to make Sims die – because it's simply not possible under normal circumstances. The more devious realized that one route to 'success' is blocking Sims into areas with no exit routes or (in later versions) removing the ladder from a swimming pool after a Sim has entered.

Although *The Sims 2* was more refinement than revolution, it did introduce the idea of 'aspirations' through a points system – the more social and networked a Sim is, the more points and aspiration they gain. Even in the virtual world, it seems, success breeds success.

here you can instruct them to interact with various household objects, go to the loo, have something to eat and arrange a daily activity schedule.

➡ Sims have a certain amount of free will (this can be toggled in the options) and will do their own thing to a degree, babbling away to each other in the delightful language of 'Simlish' or letting you know via a thought bubble when something is wrong. They will also suffer the consequences of neglect: most obviously, peeing themselves if you don't allow toilet trips, or more long-term effects like turning into lazy dropouts who spend all day on the couch.

➡ *The Sims 2* (2004) improved on its predecessor with a move to fully 3D environments, and added much while keeping the simple interactions and underlying complexity. In this version Sims have more life stages to age through, have more appearance parameters (when creating a Sim you essentially 'construct' its look) and expressions, there are more social interactions (such as Sims being able to influence one another), body shape will now be affected by diet and exercise, and following careers can result in certain rewards.

➡ This incomplete list may sound like minor tweaking, but in reality it is laser-focused on what matters most to players of *The Sims*. *The Sims 3* (2009) is perhaps the ultimate entry in the series, expanding the world in which the Sims live greatly (so you can observe and direct their daily routine) and streamlining away tasks that had come to seem like a chore (such as having to tell a Sim to pee). Unfortunately *The Sims 4* (2014) dropped the ball, angering long-term fans by removing many expected features in order that they can later be sold as expansions.

➡ All *Sims* games have featured their own websites called 'The Exchange' where players could download custom content and skins made by others, but it is the sheer number of *Sims*-focused sites and exchanges elsewhere that drives home that the series is a phenomenon. These sites are often focused on simply telling the stories of what happened to a particular set of Sims, with players creating elaborate video homages, extended sequences of captioned screenshots or simply pouring out their heart with the pretext it's about a video game.

⊘ A great example of the kind of long-form narratives players find in *The Sims* is 'Alice and Kev: The Story of Being Homeless in The Sims 3' (http://aliceandkev.wordpress.com), which follows a father and daughter with amusing personality traits as they survive, grow, and exhibit constantly surprising behaviour. (Particularly notable is when, after finishing her first-ever work shift, the perennially unlucky and downtrodden Alice gives her wages to charity.)

⊘ If *SimCity* pioneered a particular style of open-ended play, *The Sims* takes this down to the individual level and something surprising happens to some of the game's players: you begin to project. Video games chase various forms of interactive narrative, most of which are dead ends, but *The Sims* taps into a basic aspect of the human mind – we enjoy making up our own stories.

⊘ So *The Sims* may look like a 'doll's house' (another working title for the game, until Wright realized it alienated teenage boys) and can certainly be played as such, but really it's a scenario generator. This is a miniature universe where you see stories familiar to everyone play out – work, family, love, joy, sadness, anger and, hope and love (*The Sims* is notable for allowing same-sex relationships, an area in which the games industry does not have a proud record) – and it is impossible not to see small aspects of your own life refracted through the green diamond of its cursor.

The most intriguing feature in *The Sims 3* is the ability, like God, to grant your subjects free will in the form of a 'story progression' option. This means that a neighbourhood of Sims can go about their lives, get married, change jobs and move around independent of the player's control.

Doom 101

➔ The first-person shooter is currently the most commercially popular genre in the world, as well as the focus for the majority of controversy about violence in the medium. Bemoaned by sophisticates and adored by the masses, the first-person shooter is both one of the simplest forms of interaction – aim and shoot – and a consistent driving force behind innovation and technology. It all began in an empty maze.

➔ Steve Colley was a student at the NASA Ames Research Center in California, working on an Imlac PDS-1 – the first low-cost vector graphics computer. In contrast to the more typical raster scan displays, a grid of pixels updated by a sweeping CRT beam, vector displays showed clean and sharp lines from point to point. Colley was working on simple 3D displays, and at first made a rotating cube where the 'back' lines wouldn't show.

➔ 'A little later I had the idea of doing a maze where you were actually in the maze,' recalls Colley. 'I worked out how to display the halls of the maze with perspective [. . .] and it worked quite fast so you could quickly move around in the maze.' The game was simply to explore the maze, and Colley had several different layouts. There was just one problem. 'Maze was popular at first but quickly became boring,' says Colley. 'Then someone, Howard [Palmer] or Greg [Thompson], had the idea to put people in the maze. To do this would take more than one Imlac, which at that time were not connected together. So we connected two Imlacs using the serial ports to transmit locations back and forth. This worked great, and soon the idea for shooting each other came along, and the first-person shooter was born.'[26]

➔ *Maze War* invented countless features that can still be seen today: players had avatars (giant eyeballs), a secondary top-down 2D map to judge their position, could play over a network, and had an early

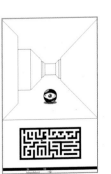

The original PDS-1 machine on which Steve Colley programmed *Maze War*, and an emulated screenshot of the game itself. Colley would later work on NASA's Mars rover technology and found his prior experience of working with a 3D perspective for *Maze War* useful.

example of online chat. The game was not a commercial release but a shared joy among computer enthusiasts with access to Imlacs, and so over the years evolved under different programmers, as Will Crowther (creator of *Adventure*) recalls. 'The interesting thing about [*Maze Wars*] was that people in San Francisco were playing against people in Los Angeles, 'cause Xerox had offices in both places, and you couldn't tell. Communications were that good.'

➡ Later versions only added to *Maze War*'s list of innovations: the original first-person shooter level editor, a version that could be played across the internet's predecessor ARPANET in 1977, an observer mode, and even the first examples of players modifying the client to cheat at the game. *Maze Wars* was ported to the day's PCs in 1986 so, although this is impossible to verify, it was probably the first video game to be played across the modern internet. The developer of *Spasim* (a contraction of 'Space Simulator'), Jim Bowery, would dispute that *Maze Wars* was first in every area. *Spasim* was released in March 1974 across the PLATO network, which was intended for educational software but turned out to be perfect for message boards, talk rooms and online gaming. Bowery had been inspired by *Empire*, a top-down 2D arena shooter also released on PLATO, and created a first-person 3D space-dogfighting simulator with wireframe ships.

➡ Thirty-two players could play *Spasim* over four planetary systems (eight players per system) and, in teams, shoot phasers and photon torpedoes at each other (*Empire* had also been inspired by *Star Trek*). A second version in July 1974 included space stations and resource management. This added complexity, and in a foreshadowing with which many big-budget developers would sympathize, halved the game's player base.

➡ *Maze War* and *Spasim* were constrained by

their technology. In the former, players moved tile-by-tile and could only turn at ninety-degree angles, whereas in the latter, positions were 'only' updated once a second. But Spasim's existence led to a PLATO-based tank simulator developed for the US Army that directly inspired Atari's *Battlezone*, the first commercial first-person shooter (see Chapter 10: The Golden Age of the Arcades).

⊘ The nature of the first-person shooter means that clear visuals and smooth movement are essential, and so although there were games throughout the 1980s and early 1990s that deserve a mention – *MIDI Maze*, *Faceball 2000*, *Hovertank 3D* – the first step towards the modern style was made by *Ultima Underworld* (1992).

⊘ Developed by the pioneering Looking Glass Studios, *Ultima Underworld* was an action-exploration game with heavy RPG elements. Players search through a huge dungeon while gradually mapping it, finding and examining items, fighting monsters and levelling up over time to become more powerful.

⊘ The RPG elements are no mere window-dressing – though the combat is realtime, there are invisible dice rolls happening all the time – and the amount of possible approaches to a given situation is extraordinarily impressive for its time. Encounters could be avoided by stealth, the player could learn spells, meet non-player characters (NPCs), get better at bartering for goods, learn to lock-pick and type in 'mantras' at certain shrines to increase their skills. The attention to detail is enormous, from weapons deteriorating over time to the player's avatar needing to eat.

⊘ History was made when a young coder called John Carmack saw *Ultima Underworld* and, without a trace of arrogance, said, 'I can write a better texture-mapper.' But then Carmack was no ordinary computer geek. A slightly withdrawn but transcendentally brilliant programmer, Carmack had started off in the industry by writing coverdisk software for magazines – where he'd met fellow programmers Tom Hall and John Romero. After several years working for other people the triumvirate, joined by Carmack's artist brother Adrian, had decided they had the talent to go it alone and formed the 'id software' company. The company's first effort was *Catacomb 3D*, a first-person shooter that featured outstanding visuals for the time and introduced the idea of a floating on-screen hand. The same technology was used to build *Wolfenstein 3D* (1992), id's first big success, which was based on an earlier series and cast the player as a Rambo-alike called B. J. Blazkowicz who specializes in blowing away Nazis.

➔ *Wolfenstein 3D* moved smoothly, was great fun to play and had bags of gore at a time when such an aesthetic was relatively unusual. The game received a rapturous reception critically and commercially and, thanks to its innovative release as shareware (a free demo, with instructions on where to send a cheque for the full game), popularized the largely unknown shooter genre on PC.

➔ *Wolfenstein 3D* also took *Catacomb 3D*'s idea of an on-screen hand to its logical conclusion by putting a gun in it. This is not a functional aspect of the game so much as a psychological one – while the first-person perspective is immersive by default (you see what the character sees), an on-screen hand clutching a weapon reinforces the point by showing the player 'their' limb. As good as it was, however, *Wolfenstein 3D* was just the starting gun.

➔ *Doom* (1993) is one of the greatest and most influential games ever, and set the course that the majority of modern first-person shooters still follow. The setup is simple: you're a space marine in hell, and lots of monsters stand between you and the

Doom is still cited by many gamers as one of the most perfect games ever made. Its influence at the time of writing is as strong as ever, and though id's stock as developers has fallen in recent times the announcement of an upcoming reboot of the series was met with frenzied excitement.

exit elevator. Get blasting. Even now *Doom*'s combination of fluid motion and speed can take the breath away, its cacophonous sound effects ringing out as yet another demon explodes into a pile of mushy pink pixels.

→ *Doom*'s visual style is a mix of science fiction and pulp horror, into which id crammed as much gore and vaguely meaningful symbology (e.g. pentagrams) into the levels as possible. What makes this style so distinctive is the bright palette and distended enemy designs, but the game's rhythm is as much about the outstanding metal soundtrack that positively hammers along as the player blasts away – it's impossible to play *Doom* slowly. No game has matched the shotgun's 'BOOM ca-clack BOOM' sound effect.

→ The weapons established a template: the starting pistol, the booming shotgun, the rattling chaingun, the hot thrum of the rapid-fire plasma rifle, the unbearably exciting

seconds as the BFG9000 charges up a death-pulse before annihilating everything ahead of it. Using them felt visceral and incredibly satisfying – thrusting a chainsaw into a bloated Cacodemon's eye and watching it collapse into scarlet guts, firing a rocket into clustered groups and watching their gibbed corpses fly away from the impact.

→ The grotesque enemies were simply begging for it: fireball-throwing Imps with faces twisted into a grimace of hate, the Mancubus's fattened flesh and chaingun arms, the bright pink musculature of the Barons of Hell and their terrifying bull cries when you're spotted. The latter are some of the toughest fighters in the game and, when you land the final shot, their bodies split in half as the beast lets out a high-pitched gurgling, leaving the top and lower halves linked only by a pool of green blood and intestines. These effects are not incidental but at the core of how *Doom* envelops

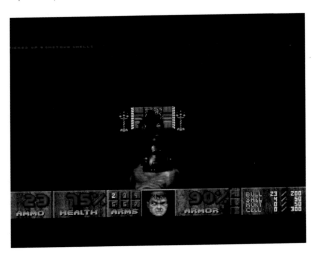

players: absolute fear and adrenalin, followed by the catharsis of an unmistakeable victory.

➲ Then there was multiplayer. Again *Doom* was not the pioneer but the first great example: up to four players could connect to a server and blow each other away, gaining a 'frag' for each kill and respawning (reviving) at a random location after death. Later improvements allowed up to sixteen players to compete at once.

➲ The appeal of competitive multiplayer in any game is simple: human opponents are more fun to play against than any AI. Humans are devious, accurate, smart, consistently surprising, and so fragging another player adds a frisson of satisfaction that single-player games can't touch. The popularity of this aspect of *Doom* would play a large role in the design of id's later *Quake* series. *Doom* was distributed online, the first third given away as shareware with players able to pay to download the rest, and demand

was such that the university network on which it was hosted crashed almost immediately on launch. Despite internal opposition, Carmack programmed *Doom* so that replacing the audio or visuals was easy and reversible, as well as making the level editor available. While id's detractors saw this as poor business sense, it is arguably the most important element in *Doom*'s longevity, fostering and encouraging an entire generation of modifiers – modders – to get involved with a game they loved and build their own on the foundations.

➲ The sequel *Doom II: Hell on Earth* (1994) did little more than refine the original's formula and add an outstanding double-barrelled shotgun but, in this case, that was exactly the right thing to do. For an entire generation the names Carmack and Romero – programmer and level designer – will forever be entwined. Although it wasn't the first first-person shooter, *Doom* is without

Doom 3 – 'ICU' by Dead End Thrills. id's third entry in the series didn't arrive until 2004, by which time the company was much changed, and although *Doom 3* was another visual showcase it never enjoyed the impact of its predecessors. (Courtesy of Dead End Thrills)

A BRIEF HISTORY OF VIDEO GAMES

exception the most important, popularizing the perspective that has since been used for everything from *Myst* to *Gone Home* – as well as its countless more straightforward followers.

◉ The immediate future for id was *Quake* (1996), which was a 'true' 3D game – the *Doom* engine uses two-dimensional floorplans to render 3D environments, which has limitations such as the fixed height of viewpoint and an inability to design multi-levelled structures. The *Quake* engine was built specifically to address these limitations and so the game features jumping, huge multi-tiered levels and physics elements.

◉ This capabilities-first approach meant that *Quake* ended up somewhat similar to *Doom* in theme, though with a more muted palette and much more of a Lovecraftian influence on enemy types. The most important change, however, was the focus on multiplayer: *Quake* offered many new modes and maps, but the

real revelation was how much more capability the player's avatar possessed.

◉ The more depth and functionality a control system has, the more players will wring out of the game. And when talking about competitive multiplayer games in particular, the community will do anything and everything for the tiniest edge. The *Quake* engine's physics, for example, led to an unforeseen consequence for movement. Players realized that if they were at the apex of a jump and fired a rocket at the ground, then the avatar would take some damage and be 'boosted' further into the air – opening up all sorts of shortcuts and previously inaccessible parts of maps.

◉ This technique is called 'rocket-jumping' and is considered the most basic of *Quake* tricks. Such potential in the controls, along with the increased options for distribution and recording, is why *Quake* popularized new ways for communities to play games:

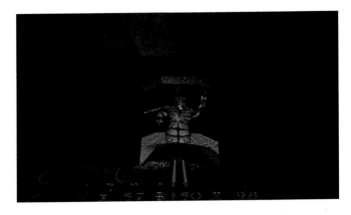

The biggest distinction between *Quake* and *Doom* is in the hands – Carmack's new engine allowed for unparalleled speed and freedom of movement. This alone meant that, even if you weren't quite taken with id's gory aesthetic, you simply could not ignore the company's games.

speedrunning and machinima.

⊙ Speedrunning had happened among elements of the *Doom* community, but the practice came to prominence in 1997 when a group of dedicated *Quake* players created a recording of themselves completing the game in record time on the 'Nightmare' difficulty level, called *Quake Done Quick*. If you owned *Quake* you could download and watch this to marvel at the skill involved and learn some tricks, so of course it wasn't long before the release of *Quake Done Quicker* and eventually *Quake Done Quick with a Vengeance*. The Speed Demos Archive (speeddemosarchive.com), a website dedicated to hosting speedrunning records and videos of any game, began as an archive for *Quake* speedruns.

⊙ Machinima is the use of a video game, or game tools, to create a movie of any length. Players had been recording straightforward gameplay for years, with limited distribution

and little in the way of self-expression, before the release of *Diary of a Camper*. Although only one minute and thirty-six seconds long, this sequence is distinguished by a text-based narrative: a 'camper' sits in one spot and waits to surprise enemies for easy kills, which is what happens here before he gets his comeuppance. The final gag is that the camper was John Romero.

⊙ Although *Diary of a Camper* is rudimentary in the context of what follows, it showed the way. In 2000 the site machinima.com codified the name for this new form of expression, and since then so many games have been used for machinima it would be impossible to list them all: well-known examples are *Red vs Blue* (*Halo*), the *South Park* episode *Make Love, Not Warcraft* (*World of Warcraft*) and Valve's magnificent *Team Fortress 2* shorts.

⊙ As all of this suggests, *Quake* was a quantum leap for both id's engine and

A BRIEF HISTORY OF VIDEO GAMES

Carmack's principles. Although the first sequel wasn't quite as special, *Quake III Arena* (1999) may be id's finest moment. This entry largely abandoned single-player and focused overwhelmingly on the multiplayer experience and the tools available for modders to recreate the game. In this it pioneered a decisive split in the first-person shooter genre between narrative (mostly single-player) games and a new breed focused exclusively on the competitive multiplayer experience.

➜ *Quake III Arena* is a precision shooter where every element is about the competitive experience. For the first time id refused to compromise on system requirements, so the game required a dedicated graphics card to run, but this allowed *Quake III* to look amazing and run at high speed without dropping frames. The quality of *Quake III*'s combat comes from so many elements that it can be hard to define exactly why the game feels so good in the hands: fans often describe it as 'crisp' or 'clean'. There is no clutter, and the openness meant that a mod such as *Challenge ProMode Arena* (2000) could deliver exactly the standardized parameters a burgeoning competitive scene required – making *Quake III*, among its many other achievements, a foundational eSport.

➜ *Quake III Arena* arguably ended id's great hot streak, though the company continues to develop games to this day (a *Doom* reboot is eagerly anticipated). And other things had been going on besides. Released a few months before *Doom*, *Myst* (1993) is a first-person game without the shooting. A real slow-burner, *Myst* presents an uncommonly beautiful island filled with puzzles and the player navigates around while trying to solve them.

➜ *Myst* is often hailed for its huge sales, which tends to obscure what a forward-thinking design the game had. There are no enemies to speak of on *Myst*'s island, the

Valve's *Team Fortress 2* shorts are brilliant comedic introductions to each class in the game – this still is from 'Meet the Sniper', where the grumpy Australian extols the virtues and pleasures of his job in-between talking to his parents.

narrative is left ambiguous and fragmentary, and there's no time limit. At the start of the game there aren't even any objectives, so the player decides of their own volition to begin exploring. Although the experience isn't quite as smooth as the visuals suggest, *Myst* established a new kind of adventure game that has recently come back into vogue: recent releases *Dear Esther* (2012) and *Gone Home* (2014), two first-person exploration games with unusual narrative mechanics, are absolutely in this lineage.

➲ So too, in a less obvious manner, is *Half-Life* (1998). Although built on a heavily modified version of the *Quake* engine, and featuring more than its share of gunplay, *Half-Life* marked a new level of narrative sophistication in how first-person shooters used environments and pacing. There are no cutscenes, and at scripted moments the player remains in control of main character Gordon Freeman.

➲ Freeman is a physicist at the Black Mesa Research Facility, and the game opens with his simply going to work on the tram. All told, this sequence lasts just over five minutes and lets the player see *Half-Life*'s world in 'normal' operation – the technology, the automation, the high security – while the tram's computerized voice runs through a standard series of announcements that provides just as much context. By the time Freeman arrives for work, a relatable chore, *Half-Life*'s semi-futuristic setting already feels familiar: a textbook example of showing, not telling.

➲ This continues even when the action begins: Freeman takes part in an experiment that goes horribly wrong, opening a rift which allows the hostile Xen aliens access to Earth. As one of the few survivors Freeman has to work his way out of the facility, battling both the Xen and the government special forces who have arrived to clean up the incident with no witnesses. The first half of the game is crammed with events to be witnessed that educate the player, whether that's seeing a scientist being killed by a headcrab or marines being pulled into air ducts.

⊙ Where Doom was a hostile universe where everything needed shooting, *Half-Life* feels like an inhabited place gone hostile: not least because you run into other survivors who help Freeman along. The Black Mesa complex feels like somewhere people actually work, rather than a series of arenas. The smart puzzles range from physics challenges to utilizing the environment against overwhelming odds, and the gunplay moves beyond *Doom*'s repertoire (great but imitated into banality) to offer grenade launchers, a crossbow, a raygun, a Xen homing gun and flesh-burrowing parasites that can be launched at foes.

⊙ If *Half-Life* indicated Valve was a special company, its subsequent attitude to mods showed it was unique. *Quake*'s engine had allowed mods to become more like complete games in their own right, and *Half-Life* was itself built using an almost completely rewritten version of these tools, GoldSrc, which innovated heavily in areas like AI – which Valve then went out of its way to promote to the modding community. *Team Fortress* (1996) was originally a Quake mod but Valve hired its designers to build *Team Fortress Classic* (1999) as an example of what GoldSrc could do, then gave them eight years to develop the outstanding *Team Fortress 2* (2007).

⊙ Valve adopted the best and most popular Half-Life mods, often hiring their creators and releasing the game as a standalone product – the most famous example of this being the peerless *Counter-Strike* (1999), the ultimate competitive shooter (more on which later). Other mods Valve brought to release include *Day of Defeat* (2003), and the company was equally happy to see popular

Half-Life emphasized the normality of Gordon Freeman's working environment in order to accentuate the horror of what was happening – and it was also great at warning the player by example. The example usually being the death of innocent NPCs.

mods like *Natural Selection* (2002) profit from its engine. Valve's influence over PC gaming would grow to even greater heights, but this is where its unique engagement with players began.

● Where *Half-Life* achieved a new standard in environmental narrative, *Thief: The Dark Project* (1998) achieved a new standard in environmental interaction. *Thief* uses a typical first-person shooter viewpoint but the mechanics are focused on avoiding detection and themed around its medieval setting. So, for example, there is no on-screen map showing guard positions – though, in a wonderful period touch, a 'hand-drawn' map of the location can be examined in fullscreen. Instead *Thief* makes the player rely on their eyes and ears, the latter to an unprecedented degree. Main character Garrett's footsteps can be heard by guards, though walking at different speeds and on different surfaces will affect the volume, while guards themselves

make noise and also tend to talk among themselves. *Thief*'s other key stealth mechanic is light, with Garrett's 'visibility' always indicated by an on-screen gem, and together these combine to form a natural rhythm of moving between shadows and spying on enemies.

● The fact that this is such an engaging way to play might seem surprising – after all, players will spend a lot of time simply standing still – but the appealing aspects lie beneath the surface. There's a voyeuristic charm to observing AI enemies, and their conversations are well written and acted while often containing useful information. And this feeds beautifully into the fact that first-person shooter enemies before *Thief* tended to have only two states – either they had noticed the player or they hadn't. *Thief* introduced a more complex style of AI that could become 'suspicious' about noises or unusual sights, and begin searching the area more carefully, rather than becoming hostile immediately.

❯ *Thief*'s locations were enormous and offered a multitude of ways to approach or avoid enemies, the perfect setting for these guards, and Looking Glass's faith in the core mechanics only stumbles when the second half of the game proves more combat-focused. The theme is also beautifully woven into objectives: Garrett is obviously a thief, and one of the most enjoyable rewards is finding a large stash of loot hidden away, and hoovering up the goodies one-by-one. This allows many levels to be built around Garrett finding a particular item, but the genius touch is that as the game's difficulty increases so do the number and complexity of the objectives in any given area.

❯ The sequel *Thief II: The Metal Age* (2000) improved on the original by focusing more on stealth, stripping away unnecessary monster encounters and toning down the supernatural vibe. The outstanding AI and sound design maintains high standards and, though it's no great departure, it is a fabulous game.

❯ *Thief II* was also the last major game from Looking Glass Studios. Although it lasted only a decade, the Massachusetts-based developer had an enormous impact on the first-person shooter genre: the pioneering *Ultima Underworld*, the psychological horror of *System Shock II*, and the spatial and AI complexity of *Thief* resonate through first-person games to this day. To take one example, in the original *System Shock* (1994) main enemy SHODAN mocks the player constantly, icily noting down details of their progress and making threats as they approach key objectives. The idea of an antagonist being a constant presence hadn't been used in a video game before – and certainly not in such an all-encompassing sense as SHODAN, who is not only your eventual goal but also the master of your environment.

With *Half-Life 2* and *Thief*, first-person shooter games moved from shooting galleries where enemies home in or fire from distance to more intricate systems that can be toyed with. The games can and do still resort to combat as a core mechanic, but the AI and environments are now complex enough to present new types of scenario for players. The advent of truly open first-person shooter is yet to come, but these are the first steps.

The first-person shooter genre is extremely well-suited to the PC controls of a mouse and keyboard – movement and any number of various commands can be assigned to the latter, while the mouse allows a speed and precision of movement that analogue sticks simply can't match. However, the greatest console shooters are built around this limitation.

One of the first and greatest is the Nintendo 64's *Goldeneye 007* (1997), developed by Rare (formerly Ultimate Play the Game). Based on the film of the same name, but exploring its world in considerably more detail, the player controls James Bond and has to work their way through various locations either based on or inspired by the movie.

Goldeneye's first great idea is implementing a semi-realistic take on stealth: Bond begins each mission with his silenced PP7 pistol, and can shoot guards before they have noticed his presence. Several neat tricks feed into this. The windows are one-way in the player's favour, allowing safe observation of enemies (and shots through the glass), while what would become one of the game's most iconic weapons, the sniper rifle, is fitted with a suppressor. The latter is hugely influential in the first-person shooter genre, being the first sniper rifle with an adjustable zoom and harder to aim at more distant targets.

Many of *Goldeneye*'s levels are structured such that they can be at least partially

The N64's *Goldeneye 007* was the first great console first-person shooter and, by putting the emphasis on the player's brain as well as their trigger finger, suited the licence perfectly. Another great pleasure is being able to explore the film's locations in greater detail, adding to the sense of 'being' Bond.

completed by stealth, but what really makes the game is its attention to detail. Adjusting the difficulty level doesn't merely increase enemy efficiency, but adds further objectives within each which change the playthrough significantly, and can often be completed in an order of the player's choosing. Enemies respond to locational damage, so headshots (the staple introduced to the first-person shooter genre by version 2.5 of the original *Team Fortress* mod in 1997) are an instant kill while a leg shot will make a soldier grasp at that area in shock. Bullets left holes in the wall, distant enemies would hear gunfire, and if Bond died blood would fall from the top of the screen (as in the famous opening sequence of every Bond movie) while the camera perspective 'collapsed' to ground level.

➲ Another reason *Goldeneye* is remembered fondly is its status as a licensed game that actually enhances the experience of the original movie. Most licensed games are awful. But *Goldeneye* presented locations that a player could explore at their leisure, and its levels were filled with 'unnecessary' details – whether that be a frightened scientist or simply a room irrelevant to the mission. *Goldeneye* is often cited as a great example of atmosphere in first-person shooters but perhaps the more accurate praise would be towards the combination of its locations and the source material: in the film you see many places briefly that, in the game, the player can explore thoroughly. This feels somehow illicit, secret agent-y, like you're seeing behind the scenes.

➲ It is perhaps hard for a modern player to appreciate *Goldeneye*'s many achievements because the frame rate is enormously variable and turns to treacle at high-action moments, but an equal issue is the relative decline of splitscreen multiplayer. *Goldeneye* featured a two-to-four player mode that was played on the same screen and, at the time, this was the best multiplayer shooter experience that could be had without the internet. It was also built around the capabilities of the N64 machine and its four controller ports, meaning an entire generation has memories of lugging pads round to a mate's house for an evening of License to Kill (one shot kills) on Facility. Although an experience of its time, it was one of the very best.

➡ It also led to Steven Spielberg taking an interest in first-person shooters. The great director had long been involved at the margins of video games and, though always a keen player himself, he had become intrigued after seeing his son Max playing *Goldeneye* with friends. In late 1997 Spielberg was in post-production on *Saving Private Ryan*, and resurrected a long-cherished idea he had previously pitched to Dreamworks Interactive (DWI) as 'Normandy Beach'. The problem was that no one at DWI thought a shooter based on a real historical war would sell: the kids

wanted *Doom* or *Quake*, they wanted aliens and green blood.

➡ Nevertheless Steven Spielberg is Steven Spielberg, and so over the course of a week a small team knocked together a very rudimentary demo based on his pitch and using mostly pre-existing assets. Spielberg had reworked his 'Normandy Beach' idea into *Medal of Honor*, named after the US Army's highest award, and wanted it to be a fun but authentic shooter that was also an elegy for the fallen. To this end he got the military advisor for *Saving Private Ryan*, Captain Dale Dye, involved.

➡ *Medal of Honor*'s locations are accurate, its dates are accurate and the constant feed of information about World War II is both fascinating and accurate. This was a new kind of immersion, almost the first non-fiction video game, except of course the player's character never really existed and these events are being reimagined rather than

Among many spooky elements in *Deus Ex* is that the New York skyline, in a game made before 9/11, doesn't have the twin towers – which is explained in-game as the result of a terrorist attack. The real reason, however, was that the game didn't have enough memory to render them in the background.

retold. The levels are structured like military missions, from infiltrating to engaging target to escaping, even letting the player impersonate a Nazi with fake papers for a short spell. It is a testament to *Medal of Honor*'s achievement that calling it a great shooter is almost an afterthought.

➲ *Deus Ex* (2000) stretched first-person shooter components about as far as they could go, offering open environments and a multitude of ways for clever players to make their way through. Although it's ostensibly a stealth game the enemies are almost blind and, really, the fun in *Deus Ex* is messing around with its systems: turrets can be reprogrammed to attack the baddies, patrol routes are so predictable they're begging for proximity mines, and most objects can be picked up and moved around.

➲ The magic of *Deus Ex* is in how much redundancy there is: levels can be played through in countless ways and the player can choose to follow orders to the letter or, by messing them up, unlock new dialogue and situations. This is a perfect fit for its open-ended style of progression, and the simple fact that the best-laid plans of cyberpunk avatars often go wrong (with pretty amusing results) means *Deus Ex* offers a freedom of approach that, even today, is extremely uncommon for games in general.

➲ By the turn of the millennium the first-person shooter had evolved beyond *Doom*'s template, though the impact of id's design could still be felt in every shotgun blast and corridor full of cannon fodder. The genre had proven itself to have the room for big ideas and smartly controlled narratives, as well as headshots, and its popularity meant it had become one of publishers' favourite bets. Although there's still a long way to travel, the modern first-person shooter had arrived.

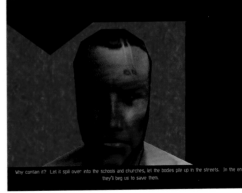

Why contain it? Let it spill over into the schools and churches, let the bodies pile up in the streets. In the end, they'll beg us to save them.

Deus Ex: Human Revolution –
'Activity of Hive' by Dead End
Thrills. Eidos Montreal's 2011
successor reintroduced some
of the original's ideas, but
more than anything shows
the visual progress made in
under a decade. (Courtesy of
Dead End Thrills)

The Console War

Genesis does what Nintendon't.

Sega of America marketing slogan

> The problem faced by Nintendo in the late 1980s is a theme for platform-holders. The company had begun thinking about a successor system, but the NES was still selling as well as ever, and the money from software licensing simply didn't stop coming. How to turn your back on that?

> For a long time Nintendo couldn't and focused on supporting the NES market as much as possible. In 1987 NEC had begun the 16-bit era of home consoles with the PC Engine, a console co-developed with Hudson Soft. Although it had an 8-bit CPU, the machine had a dual 16-bit GPU that allowed it to display 512 colours, over ten times what the NES and Master System could offer. The PC Engine was successful enough in Japan to warrant an international release but, by this stage, Sega was ready for battle.

> Sega's R&D team, led by Masami Ishikawa, had been working on the next console ever since finishing work on the Master System, and this time the arcade side of the business paid off. One of the earliest 16-bit arcade boards was 1985's Sega System 16, and falling microprocessor prices meant adapting this design for a home console was now feasible. It is impossible to overstate how important this decision was. The System 16 had powered arcade games like *Altered Beast*, *Golden Axe* and *Shinobi*, and so the new console could deliver near arcade-perfect versions.

> Although the hardware was called the 'Mark V' during development, Sega realized that the Master System's successor deserved a little more flair in the name department. The classic Mega Drive was chosen, though in North America this was changed to Genesis for legal reasons. The system was launched on 29 October 1988 in Japan and started slowly, racking up 400,000 sales in the

first year – among other things, the near-contemporaneous launch of the incredible *Super Mario Bros. 3* had taken some of the shine off the 'next generation' of consoles.

➜ The Mega Drive would never quite catch on in Japan, eventually being outsold by both the PC Engine and Super Nintendo Entertainment System (SNES), but Sega's main target was the American market. Dissatisfied with the Master System's marketing under partner Tonka, Sega started casting around for alternatives – one of whom was Atari. Although CEO Jack Tramiel would eventually turn the deal down, the president of Atari's entertainment division Mike Katz was more interested – so much so that, one month after the American launch of Genesis in January 1989, Katz was hired as Sega of America's CEO.

➜ Although Katz's reign would be brief, he certainly made it memorable and laid the foundations for the success of Genesis. His most inspired decision was to stigmatize Nintendo as a company that made children's games, leading to the advertising slogan 'Sega does what Nintendon't'. A bizarre TV commercial shows Genesis games running while a chorus line sings 'You can't do this on Nintendo', followed by glimpses of men shooting at a building, a Genesis blimp, Michael Jackson and a pro football player. Somehow this campaign instantly redefined Sega as the 'cool' video-game company, in opposition to Nintendo's family-friendly image.

➜ Katz also took extremely smart steps towards solving Sega's software problem. Inspired by Electronic Arts (EA)'s adoption of real-world personalities to shift titles, Katz signed up professional athletes including Joe Montana (American football), Pat Riley (golf) and Evander Holyfield (boxing), thus giving Sega's 'own brand' software an instant dusting of credibility.

➔ But Sega of Japan was impatient. Despite only shifting 400,000 units itself in the first year, it expected Sega of America to sell a million, and among other things mandated that Katz and his staff should chant *Hyakumandai* (Japanese for 'one million') every day. Surprisingly this strategy didn't work and in its first year in the states the Genesis sold 500,000 – which Katz considered 'damn good'.

➔ Shortly afterwards Katz was gone, cast aside by Sega of Japan's president Hayao Nakayama in favour of industry newcomer Tom Kalinske. Kalinske had firm ideas for how Sega could make Genesis a bigger success, prime among which were a price cut, prising third-party developers away from Nintendo and ramping up the competitive advertising.

➔ 'Oh and the other thing was that we [had] to take *Altered Beast* out and put our own character in,' says Kalinske. 'There was a combined US/Japanese team working frantically on what became *Sonic the Hedgehog*, which wasn't called that at the time. I said we have to put that in with the hardware, and that really pissed [Sega Japan] off, because they said I was nuts to want to put our best software title in with the hardware . . . They felt it made no sense whatsoever.'[27]

➔ Kalinske was certainly right on *Altered Beast* (1988). Designed for the Sega System 16 board, so clearly intended to be a killer title for both arcade and Mega Drive, *Altered Beast* is a side-scrolling beat-'em-up where the player's centurion character can change into various beasts with power-ups. The main selling point turned out to be the combination of large sprites and some inspired enemy designs because the action stank – the combat was repetitive and simplistic, with the beast forms barely improving things.

➔ Then there was the hedgehog. Mario's success led to a host of imitators over the late

One of the most unusual aspects of the Sega Mega Drive's marketing, though by some lights it is genius, was the emphasis on 'blast processing' – a minor and obscure programming trick on the console's graphics chips that was blown up into a major differentiator with the SNES. It was nothing of the sort. (Photo credit: Evan Amos)

1980s and 1990s, most of them starring in woefully designed platformers like the *Bubsy* series, *Zool* and *Cool Spot*. Not only were Mario's clones lacking in the visual design department but, much more importantly, the games simply didn't compare.

→ The origins of *Sonic the Hedgehog* are perhaps no different – Sega ordered its crack AM8 development team to come up with a character that could fill the Mario role of console mascot. But Sonic was different. First of all he was born out of an idea for unique gameplay – young programmer Yuji Naka had created a tech demo featuring a sprite moving smoothly on a curve, which became a prototype of a speedy character moving through a winding tube. Naka's prototype required an animal that could move fast and roll up into a ball. Rather bizarrely this thought process led to the selection of a hedgehog, designed by Naoto Ōshima, an animal that isn't exactly known for speed

but had the additional benefit of spikes (for attacking).

→ '*Mario* was already on the market,' says Naka. 'So obviously I played it a lot and studied it, but the important idea about *Sonic* was trying to create something that was completely different from *Mario*. So the way the idea was developed was away from the *Mario* paradigm which was already well-known and copied.'

→ Naka looked at the fundamentals that made the *Mario* games so good – noting with particular admiration how fluid movement was achieved with just a D-pad and two buttons. He also noticed that the levels' structure often stopped *Mario* in full flow, forcing the player to work their way up vertical platforms, bash bricks or enter a pipe.

→ 'Rather than being simply about trying to communicate the power of the Mega Drive, it was trying to do something that *Mario* didn't,' says Naka.

Sonic the Hedgehog's bright visual palette and large sprites distinguished it from the vast majority of SNES games, but the real selling point was the speed at which Sonic could move through the levels – which the designers emphasized with features like loops that required Sonic to be moving quickly.

The cornerstone of Sega's US strategy was comparing the Genesis directly to the SNES, and crimes against the English language were a small price to pay. This advert is one of the most impactful in video game history, with its sheer attitude the foundation for countless schoolyard arguments.

For example when you play **Mario**, however good you are, it always takes let's say 30 seconds to go through a level. Now my idea with **Sonic** was that as you get better you can learn where things are and clear the stage quicker. So when I was programming it I thought about how to push that speed factor, so it was more about trying to make it feel different from **Mario** in the hands, and having a more fluid movement than in **Mario** which can occasionally feel a little jagged, stop-start.

➔ *Sonic the Hedgehog* was released on 23 June 1991 for the Mega Drive in both the US and Europe, with the Japanese release a month later. It was a stunning game to look at, featuring huge, brightly coloured sprites moving at speeds no other console could match, and it was a new spin on the 2D platformer too.

➔ *Sonic*'s stages could be raced through, with tricks for experienced players to improve their times, or the vertical expanses could be explored. Environmental features like loop-de-loops were simply fun to trigger, power-ups littered the landscape and every stage had areas you would miss if simply blazing through. This meant that *Sonic* could withstand multiple playthroughs, and the world had a simple but charming personality: destroying the Badnik enemies saw a fluffy animal escape, while the moustachioed Dr Robotnik would turn up at the end of each world with a diabolical new boss machine.

➔ Best of all, under Kalinske's plan *Sonic the Hedgehog* became the new pack-in title for Genesis: now the console had a 'must-have' title and a reduced price of $129. *Sonic*'s 'cool' factor among the young audience saw Sega strike the first big blow of the console wars, outselling Nintendo's newly released Super Nintendo almost two to one during Christmas 1991.

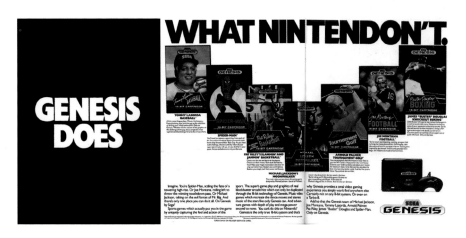

➡ Nintendo had waited on the sidelines as the PC Engine and Mega Drive made the running in the 16-bit race, both confident in its market position and unwilling to leave the lucrative NES behind. In a sense this confidence was well-placed: by the time the Super Nintendo launched in Japan in November 1990, anticipation was at fever pitch and the initial shipment of 300,000 units was gone within hours.

➡ If *Sonic* had the slightest whiff of style over substance, that was mainly because the Super Nintendo had been launched with *Super Mario World* (1990). Where *Super Mario Bros. 3* had marked a giant leap for the series, this was more of a refinement – but on a much more powerful console with commensurately superior visuals. It is simply one of the best 2D games ever made.

➡ *Super Mario World*'s main innovation is Yoshi, a ride-able green dinosaur that gulped down enemies and in almost any other game would make things a doddle. But *Super Mario World*'s levels are something else, a collection of clockwork obstacle courses designed to bamboozle and delight in equal measure. The open structure and world map were familiar but polished to a shine – Super Mario's world connects together in one long sequence of bobbing landmarks, allows replaying levels to find 'secret' exits, and hides even more secrets beyond these.

➡ *Super Mario Bros. 3*'s brilliance meant that Nintendo's designers didn't need to reinvent the wheel – they could simply build the best possible game. This shows in the intricacy of the Ghost Houses, which fiendishly toy with players and hide their solutions, or the Forest of Illusion where every 'normal' exit is a fake. Most of all it's in the Star Road, a group of secret levels that would be found only by the dedicated and offered an extreme challenge (and at the end of the final one, the legend 'You Are A Super Player' spelt out in coins).

A key SNES feature for young children everywhere was the gorgeously clacky 'eject' button – which was in fact totally unnecessary, but Nintendo's designers felt it might be fun to play with. The Japanese Famicom also had an eject button, although not the NES. (Photo credit: Evan Amos)

Super Mario World also pared back *Super Mario Bros. 3*'s power-ups and concentrates on wringing as much as possible out of the feather. This grants Mario a cape and flight just like the Raccoon Suit, but after running out of juice the player can then divebomb towards the ground or hold the cape like a parachute, and alternating the two lets Mario hang-glide through levels. It's a gorgeously tactile system to be mastered and the best power-up in the series.

The most unusual thing about *Super Mario World*, and a major contrast to *Sonic the Hedgehog*, is that it wasn't really designed to show what the hardware could do. The demonstration of technical prowess took a back seat to perfecting the game, and this is one of the reasons why *Sonic* made such an impact – Sega's title was a brash technical showcase, where *Super Mario World* looked like more of the same but a bit prettier. It may have been a much better game but,

as Nintendo was learning, software was no longer everything.

The all-consuming NES had made Nintendo complacent, and the company had underestimated both Sega and third-party publishers. Nevertheless the SNES was a hit from the start, shipping four million in its first year on sale in Japan. Just under a year later, on 23 August 1991, the SNES was released in North America and began quickly making up ground on the Mega Drive (Europe, rather typically for Nintendo, would have to wait until the summer of 1992).

Nintendo no longer had a monopoly on third-party developers, with companies like Electronic Arts throwing their weight behind the Mega Drive, and Sega drove home its advantage by establishing the Sega Technical Institute (STI) in San Francisco – a developer dedicated to making games that would appeal to the US market, with star talent like Yuji Naka imported.

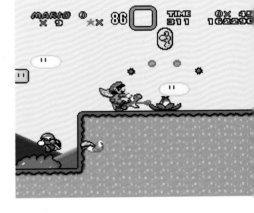

Super Mario World is one of the greatest 2D games ever made, its many worlds packed with new ideas and objects for Mario to interact with. *Sonic* had style, but *Mario* had substance. *Super Mario World* also demonstrates a larger theme with Nintendo: packaging your console's best game with the hardware.

SCORE   33500
TIME 1:34
RINGS   16

SONIC x 2

Sonic the Hedgehog 2 is probably the best of the original Sonic games, with Sega's developers given all the time they needed to produce a follow-up of extremely high quality. Especially notable were the faux-3D bonus stages, which saw Sonic and Tails running 'into' the screen to try and nab Chaos Emeralds.

The studio produced hits like *Sonic the Hedgehog 2* (1992), which greatly improved on the original and added *Sonic*'s buddy Miles 'Tails' Prower – and, in a dig at Nintendo's release habits, was released almost simultaneously worldwide, with Tuesday 24 November 1992 dubbed 'Sonic 2sday'. Other STI games like *Kid Chameleon* (1992) filled a *Mega Man*-shaped hole with a shape-shifting hero, while oddities like *The Ooze* (1995), a 2D platformer built around the character's size, tried to craft more offbeat icons.

Perhaps the studio's finest work, outside of the Sonic sequels, was *Comix Zone* (1995). A brutally difficult 2D beat-'em-up, *Comix Zone* was distinguished by its concept and presentation, which featured illustrator Sketch Turner being sucked into his own work. The game takes place over a series of panels, creating the effect of being inside a comic book, and at certain stages Turner can bash through panels to find alternate routes and secrets. To this day, no game has mimicked this winning concept.

Sadly many of the best titles on the Mega Drive suffered neglect, overshadowed by the more obvious charms of Sonic and co. One of the console's finest was *Herzog Zwei* (1990), which combined realtime strategy (RTS) and shooter mechanics – the player controls a flying mecha that can purchase, deploy and give orders to ground combat units. The limited AI makes single-player something of a walkover, but multiplayer is genuinely thrilling thanks to the depth of its mechanics: production bases have to be controlled to keep your army supplied, units will run out of fuel and need repairing, and the position of your mecha on the map is always crucial. *Herzog Zwei* was an enormous influence on *Dune II* (1992), often considered the 'true' starting point of RTS games, but sadly never went further as a series.

Sega had a knack for finding more offbeat

Comix Zone took three years to develop and arguably had little impact, but remains a stylish implementation of a truly brilliant concept: multiple routes through the panels can be chosen, characters communicate through speech bubbles and hero Sketch can 'rip' bits of the background to use as paper planes.

titles, the best of which was *Toejam & Earl* (1991) – developed by Johnson Voorsanger Productions, a tiny studio. Sega funded and published the game as an exclusive. *Toejam & Earl* are hippie-ish aliens trapped on Earth who have to escape by finding ten spaceship parts, while being pursued by various nightmarish 'Earthlings' – packs of nerds, ghostly ice-cream trucks and chickens armed with tomato mortars among others.

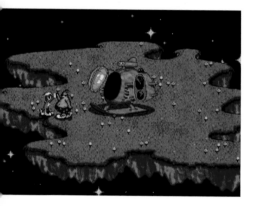

The deeply funky *Toejam & Earl* was filled with nice touches, including a co-op mode that would smoothly switch between one screen and splitscreen as players moved independently of one another. It also, when you were playing solo, claimed the other character was on vacation.

● This surreal aesthetic was combined with a roguelike structure which randomized the levels in every game, something new for consoles. But it was the care and attention put into the world that made *Toejam & Earl* a classic, particularly in two-player mode: the aliens would chat and bicker with each other, while the screen would split when players were apart and come back together when they were close enough. The sequel *Toejam & Earl in Panic on Funkotron* (1993) was an excellent side-scrolling platformer, with the same mischievous sense of humour, but it's nowhere near as original or memorable as the first game. (This was down to Sega, which considered a 'straight' sequel unmarketable and pushed the developer towards the more standard platformer archetype.)

● In the face of such originality Nintendo had beloved franchises and its own technical showcases. Futuristic racer *F-Zero* (1990) was created as an SNES launch title to demonstrate the console's 'Mode 7' ability, which rotated and scaled backgrounds to create pseudo-3D environments. *F-Zero* is blisteringly fast with tough AI opponents, and its tracks are filled with hairpin bends that test skills and showcase the sweetly gaudy visuals at incredible (for the time) speeds. If that didn't appeal there was the quietly brilliant *Pilotwings* (1990), a kind of 'lite' flying simulation with superb controls and Mode 7 scaling, where the player simply had to complete tests by flying through markers in the sky. As peaceful as it is challenging, *Pilotwings* is unique.

Nintendo also managed to improve the capabilities of the SNES through a cartridge-held coprocessor called the 'Super FX' chip. Developed by the British Argonaut Games, who were swiftly bundled over to Japan, the chip allowed the SNES hardware to render polygons and advanced 2D effects, with most of the games that used it combining the two.

The first game to contain the Super FX chip was *Starfox* (1993), co-developed by Argonaut and Nintendo. The player pilots the Arwing assault ship in a 3D on-rails shooter, snaffling power-ups, blasting enemies and dodging obstacles. The game's polygonal visuals remain one of the 16-bit era's defining achievements, but these are matched by an outstanding soundtrack and the Nintendo touch of these space pilots being talking animals – Fox McCloud, Peppy Hare, Falco Lombardi and the useless Slippy Toad. Along with the jabbering bosses this imbued the sharp edges of *Starfox*'s world with personality, and the multiple routes through the game (many of which were extremely well-hidden) gave enormous replay value.

The reason the SNES is remembered so fondly, however, isn't for the technical showcases so much as the spectacular versions of Nintendo's classics, and the blooming of the JRPG genre. *Super Mario*

F-Zero set a new standard for the racing genre and spawned a sub-genre of 'futuristic' racers of which the most notable is the PlayStation hit *Wipeout*. It was an early example of the 'Mode 7' technology of the SNES, which allowed the track to be scaled and rotated around the player's hovercar to create the illusion of breakneck speed.

A BRIEF HISTORY OF VIDEO GAMES

World refined the 2D platformer to near-perfection, and on 21 November 1991 *The Legend of Zelda: A Link to the Past* did the same for the action-RPG.

➲ Often cited as one of the greatest games ever made, *A Link to the Past* abandoned *Zelda II*'s side-on combat in favour of an angled, top-down 2D experience. The major difference was atmosphere. The game begins on a dark and stormy night with Link waking to see his uncle – who warns the boy to stay in bed – venturing outside. As soon as he leaves, the player naturally hops out of bed and leaves the house, entering a world dashed with rain and filled with worried soldiers. Exploring further they find a route into the castle's basement, where Link's dying uncle bequeaths his sword and shield to the boy. This may not sound like an especially original narrative, but its telling through the player's actions gives the opening a queer and unforgettable power.

➲ *A Link to the Past*'s greatest achievement is the combination of overworld, dungeons and the structure that gently guides the player between them. The world of Hyrule has many elements: a large town filled with NPCs and minigames, odd little cabins in faraway corners and secrets dotted around. The dungeons are each constructed around one of the game's items: at first progress is slow and painstaking as the player acquires a map and a compass, but is unable to face most of the dungeon's challenges. Then a turning point comes when the player finds and defeats a midboss to acquire a new item, the capabilities of which feed into previously unsolvable challenges, and the second half of any dungeon speeds up in pacing.

➲ This alone is a great structure, but *A Link to the Past* has a magnificent twist. After completing the first three dungeons Link is banished by main baddie Agahnim to the Dark World, a warped version of Hyrule where

A Link to the Past's central innovation was the light and dark world, whereby after a certain point in the plot Link could travel back-and-forth between Hyrule and an alternate Hyrule ruled by Ganondorf. It was such a brilliant twist that most subsequent *Zelda* games have featured some variation on the idea.

the ultimate villain Ganondorf is imprisoned. The game then continues with Link having to complete seven dungeons in the Dark World, while warping back and forth between the two settings and solving mysteries that seem to cross the boundaries of both.

➜ In this *A Link to the Past* more or less codified the structure that *Zelda* games would have in the future. It introduced multi-level dungeons, allowing Nintendo's developers to create correspondingly fiendish puzzles that almost forced the player to think in three dimensions, and the dual-world structure that has since become commonplace. The huge world, doubled in size by that Dark twist, also captures the sense of exploration and mystery for which Zelda strives – ask any player for memories, and you're as likely to hear about a strange flute boy or secret cave as a daunting dungeon.

➜ *The Metroid* series experienced an equally revolutionary upgrade with *Super Metroid*

(1994). This would be Gunpei Yokoi's final hurrah with the franchise he had created, and something of a return to the first game in the series. The narrative of *Super Metroid* is built around lurid energy-sucking aliens and space pirates, but the game rises far above such schlock by keeping its focus on the environment and the player character. The real story of *Super Metroid* is in how Samus's abilities – and so those of the player – increase throughout.

➜ The main location, Zebes, is an enormous 2D maze where most routes are blocked until a certain item is acquired, meaning that as Samus becomes more capable the planet begins to open up for exploration. Finding closed doors may be frustrating at first, but it's tinged with the delicious knowledge that soon you'll return with the means to make it through. One of Super Metroid's intangible pleasures is the mental map a player begins building to complement the in-game one

– making a note of a gap you can't quite get into or out-of-reach items that you'll come back for later. And the reason this is a pleasure is that the game delivers, bending to your will as you blaze back through with a buffed-up Samus.

➡ *Super Metroid*'s structure popularized the *Metroidvania* subgenre, the other half of this portmanteau coming from Konami's *Castlevania* series. The latter's focus was on gothic castles and vampires rather than aliens, but as early as *Castlevania II: Simon's Quest* (1987) it was adapting the original *Metroid*'s structure into a more non-linear overall design.

➡ The SNES benefited greatly from certain smart licences, such as a classic conversion of Capcom's *Street Fighter II* (1992). This had almost single-handedly revived the arcade industry by bringing a new complexity and flair to two-player fighting games, including hard-to-execute special moves and a colourful roster of fighters from which to choose. The SNES conversion captured the arcade game's feel and was followed by several updates (the best of which is *Street Fighter II Turbo*). This was one of Nintendo's major third-party victories, as an exclusivity deal significantly delayed release of a Mega Drive version.

➡ There are many, many more great games across both consoles. Squaresoft's *Final Fantasy* series had began on the NES, but *Final Fantasy VI* (1994) marked a new level of storytelling sophistication in a brilliantly realized steampunk world that pushed the SNES to its absolute limits. Although its turn-based battling was familiar, *Final Fantasy VI* added a huge number of customization options, allowing players to personalize characters, and its thematic scope was more mature than its predecessors, encompassing issues as varied as sexuality and suicide.

➡ Nintendo's own *EarthBound* (1994) is something of a counterpoint to this, an RPG

Street Fighter II marked the real beginning of the greatest fighting game series ever, with Ryu and Ken its classic match-up. Capcom took advantage of *Street Fighter II*'s popularity by releasing several versions across formats with minor tweaks, all of which sold like hotcakes.

that takes as its setting a typical suburban American town – starring a young boy called Ness who has to phone his mother every so often to avoid getting homesick. The game's RPG systems are well-executed if unoriginal, but it's the world crafted by Japanese writer Shigesato Itoi that is singular. The typical RPG structure is a perfect metaphor for a narrative about growth, and *EarthBound* is a game about growing up and finding your own identity in the world. Self-aware and slightly warped, personal in focus but epic in its sweep, poignant and profound, *EarthBound* is a masterpiece.

➔ Other great titles include the isometric RPG *Shadowrun* (1993), based on the pen-and-paper RPG series, which blended a dark story and noir-ish visuals with an excellent upgrade system. LucasArts's *Zombies Ate My Neighbours* (1993) was an irreverent top-down shooter that excelled in cooperative gameplay, while *Uniracers* (1994) was an

off-the-wall stunt-racing game that remains unique. Definitive arcade conversions like *Super R-Type* (1991), system exclusives like *Contra III* (1992), excellent licences like *Super Star Wars* (1992) and quality platformers like *Plok* (1993) were all a part of one of the most wide-ranging and high-quality game libraries a console has ever had.

➔ Not that the Mega Drive was any slouch. Sega's partnership with Electronic Arts resulted in a regular series of superb sports titles, and the platform-holder went further in commissioning direct competition for other popular titles tied up in Nintendo's exclusivity deals. The best example of this is *Streets of Rage* (1991), based on Capcom's popular side-scrolling, beat-'em-up Final Fight. *Streets of Rage* simply cloned the mechanics, down to having three selectable characters, health-regenerating food items and temporary weapons. The sequel *Streets of Rage II* managed to surpass its inspiration,

EarthBound oozes charm and the designers clearly lavished attention on even the most incidental parts of the game. An interesting footnote is that Satoru Iwata, later president of Nintendo, was one of the core programmers on the team.

introducing a more complex combat system, a wider range of enemies, a fantastic techno soundtrack and more differentiated characters.

➡ The Mega Drive's most infamous victory in the console war was the uncensored version of *Mortal Kombat* (1992). This was a *Street Fighter II* clone designed to attract publicity (which it managed very successfully) by ending each bout with a Fatality – the losing player's character would stagger upright for a few seconds, during which time the winning player could input a complex button sequence to execute a grisly finishing move. These ranged from the winner morphing into a dragon and biting their unlucky opponent in half to burning off their face or freezing and then shattering their body.

➡ *Mortal Kombat* was an appalling game compared to *Street Fighter II*, but its extreme violence and gore led to success and notoriety. When it came time for the home conversions Nintendo insisted that this aspect be toned down or removed entirely, conscious of its family-friendly image, while Sega was happy to have everything on show. This, of course, fed straight into Sega's overarching marketing strategy, made Nintendo seem out-of-touch and resulted in the Mega Drive version outselling the SNES game by more than two to one.

➡ This also meant that *Mortal Kombat* played a key role in the 1992–3 US Senate hearings on video-game violence. These hearings, led by Senators Joseph Lieberman and Herb Kohl, were based on fundamental misunderstandings of what games were and what they allowed, which means that with hindsight it's hard to see them as anything but slightly comical. In a nutshell Lieberman's understanding of what games allowed their players to do did not match up with reality (he never bothered to go as far as playing one) but the fact of his position as a senator

Streets of Rage II vastly improved on the original and introduced characters with much more variety – as well as special moves that cost health but were extremely useful, a nice risk/reward mechanic.

led to the hearings and through these the industry voluntarily establishing the Entertainment Software Rating Board (ESRB) – the situation was not helped by witnesses from Nintendo and Sega who were more concerned with taking potshots at each other than correcting misperceptions.

⊙ The most important difference between Nintendo and Sega, however, was in how they treated hardware upgrades. Nintendo managed to revitalize the SNES by first introducing games made with the Super-FX chip, and later Rare's *Donkey Kong Country* series – these featured 3D models and textures pre-rendered on SGI workstations

then converted to the SNES hardware, resulting in truly outstanding visuals that many compared favourably to contemporary 32-bit games. The *Donkey Kong Country* games were very average platformers under this visual sheen, but the visual sheen was what mattered – the first sold over nine million copies globally. The important point is that Nintendo's improvements were included on the cartridge the consumer buys.

⊙ Sega, on the other hand, adopted and then abandoned two major hardware upgrades for the Mega Drive. The Mega-CD, released in Japan in 1991 and the States in 1992, was a CD-ROM unit that attached to the base Mega Drive console and allowed for, among other things, full motion video (FMV) sequences. Sega saw FMV as a major selling point and bought up several old laserdisc games that had never seen release, such as *Sewer Shark* and *Night Trap*, as well as working on its own exclusive titles like *Sonic CD*. But this was

The Genesis version of *Mortal Kombat II*. The game's 'fatalities' were one of the marketing triumphs of the 1990s, and arguably in video-game history, both enticing impressionable youth and scandalizing their parents.

as far as Mega-CD support ever went, and outside of *Sewer Shark* the FMV games were pretty pathetic productions.

→ If the Mega-CD was an expensive add-on that fractured the Mega Drive audience, then 1994's 32X showed Sega had learned nothing from the experience. This add-on was designed to bridge the gap between the Mega Drive and the upcoming 32-bit generation of consoles, therefore allowing Sega more time to perfect the troubled design of its own Saturn. The 32X software had its highlights, including a great port of *Virtua Fighter*, but it mostly played host to barely enhanced Mega Drive conversions. And shortly after release, in an unforgiveable act of foolishness, Sega abandoned it in favour of the newly released Saturn.

→ The 16-bit era made Sega a household name, and by 1992 it had a previously inconceivable 55 per cent share of the market, but the Mega-CD and (especially)

the 32X created serious problems for the company. Consumer confidence took an enormous hit after two add-ons that were poorly supported, and the uneasy relationship between Sega's Japanese and American arms led to the Genesis audience being largely abandoned in 1995 as the company's focus switched to the Saturn. As Sega's audience fractured, the SNES kept on selling.

→ When the dust settled Nintendo had shifted forty-nine million SNES consoles worldwide, compared to forty million Mega Drives – which may not sound like a victory for Sega, but certainly was in terms of the previous generation's market share. (The NES sold sixty-two million units in its lifetime to the Master System's thirteen million.) Both Nintendo and Sega believed they had won the 16-bit console war and prepared for more of the same. What neither understood was that their little rivalry was about to be blown apart by a new challenger.

The 'Nintendo' PlayStation

The 32-bit generation begins with two failures: one was the last throw of the die for a wizened competitor, and the other simply too far ahead of its time. By the mid-1990s the Atari Corporation was unrecognizable from the industry-defining company of the 1970s, reeling from a series of home-console misfires and the failure of its Lynx handheld device. The Atari Jaguar was designed to put it back on top.

Marketed as the first 64-bit gaming system the Jaguar, like almost all of Atari's later products, was developed by external talent. Flare Technology was a British team that had raised industry eyebrows with its proposed Konix Multisystem console and, though that design never made it to market, its potential was enough for Atari to fund development on what would become the Jaguar.

A priority with the Jaguar was getting the machine to market as quickly as possible, in the hope that its comparative grunt would tempt players away from the Mega Drive/SNES duopoly. The machine launched in the USA for $249 in November 1993 with one of the most bizarre controllers in history: a gigantic plate-shaped plastic mould with a standard layout (D-pad, three buttons) on the top half, and what looked like a twelve-button switchboard on the bottom.

A dodgy controller turned out to be the least of Jaguar's problems. Although a powerful machine overall, its CPU had severe issues that, combined with a lack of documentation, turned many developers off. Atari claimed that it had shipped 100,000 Jaguars by the end of 1994, but this did little to allay fears among both consumers and developers that it would falter badly against upcoming machines from Sega and Sony.

In 1995 Atari's revenues dived as, despite a price cut, the Jaguar stopped selling. In a 1996 filing to its stockholders the numbers were

The Atari Jaguar: in an odd quirk of fate the console's dimensions were later found to be ideal for housing a dental camera, and the moulding plates were sold to Imagin Systems, a manufacturer of dental imaging equipment. (Photo credit: Evan Amos)

laid bare: 'From the introduction of Jaguar in late 1993 through the end of 1995 Atari sold approximately 125,000 units of Jaguar. As of December 31 1995 Atari had approximately 100,000 units of Jaguar in inventory.' [28]

➡ The Jaguar would be Atari's last console, and at least it had a few decent games. Its ports of *Doom* and *Wolfenstein 3D* were far beyond what the 16-bit competition could achieve, and among the exclusive titles *Alien vs. Predator* (1994) offered a unique take on the first-person shooter. Developed by the UK's Rebellion, who would never hit such heights again, *Alien vs. Predator* allowed players to take on the role of an Alien, a Predator or a human marine – each of whom had different abilities, objectives and a unique user interface. As much a horror game as a shooter, *Alien vs. Predator* was the machine's bestselling game.

➡ A more unusual highlight was Jeff Minter's *Tempest 2000* (1994). The original *Tempest* was a wonderful vector-based shooter, full of bright colours, neat perspective tricks and extremely fast. *Tempest 2000* dials this up to eleven with trippy special effects and warping backgrounds, backed up by blasting techno music. It's a superb shooter, a fitting follow-up to Dave Theurer's original, and in its own way brings Atari's early creativity full-circle – going out not with a whimper, but a bang.

➡ The Jaguar's equally ill-fated contemporary was the 3DO Interactive Multiplayer, a console conceived and brought to market by Electronic Arts founder Trip Hawkins. The 3DO is often derided for its commercial failure, though it did sell around two million units, and lack of software (which is certainly true).

➡ The 3DO was, however, an interesting idea – a unified platform that could be manufactured by any licensee, with much lower royalty rates on software than contemporary home systems. This business model depended on large electronics

Alien vs. Predator was a rare highpoint for the Jaguar, though its atmosphere arguably owes a lot to the console's limitations – the sound is minimal and the environments are in places desolate. The animations are also impressive for the time, achieved by taking stop-motion photographs of character models then digitizing them.

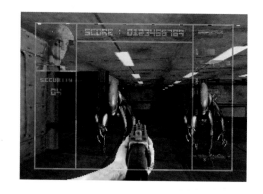

A BRIEF HISTORY OF VIDEO GAMES

companies like Panasonic or Sony licensing and selling the 3DO hardware. Hawkins had extensive industry contacts and, though Sony declined to get involved for obvious reasons, Panasonic signed up.

➡ The real problem was the price. Manufacturers had to make a profit on any hardware sold and this, along with the 3DO's powerful specs, meant an astonishing launch price of $699. Even retailers balked at this, quickly arranging a new price point of $599, but such an upfront cost combined with the lack of truly must-have games sealed the machine's fate. The 3DO did offer good conversions of PC games like *Alone in the Dark* and *Myst* but, starved of exclusive software and oversaturated with awful FMV games like *Mad Dog McCree*, it died a death and was discontinued by the end of 1996. The 3DO's successor M2 would, according to Hawkins, have been all things to all men. Unfortunately the 3DO's failure saw the nearly completed M2 design sold to Matsushita, who did little with it.

➡ Change was coming. It had its origins in 1990 when Nintendo was considering a response to Sega's Mega-CD add-on and had approached Sony about a partnership. The companies agreed to work on a similar CD add-on for the SNES (which already used a Sony-engineered sound chip), the original idea being that Nintendo would sell the add-on and Sony would sell an integrated unit called the PlayStation.

➡ Sony's engineers, led by Ken Kutaragi, worked hard on this project. Kutaragi had joined Sony in 1975 and was a brash, dynamic and creative engineer intrigued by the possibilities of video games – which he felt weren't progressing as fast as they should (as far back as the 1980s, Sony colleagues remember him talking about a realtime 3D game system). But Sony's CEO Norio Ohga had told Kutaragi in no uncertain terms

The Panasonic 3DO, produced in 1993, was heavily promoted and even named as *Time* magazine's '1994 Product of the Year'. The 3DO was truly a forward-thinking product, but its price was also from the future. (Photo credit: Evan Amos)

that Sony was not going to get into the 'toy business' and so collaboration with Nintendo looked as good as it would get.

➡ Nintendo began having second thoughts about the unit well before its announcement, primarily because it would be ceding a huge amount of control – the design and manufacturing rights to the CD unit would belong to Sony. Used to controlling every aspect of his business, and seeing this as crucial to its success, Hiroshi Yamauchi decided that the Sony deal would not do. And so Nintendo approached Sony's arch-rival Philips about making an alternative product – without telling Sony.

➡ At the 1991 Consumer Electronics Show Ken Kutaragi proudly announced the Nintendo PlayStation, the culmination of his team's efforts. Almost immediately Nintendo announced that it would not be partnering with Sony but Philips. Kutaragi and Sony had been humiliated in front of the world's press.

➡ Norio Ohga was incandescent with rage. A failed project was one thing, but the way Nintendo had conducted itself was tantamount to betrayal. Kutaragi was equally furious, but used the opportunity to press Ohga on Sony's own future in video games. Kutaragi explained that Sony now had the expertise, the global reach and the resources to become a major force in video games, and perhaps strike a blow back at Nintendo. The seething Ohga had two words for his young engineer: 'Do it.'

➡ In 1992 Sony would produce 200 of its SNES-based CD-ROM PlayStations, but internally had already decided to wait until the next generation to make its debut and capitalize on CD-ROM technology. Kutaragi designed the CPU for the machine himself, focusing on realtime 3D graphics and speed. In October 1993 the PlayStation X – the PSX – was announced.

➡ Sony had carefully observed its

competitors, and took particular note of the 3DO's failure. The 3DO's biggest problem was a chronic lack of software, and so Sony began a global charm offensive with developers and publishers. Many were wary of the PlayStation, not so much because of Sony itself but because of the higher costs associated with 3D development – at the time, most were making 2D games. The success of Sega's *Virtua Fighter* (1993), ironically enough, was a turning point in industry perceptions of 3D – Yu Suzuki's brilliant arcade game used fighters constructed from 3D polygons, and demonstrated that 3D was both viable technically and the underlying game could be as well-designed as anything in 2D.

➤ A crucial part of the PlayStation's success in this context was the creation of a general software library – a set of tools for all developers to use when developing for the machine. It meant that common functions, such as saving, could simply be 'plugged in' to each game. Shinichi Okamoto, who developed the library under Kutaragi's direction, compares it to a car factory. 'When you make an automobile, you use screws in many different places. You use the same screws for different models. It's the same principle.'[29]

➤ Thanks to such forward-planning, by the time of the PlayStation's Japanese launch Sony had over 250 studios committed to developing for the machine. Soon after launch Sony would also begin buying up pre-established global studios like the UK's highly respected Psygnosis, which became Sony Interactive Entertainment. In the lead-up to release Sony encouraged comparisons with Sega, believing that not only did it have a better machine, but that the 'vs' narrative would help keep the PlayStation in the news.

➤ Sega had been caught napping. Its Saturn project had initially been designed as the ultimate 2D machine and, though it was

The PlayStation was named the PSX right up until launch, to the extent that early advertising in the USA used the latter. Years later Sony would release an integrated PS2/digital video recorder called the PSX, though this gained little traction and was never released outside of Japan. (Photo credit: Evan Amos)

capable of 3D visuals, it simply wouldn't be able to compete with the PlayStation's capabilities. This meant a last-minute redesign and something of a botch job: the Saturn's CPU lacked the grunt to perform the complex calculations 3D visuals required, so Sega simply added another CPU.

⮕ In comparison to Kuturagi's PlayStation design, which emphasized simplicity and ease of manufacture, this meant that the Saturn's internals were a mess of wires and connections. Sony's team instinctively understood that this meant the Saturn was more expensive to make and assemble than the PlayStation. In other words, it was an invitation to start a price war.

⮕ The Saturn was launched in Japan on 22 November 1994 and its initial shipment of 200,000 units sold out on the first day – largely thanks to the arcade-perfect port of *Virtua Fighter*, which sold at a nearly 1:1 ratio with the machine. Sega then held back stock

until the PlayStation's launch date of 3 December 1994, and put the machines head-to-head.

⮕ Initially the Saturn outperformed the PlayStation but it rapidly ran out of steam. Three months after the PlayStation's launch Sony had sold one million units with no signs of a slowdown (Nintendo's Hiroshi Yamauchi had vowed to resign if Sony sold more than 300,000; unsurprisingly he didn't, but no journalists were brave enough to raise the matter). The Saturn, starved of non-Sega software, had already peaked. Sega's disastrous management had cut off the company's support for the Mega Drive and its add-ons, which still accounted for a huge part of the market, and focused exclusively on Saturn software.

⮕ The Saturn's design came to the fore when Sony initiated a price war, and Sega had no option but to respond. In June 1995 Sony reduced the PlayStation's price by $100,

The Saturn performed well initially against the PlayStation but by the end of 1996 was lagging badly, and the launch of the Nintendo 64 sharply reduced sales. Although it had several tough competitors, the real enemy was Sega's corporate disorganization, with senior management changes and an overall lack of strategy contributing to a lack of consumer faith in the hardware. (Photo credit: Evan Amos)

A BRIEF HISTORY OF VIDEO GAMES

and shortly afterwards Sega did the same – a pattern that would continue in small increments until 1998, when Sega was forced to stop price-cutting and write off Sega of America's cumulative losses of $4.3 billion.

❯ The most iconic moment came with the American launch of both consoles. Saturn was announced at the first-ever Electronic Entertainment Expo (E3) in May 1995 at $399, including *Virtua Fighter*, and in a surprise twist was available immediately at certain retailers (which of course alienated those retailers left in the cold, some of whom responded by refusing to stock the Saturn at all). Sony representative Steve Race took the stage at E3 for the PlayStation presentation, said only '$299', and walked off to huge applause.

❯ Sega's marketing ideas had been built around the concept of 'cool', but Sony's thinking was much more profound. The PlayStation was targeted at young adults who had grown up playing games, but this was lifestyle marketing – aspirational, slightly edgy, the backing tracks familiar and the faces hip. The tactics went far beyond 'normal' advertising. PlayStation demo pods were set up in London's Ministry of Sound nightclub, for example, and a leaflet distributed at festivals was made out of perforated cardboard that was perfect for constructing marijuana roaches (although Sony has always claimed this was a coincidence).

❯ The best example of the distinction between Sega and Sony is *Tomb Raider* (1996), an iconic game synonymous with the original PlayStation – yet launched on the Saturn roughly a month before the PlayStation version in both Europe and Japan. Sony immediately recognized that Core Design had developed not just a great game, but in Lara Croft had a character with mainstream media potential – a tough, sexy

Virtua Fighter was the first fighting game to feature fully 3D polygon graphics, but it was amazing because of the detailed and in-depth fighting system Yu Suzuki and his team had crafted around this. Even more impressively, this system was built around a control stick and three buttons, with moves dependent on situation and positioning.

female adventurer in the Indiana Jones mould, distinct from the gruff marines and cartoony mascots people traditionally associated with video games.

◉ Much of the attention paid to *Tomb Raider* centred on Lara's sex appeal, rather odd given that her (gigantic) breasts resembled jutting triangles rather than anatomy. This means that she is alternately considered either a feminist icon or – perhaps more accurately – a chauvinistic stereotype masquerading as such: nevertheless Lara remains to this day one of video gaming's most recognizable heroes.

◉ This also overshadows the fact that the original *Tomb Raider* is a great game and innovative in its focus on environments over combat. The game is built around simply negotiating its huge (for the time) levels, and mastering Lara's capabilities – she can run so fast, jump so far and grab certain surfaces. Entering a cave and having to find your way to

an opening visible far in the distance, plotting an achievable route before taking a step, was a new way to play in 3D environments.

◉ The game received criticism for its so-called 'leaps of faith' but, in fact, patient inspection of the surroundings rewarded players. The lack of allies and infrequent human enemies made it an even lonelier trek, while the focus on irritating animals like bats and wolves served to mask the basic AI of this era. The advantage of this is that *Tomb Raider*'s major moments stick in the mind. At the start of the third area the skeletons and huge footprints may be noticed by more observant players, but are still scant preparation for a gigantic T-Rex bursting onto the scene that, given the chance, will eat Lara in a single bite. It's one of the most memorable moments of the PlayStation era in size and imagination. Beyond the fact that Lara, ironically enough, doesn't look that good anymore, *Tomb Raider* still stands as

Tomb Raider has become a bona-fide cultural phenomenon, not least thanks to a pair of awful and yet bewilderingly successful Hollywood movies starring Angelina Jolie. In recent years Square Enix has rebooted the series, taking heavy inspiration from the *Uncharted* games, themselves inspired by Lara Croft's original adventures.

the first of a new breed of 3D adventure and a defining influence on contemporary series like *Uncharted*.

➔ Sega had worthwhile exclusives but simply couldn't compete with the mainstream awareness Sony had created for PlayStation. *Panzer Dragoon* (1995) was a stunning rail shooter that cast the player as a dragon-riding hunter, swiftly followed by *Panzer Dragoon Zwei* (1996) – which introduced multiple routes and a morphing dragon – and *Panzer Dragoon Saga* (1998). The latter was an RPG that adapted the series' on-rails shooting into cinematic turn-based battling, allowed the dragon to morph into hundreds of forms, and gave the vivid art direction space and time in which to breathe. Sadly *Panzer Dragoon Saga* was released at the tail end of the Saturn's life in extremely limited quantities and has never been ported, making it something of a lost classic.

➔ *Dragon Force* (1996) is a fantasy RTS that combined tactical battles with managing a camp and gradually expanding across a world map. It is a much less well-known contemporary to the likes of *Vandal Hearts* (1996) and the PlayStation's genre-popularizing *Final Fantasy Tactics* (1997). Slightly more bizarre was *Sakura Wars* (1996), which combined this style of combat with a relationship sim. This is most notable for its branching storyline which, depending on your interactions with other characters, can go in different directions and affect your capabilities in battle.[30]

➔ The Treasure-developed *Guardian Heroes* (1996) is something of a spiritual successor to *Golden Axe* that improves immeasurably on its simplistic forebear: prime among its innovations was composing the battlefield of three 'planes' that could be switched at will, meaning the player always knew when they were lined up with an enemy. In addition to this *Guardian Heroes* features an RPG-like levelling system, multiple story paths and a stiff challenge.

→ Treasure also ported its arcade title *Radiant Silvergun* (1998), one of the Saturn's finest moments, a side-scrolling shooter with a unique weapon system that gave the player full control – and looked incredible. Sega never released it in the west. You could argue, in fact, that Sega didn't have a clue what to do about the changing audience that Sony seemed so adept at targeting. The brilliant RPG *Grandia* (1997), which many considered superior to *Final Fantasy VII*, didn't see a western release until Sony published it for the PlayStation, two years after the Saturn release. Similarly *Shin Megami Tensei: Devil Summoner* (1997), part of a major RPG series, was first released on the Saturn then ported two years later to PlayStation.

→ The elephant in the room was a blue hedgehog. Sega's attempts to develop a system-selling Sonic title for the Saturn met disaster, not least because Nintendo's *Super Mario 64* had set such a high bar. The Sega Technical Institute worked on a concept called 'Sonic X-Treme', the best part of which was an innovative 'fish-eye' lens that bent the surroundings at the edges of the screen – allowing more of the level to be shown as the focus remained on Sonic.

→ But 'Sonic X-Treme' was torn apart by Sega's internal factions. Over 1996 the developers were worked to death and given new objectives on a regular basis, while promises like the use of Yuji Naka's new Saturn engine were quickly revoked. 'We had artists doing art for levels that hadn't even been concepted out,' says executive producer Mike Wallis. 'We had programmers waiting and waiting until every minute detail had been concepted out, and we had designers doing whatever the hell they wanted. It was a mess.'

→ In early 1997, following the departure of

several key team members, 'Sonic X-Treme' was finally cancelled. The lack of a Sonic title is often cited as key to the Saturn's failure, but this is wishful thinking – Sega's problems ran far deeper than one cancelled game, even if it did star a bankable character. And what were Yuji Naka and Sonic Team doing?

➡ Making the Saturn's greatest game: *Nights into Dreams* . . . This was a game played in 2D on 3D backgrounds, and the concept is simply the joy of flying. Players initially control one of two children, who are dreaming but troubled by nightmare manifestations of their insecurities – whether they're smart enough or pure enough. The game really begins when they merge with a jester-like character called Nights.

➡ Nights soars into the air, flying a predetermined route around each nightmare, and can use boosts, grab onto other characters and perform acrobatic moves as stars trail in its wake. A combo system encourages the player to fly quicker, which in turn encourages the use of as many stunts as possible, and a strict timer counts down from the moment Nights is given to your control – when it ends, you come back to 'Earth' with a bump as one of the children. If *Sonic* was about speed, *Nights* was all about momentum.

➡ The final stage is one of the great gaming moments. Previously the children have to find Nights to fly, but this level is a flat miniaturized version of their hometown Twin Seeds with no jesters to be seen. After a few minutes, the player realizes that the only thing to do is take a leap of faith and jump off the level's edge. The child falls out of sight. The camera pans down and seconds pass with nothing.

➡ And then the music kicks in, and the child soars into the sky – Nights is no longer required to take flight. It's a magical little twist, all the better for being communicated

Nights into Dreams was launched in Japan alongside the Saturn 3D controller, which featured an analogue stick. The game was always about flight but in the initial stages the main character was intended to be a bird – Yuji Naka and his team decided that any animal character would lead to comparisons with Sonic (which Nights received regardless).

through the player's choice. *Nights* is so original it has never been copied, and was sadly too singular to bring the kind of commercial success Sega craved.[31] Sonic Team couldn't save the Saturn. But at least they created a masterpiece.

● The PlayStation's library had much more mainstream appeal and, thanks to Sony's wooing of third-party developers (partly by introducing a simple licence fee of $10 per game, much-reduced from the money demanded by Nintendo and Sega),[32] this was the main nail in the Saturn's coffin. By the end of its life Sony's console had 2,418 officially licensed games, making a comprehensive overview more or less impossible. Key to the PlayStation's early success was developer Namco, who contributed both *Ridge Racer* (1994) and *Tekken* (1994) as launch titles. Heavily inspired by *Outrun*, *Ridge Racer* was a fast and furious arcade racing game that, despite having limited tracks, was endlessly replayable thanks to its own take on drifting and vicious higher difficulty modes.

● *Ridge Racer* wowed with its 3D polygon visuals, which had previously been the preserve of the arcades, and established the power of the PlayStation – nevertheless it received criticism for offering an arcade rather than a home experience. This criticism is true, as far as it goes, but *Ridge Racer* is an arcade game. Nowhere is this better seen than in the semi-sequel *Ridge Racer Revolution*, which seemed to offer little more in terms of hard data – no new courses, for example – but amped everything up, made the whole world brighter and added crazy extras to test the player's mastery of its bucking drift controls. Its 'Spinning Point' mode challenges the player to execute multiple turns in midair. Turning this feature of its controls, really more of a quirk, into a point-scoring mechanic showed an intimate

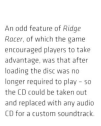

An odd feature of *Ridge Racer*, of which the game encouraged players to take advantage, was that after loading the disc was no longer required to play – so the CD could be taken out and replaced with any audio CD for a custom soundtrack.

A BRIEF HISTORY OF VIDEO GAMES

understanding of what players enjoy.

◉ *Tekken* was Namco's answer to *Virtua Fighter* but, in its focus on button-mashing combos and fighters who moved spectacularly regardless of what you did, was much more enjoyable for a mainstream audience. This is not to say *Tekken* lacks depth, and indeed among its later sequels *Tekken 3* (1998) is superb, but it was a deliberate move away from the audience that was happy to memorize long combos and precise timings; where the *Street Fighter* series was evolving to accommodate such hardcore play, *Tekken* wanted to appeal to those who just wanted to (virtually) beat up their mate every so often.

◉ No single title defined the PlayStation, but certainly one of the most important for the console's image was the F-Zero-inspired *Wipeout* (1995). Developed by Psygnosis, the game itself was a super-fast and precise futuristic racer that was difficult to master – due primarily to its highly suspect physics.

But the game didn't matter so much as the box and ad campaign, put together by the Designers Republic, and a soundtrack from artists like Leftfield, the Chemical Brothers and Orbital. Sony and Psygnosis smartly crafted the game's reputation, including a place in the film *Hackers* and overt associations with the drug ecstasy, and in the same month as the game's release Psygnosis became a Sony studio.

◉ *Wipeout* had style but the wait for a revolutionary driving game would take a little longer. The Sony internal team behind *Motor Toon Grand Prix* (1994), an excellent *Mario Kart* clone, had been simultaneously working on a much more ambitious project since 1992: the most realistic driving game possible. *Gran Turismo* (1997) was such a leap for racers that it created its own genre of hyperrealistic driving games, where everything from tyre choice to engine tuning fed into the car's performance – and controlling the thing was more akin to simulation than ever before. Because of this *Gran Turismo* is a difficult game on which to get a grip but, once it makes sense, recreates the feel of driving in a manner unmatched.

⊙ A more delightful note is struck by NanaOn-Sha's *Parappa the Rapper* (1996), a colourful music game where the player hits buttons corresponding to an on-screen beat as the titular Parappa goes through a variety of surreal situations. An early example of the rhythm genre, *Parappa*'s visuals and funny tunes elevate its rather simplistic system above pedantry – the wildly inconsistent 'freestyle' mode would have frustrated in many other games, but here it is somehow charming and moreish.

⊙ Konami's *Castlevania: Symphony of the Night* (1997) updated the platforming series with a more *Metroid*-style structure, and rather than attempting a transition to 3D visuals concentrated on creating a lushly animated and rich 2D world. Its empowering upgrade path and winningly arch dialogue ('What is a man? A miserable pile of secrets!') are perhaps no more than is to be expected, but it upset expectations with a marvellous 'final' twist – as the player thinks the game is ending, the castle setting is flipped upside-down and filled with new opponents, meaning they are only halfway there.

⊙ *Oddworld: Abe's Oddysee* (1997) is one of the best cinematic platformers ever made, using pre-rendered backdrops to bring the grim world of Rupture Farms to life. Abe is a Mudokan, a factory slave, who learns that his species is next in line to be turned into a tasty snack and so resolves to escape. The mechanics are clever if not quite revolutionary, but it's the world that is special – Rupture Farms is a dark parody of our own meat-obsessed consumerism, and its blood-caked treadmills and festering corners tell more of a story than any cutscene could.

NanaOn-Sha's *Parappa the Rapper* was an enormous PlayStation hit, enough to inspire a spinoff game, a TV series, various merchandise and, further down the line, a direct PlayStation 2 sequel. The unique visual style was created by Rodney Greenblat, an American graphic designer, and shows the characters as 2D cutouts on 3D backgrounds.

Abe's Oddysee tells the story of a slave named Abe, right, who discovers that his race is slated to be the next big food product and resolves to escape. Still fun to play now, the game remains exceptional in its use of the environment to imply the world's depressing history.

◆ The *Grand Theft Auto* series would go on to much bigger things, but its beginnings were here in a fun top-down game that crossed driving and shooting. *Grand Theft Auto* (1997) was originally called 'Race and Chase' by developers DMA Design and that knockabout spirit infuses the three titles released on the original PlayStation – though it would be revisionist to describe them as classics. There were hints of the greatness to come, not least in the sprawling city itself, but at this stage *Grand Theft Auto* was waiting for its own 3D moment.

◆ Among the early 3D titles two stand out. Capcom's *Resident Evil* (1996) used pre-rendered 3D backgrounds and fixed camera angles in creating what was termed a 'survival horror' game. Playing as either Chris or Jill, who had slightly altered routes through the game, *Resident Evil* specialised in jump scares and forcing the player to carefully manage their resources. Its mansion setting

was the real star, however, a vision of faded opulence with sinister secrets lurking around almost every blind corner. Although the atmosphere was somewhat undone by Z-list voice-acting, *Resident Evil* crafted such a potent mix of fear and claustrophobia that it began the most successful series in Capcom's impressive history.

◆ Then there is *Final Fantasy VII* (1997). One of the most beneficial side-effects of Sony's decision to use the CD-ROM as a storage medium was that it attracted previous Nintendo stalwarts Squaresoft to the platform, and *Final Fantasy VII* is the defining entry in the world's grandest RPG series. The scope and complexity of *Final Fantasy VII* is incredible. Its world is enormous and filled with distractions. Its turn-based battling is given a meta-game in the form of the Materia system, which opens up characters to pursue whatever expertise the player wants, making levelling a secondary consideration to the

Resident Evil was directed by Shinji Mikami, who would go on to direct many classic titles, and its unique visual style is down to using 3D polygonal characters on pre- rendered backdrops viewed from fixed angles – when a character reaches the screen 'edge' the camera angle changes to a new position.

pursuit of an ultimate loadout.

➤ Following the adventure of a bunch of eco-warriors as they battle to save their world from resource-stripping corporations, *Final Fantasy VII* also had something of a message. But this went hand-in-hand with a new level of ambition: *Final Fantasy VII* is a $45 million production that had a US marketing budget of over $100 million. It is often credited as the RPG that cracked the western market, but it sure had a lot of help doing so. And in this it represents something of a fork for RPGs in general and the *Final Fantasy* series in particular.

➤ Here is where the fetish for cinematography, as opposed to cinematic experiences, really took hold. *Final Fantasy VII*'s most iconic moment, the death of Aeris, occurs in a non-interactive cutscene – something of a failing for a piece of interactive entertainment. This separation of main narrative from the game's body,

with that big-budget ad campaign based on non-playable CG footage, meant that *Final Fantasy VII* became a watershed. The concept is genius in a way, and very PlayStation: make an RPG with deep systems, as Squaresoft always had, but sell it as an action movie.

➤ *Final Fantasy VII* has sold over ten million copies since release, the most successful entry in the series, and was the precursor to a golden PlayStation era for Squaresoft – games like *Final Fantasy Tactics*, *Final Fantasy VIII*, *Vagrant Story*, *Xenogears* and *Ehrgeiz*. It is a marvellous RPG but, in its emphasis on non-interactive cutscenes, created an albatross that hangs over the *Final Fantasy* series to this day.

➤ There are many more titles that deserve at least a brief mention, some of which suffer through no fault of their own – no era of gaming has aged quite as badly as early 3D titles, which often have visuals and draw distances to make a modern gamer wince.

Final Fantasy VII begins with the story of Avalanche, a terrorist group in the dystopia of Midgar, but soon broadens out into a world-spanning epic that takes as its central themes environment and memory. It is a captivating and singular achievement.

Jumping Flash (1994) was a first-person 3D platformer where the player's rabbit would jump huge heights then look to the ground to assist landing (still an under-used mechanic). Sony was on the search for a mascot during the PlayStation's early days, but would soon row back from this: Naughty Dog's *Crash Bandicoot* series were well-made but uninspired 3D platformers, while Insomniac's *Spyro the Dragon* (1998) was another attempted mascot with nice visuals but no real depth – both achieved great commercial success.

❯ *Legacy of Kain: Soul Reaver* (1999) offered a moody third-person adventure, notable for its streaming technology, which meant no loading screens (but lots of empty corridors). *Driver* (1999) winningly aped the classic car-chase films of the 1970s, while *Twisted Metal* (1995) offered a more gothic take on vehicular combat.

❯ While the battle between Sega and Sony raged, Nintendo's successor to the SNES faced one familiar problem and a few new ones. Despite the success of the Mega Drive the SNES was enormously profitable for the Kyoto giant and, unlike Sega, Nintendo would continue to support its machine well into the PlayStation era. This made sense from every perspective, but meant that Nintendo would launch its successor well after the competition. This wasn't necessarily a big deal – after all, the SNES did the same – but Sega and Sony were also enticing alternatives for third-party developers. Nintendo's iron grip on the industry had gone for good.

❯ The company's codename for its next console was 'Project Reality', stemming from the belief that a 64-bit processor capable of producing high-quality 3D visuals would surpass anything that its competitors could dream up. The console was based on a realtime 3D graphics chipset designed by Silicon Graphics, which had initially been offered to Sega, and in early 1993 work began.

➡ By far the biggest and most controversial decision with what would become the Nintendo 64 was the decision to stick with game cartridges rather than CD-ROM. Developers were horrified that they wouldn't have access to the ample storage and audio quality possible with CD-ROM, but Nintendo insisted that an experience without loading times would be preferred by players.

➡ This has been an important aspect of Nintendo's design philosophy throughout its history: it always considers the player experience as the highest priority. Whether that made cartridges the right decision is debatable, but a better example would be the N64's controller: a three-pronged hunk of grey plastic with an analogue stick in the middle, giant shoulder buttons and an underside 'trigger'. The design may look questionable but in the hands it felt even better than Sony's deservedly praised PlayStation pad[33]

and certainly trounced the Saturn's bloated effort. The N64 also featured four controller slots, making four-player splitscreen a feature of many of its defining titles – hardware design enabling software design.

➡ The N64's launch was originally set for Christmas 1995 but was delayed to May 1995 because Shigeru Miyamoto's team needed more time to perfect the machine's most important asset: *Super Mario 64*. Then it was delayed again, by almost a year, to April 1996. Rather than dampen enthusiasm, this drove anticipation for the machine.

➡ The Nintendo 64 finally launched in Japan on 23 June 1996, North America on 29 September 1996 and the poor relations of Europe got theirs on 1 March 1997. Despite the delays it had only two launch titles: *Super Mario 64* and *Pilotwings 64* (Japan had a third, based on the board game Shogi, which sold at a rate of about 1 per 100 N64 consoles). The latter was a fantastic update to the SNES

The controller was the key to the N64's appeal, and there are rumours that the design itself was changed to better serve Shigeru Miyamoto's vision for *Super Mario 64*. If true, and there's no way of knowing, it was a great decision. (Photo credit: Evan Amos)

original and ably demonstrated the N64's capabilities. But *Super Mario 64* showed that Nintendo was absolutely right to delay the console and trust its developers – it was the pack-in title for most of the console's life and may be the best game ever made.

◉ *Super Mario 64*, rumour has it, was for months nothing but a controllable cuboid. Miyamoto was adamant that, before Nintendo's designers even started constructing a 3D world around Mario (never mind giving him a moustache) it had to be fun to simply move him. After this stage came Mips the rabbit, a quick-hopping object to chase – letting the team study camera angles, momentum, character animations and cartoony-but-consistent physics. Before a single world of *Super Mario 64* was built, Mario himself was reborn.

◉ There is no comparison between *Super Mario 64* and contemporary 3D platformers like *Crash Bandicoot* because where those studios simply took their cues from 2D platformers and created a 3D version of such structures, *Super Mario 64* started from first principles. Why, for example, does a level need a fixed end point? Why should you go from one level to the next in a linear progression? Why should you have to finish them all to finish the game?

◉ *Super Mario 64* introduced a hub structure, Princess Peach's castle, which is itself one of the game's largest levels – full of paintings, crannies, an extensive basement, countless rooms hung with paintings and more secrets than most players will ever know. The castle has many wide-open spaces and it's no mistake that *Super Mario 64* starts the player off in the grounds, letting them feel the simple joy of making Mario run, jump and climb in his new playground.

◉ The many worlds are (mostly) accessed through the brilliant conceit of jumping into paintings, and then *Super Mario 64* starts to take flight. The first world, Bob-Omb Battlefield, has a twisting hill at its centre that spills down into a huge open space where Mario begins. There are cannons from which to fire him, mysterious floating islands to explore, gigantic balls rolling down hills, goombas waddling around and posts to hammer into the ground. It's packed with brief flourishes, like a half-pipe filled with swerving cannonballs, as mesmerizing as they are challenging and – more importantly – it's full of details that are nothing to do with the challenge at all.

➡ If Super Mario 64 is defined by any one thing, and that's a tall order, it is this sense of playfulness. The title screen is Mario's face, which can be pulled out of shape and twanged back into position as often as you like. Tiny-Huge world has two entrance paintings, one of which makes Mario a giant and the other a pygmy. Bop a koopa out of its shell and, rather than booting it, Mario can jump on

top and start surfboarding around the level. Find a never-ending staircase in the castle's centre, run up there for five minutes and turn around to find yourself at the bottom. Look up at the sun in the castle's lobby and you'll be transported to a secret world in the clouds. Go down to the castle's basement, and you'll find a familiar rabbit. If you can catch Mips he'll give up one of the game's 120 stars, and these are the revolutionary structure that underpins this world – a progress marker that can be associated with just about anything, allowing Super Mario 64 to be as freeform and directionless as it is. You can get one by doing almost anything: flying through hoops, bringing a ghost ship up from the ocean's bottom, swinging Bowser by the tail, thrashing a cocky penguin in a downhill ice race or even just catching a rabbit. The game never tells you to catch Mips – it just seems like a fun thing to do.

➡ Super Mario 64 is sometimes called the

Super Mario 64 uses a brilliant conceit to introduce the idea of a 3D camera – which of course would have been new to many of its players. Former antagonist Lakitu, a turtle who floats on a cloud, is reimagined as a hovering cameraman following Mario's adventure. A delicious touch, in a game full of delicious touches, is that when you find a room of mirrors he can be seen behind Mario.

A BRIEF HISTORY OF VIDEO GAMES

best translation of a 2D series into 3D, but this is simply untrue: there's almost nothing in common between the 2D Mario games and the world created for *Super Mario 64*. It is the real beginning of 3D game design that, in its blazing creativity and wide-ranging generosity, almost seems to have finished things at the same time – few games have approached it nearly two decades after its release.

⊙ Critics often discuss games as though they are simply vehicles for creators' expressions, whether that's the homilies of a BioWare RPG or the anti-war message of a *Metal Gear*. *Super Mario 64* isn't about expressing anything. It is about creating specific feelings in a player – the simple joy of motion, the satisfaction of discovering a secret, the pride in overcoming a challenge and the wonder at how a new world unfolds in ways you never thought possible. It is a game designed by a genius to make even the dullest player

feel special – an interactive universe that coaxes the child out of anyone, leads them to a thousand tiny discoveries, and somehow leaves them in control every step and jump of the way.

⊙ If *Super Mario 64* showed Nintendo's mastery of the 3D frontier, it was *The Legend of Zelda: Ocarina of Time* that cemented the N64 in a million hearts. The winner of more 'best game ever' awards than can be counted, *Ocarina* is almost as special as *Super Mario 64* but takes a different approach to recreating Link's world – logical enough, given that the previous *Zelda* games had a tilted top-down viewpoint. This didn't slow down the creativity. Prime among *Ocarina*'s inventions is 'Z-targeting' (so-named after the N64 controller's trigger button), which with a click centres the camera on a specific enemy and tracks their movements – perfect for 3D combat and filched by nearly every 3D combat game since.

◉ *Ocarina*'s structure is familiar, but now the mechanics are able to fill out into patterns of cause and effect more complex than ever: Link's inventory is designed for experimentation. The hookshot's main use is to shoot at targets and pull Link towards them, but it will sink into wooden surfaces and clang off stone. In combat it kills bats, stuns sword-wielding lizards, or sinks into the glutinous body of a Yum-Yum and pulls Link in. When underwater Link can't swing his sword or hammer, but the hookshot becomes a makeshift harpoon. This is a world with an immediately graspable internal logic.

◉ The 'Dark World' idea becomes time travel in *Ocarina*: you begin the game as child Link but later become adult Link (and can switch between the two). This is used as both narrative and mechanic. As a child, for example, you defeat the dragons infesting a cave on Death Mountain, home of the Gorons. After this you return to the Goron Village as

an adult, yet find only a single occupant, who tries to run away. When you work out how to stop him the terrified Goron shouts 'Hear my name and tremble! I am Link! Hero of the Gorons!'

◉ This is a simple idea: *Ocarina*'s dungeons are stories themselves that tie into the game's world, and Link's actions do not go unnoticed. Hyrule field may look a little bare to modern eyes, but its coherence as a place remains absolute. Perhaps the most surprising aspect of *Ocarina* is its main theme of failure and persistence. At the start of the game Link fails to save the Deku Tree and is blamed for its death by his friends. Later, child Link opens up the Sacred Realm for Ganon and can't stop him destroying Hyrule. You have to watch impotently as Princess Zelda is captured. Link's friends become sages, necessary to stand against Ganon but removing them from the world permanently. Link's destiny is that brutal twist between

Perhaps what is most surprising about *The Legend of Zelda: Ocarina of Time* is how many elements of the 2D elements transition to 3D and work perfectly with the new dimension – most of *Super Mario 64*'s basics, for example the Goomba enemies, had to have their behaviour and role completely altered.

A BRIEF HISTORY OF VIDEO GAMES

child and adult: *Ocarina* is set in a world that he's already failed to save.

❯ The majority of great N64 titles were developed by Nintendo itself, including the killer *Mario Kart 64* (which of course supported four-player splitscreen) and the debut of what would become a long-running and popular series, *Super Smash Bros*. This irreverent fighter saw Nintendo's iconic characters battling each other on floating arenas and trying to smash each other off the sides of the screen – but its simple controls and deep system made it much more than a variety act. Most fighting games are serious business or are at least treated as such by their players, but *Super Smash Bros*. almost feels like more of a party game, all about enjoyment and laughs rather than memorizing combo strings.

❯ Nintendo had bought a 49 per cent stake in Rare in 1994, after seeing the technology that would lead to *Donkey Kong Country*, and the Leicestershire-based developer had its finest years on the Nintendo 64. Following *Goldeneye 007* (see Chapter 13: *Doom 101*) Rare released a quickfire series of high-quality titles that straddled multiple genres and even invented a few new ones.

❯ *Blast Corps* (1997) is about destroying buildings and instantly latches onto that Lego-smashing child in all of us. In its main mode a truck with nuclear missiles moves slowly on a set route, which happens to go through many buildings, and the player has to bring them all down by bulldozing through the structures, switching vehicles to change abilities and generally causing as much havoc as possible. Simple as this seems, *Blast Corps* was packed with additional modes and secrets, and is such a perfect realization of the concept that it never saw a sequel.

❯ *Banjo-Kazooie* (1998) was a 3D platformer that took much inspiration from *Super Mario 64*, but added its own twist in the main

characters' abilities – Kazooie lives in Banjo's backpack and can flap its wings to grant a little more airtime. This solved one of the main problems with 3D platforming, which is that it's sometimes difficult for players to judge distances, and added the capacity for puzzles to be built around clever use of the ability. *Banjo-Kazooie* doesn't have the constant invention of *Super Mario 64*, but that's no great criticism.

➜ Rare would go on to produce several 3D platformers in this mould: *Donkey Kong 64* (1999) was an absolute collectathon notable for an appalling opening rap and the ability to play as five very different characters; *Banjo-Tooie* (2000) offered larger environments than its predecessor and again showcased Rare's weakness for stuffing games full of collectables. The upshot of this platformer apprenticeship is one of the best games Rare ever made: *Conker's Bad Fur Day* (2001). Designed in response to (entirely justified)

criticisms of the company's over-reliance on cutesy characters, Conker is an alcoholic squirrel that makes constant lewd jokes. But the game's great because Rare finally learned to strip back the infinite collectables and gimmicky mechanics: Conker has fewer abilities than his cutesy predecessors but the game is much snappier for it and, despite a dodgy camera, maintains momentum to the fourth-wall-busting finish (in which the game 'crashes' and Conker rudely bemoans the low-quality standards of Rare for failing to test the game properly).

➜ Finally, there is *Perfect Dark* (2000), the spiritual successor to *Goldeneye*. This is a shooter brimming with ideas that throws them all out just to see what sticks – like a laptop that can become an submachine-gun or a sentry gun, enemies that can be disarmed, and a gun that can see and shoot through walls. *Perfect Dark* was jam-packed with multiplayer options and a lengthy campaign but was maybe a smidgen over-ambitious technically: single-player was fine, but multiplayer often saw the game's framerate crawl.

➡ Among third parties Dundee's DMA Design stands out for two games. *Body Harvest* (1998) had a great concept, a free-roaming 3D shooter following a time-travelling soldier across different Earth eras, but it couldn't quite squeeze enough out of the hardware. The levels were huge and open, featuring towns that had to be saved from invading aliens that would try to cart away the occupants (hence the title), but were mostly bare and boxy with it – nevertheless the ability to drive vehicles across these great plateaus was special for the time. DMA also produced a true gem in *Space Station Silicon Valley* (1998), a game where you played a microchip on a space station full of abandoned robot animals that could be controlled. Every animal had its own abilities

and control kinks, and the many levels were little playparks filled with cleverly constructed stunts and a winning sense of humour.

➡ Nevertheless Nintendo would end this generation firmly deposed from pole position in the industry. Where the N64 sold around thirty-three million units by the end of its life, the PlayStation would continue to be manufactured until 2006 and become the first console ever to sell over 100 million, the final number being 102.5 million units. The Saturn's good start had turned into a disaster, with its final sales being around 9.5 million, and Sega quickly began working on a comeback strategy. For the old guard, everything had changed. PlayStation was here to stay.

A Dream Dies

16

● The history of Sega consoles is something of a tragedy. The Master System was a good start, and the Mega Drive was wonderful. But it is hard to excuse the company's decision-making when it comes to the Mega-CD and 32X add-ons, swiftly followed by the poor Saturn being steamrollered by Sony.

● It could be argued that Sega deserved what happened next, but what makes it awful is that, finally, lessons had been learned: the Saturn's successor was Sega's finest console and it was accompanied by the company's greatest-ever software hot streak.

● In 1996 Sega of America had a new president, Bernie Stolar, who had moved from the PlayStation business. 1997 saw Sega of Japan also gain a new president, Shoichiro Irimajiri. Both understood that the Saturn was a failed product and pushed for the development of a new console, and two distinct teams began working on separate designs.

● An American team led by Tatsuo Yamamoto settled on hardware that used graphics processors made by a company called 3dfx – Sega apparently agreed to this design, before 3dfx blew everything out of the water by revealing details about the (still unannounced) console during its own public offering. The architecture proposed by the Sega of Japan team, led by Hideki Sato, was then preferred – a decision with which some of Sega's partners, including EA, disagreed.

● But the design produced by Sato's team was outstanding – a forward-thinking console with a built-in 56K modem that would connect to the online gaming portal SegaNet. It used proprietary GD-ROM discs, which could hold more data than a CD-ROM, and was capable of visuals that were a true leap beyond the PlayStation.

● Conscious of the damage done to Sega's image, the decision was made to minimize the machine's association with the company

The Dreamcast was a beautiful piece of hardware but what really made it sing was the reorganization of the previously chaotic Sega internal teams into nine semi-autonomous studios headed by the company's top designers. It was a hell of a way to go. (Photo credit: Evan Amos)

name. The Dreamcast was born, its logo an orange swirl (blue in Europe) that apparently symbolized 'the universe and the infinite power of human beings'.

➡ The best laid plans of mice and men, however, were waylaid at the Japanese launch by a shortage of NEC chipsets – severely limiting stocks. The launch lineup wasn't spectacular either, but was saved by the arrival one month later of *Sonic Adventure* (1998). This marked the return of Sonic Team to the company's mascot, after the disastrous 'Sonic X-Treme' project, and while the game couldn't quite hold a candle to *Super Mario 64* it was fast, gorgeous and packed with spectacular sequences – Sonic speeds across rickety platforms atop the ocean in the first level before the camera pans to show a giant killer whale destroying the track behind.

➡ Dreamcast's first Japanese hit gave an indication of the original software for which the machine would become known. Developer

Yoot Saito, conscious of the contemporary craze for *Tamagotchi* and other virtual pets, decided to develop a 'life simulator' called *Seaman*. But this wasn't like the others. *Seaman* had the bizarre appearance of a man's face on the body of a fish and, using the pack-in microphone, players could talk and hold entertaining conversations with this odd creature.

➡ Dreamcast had problems in Japan, where the audience was still smarting from the Saturn's abandonment, but Sega's real target was the lucrative American market. The major lesson learned from the Saturn's US launch was that consumers wanted quality and quantity of launch software, and so Dreamcast launched with seventeen titles including *Sonic Adventure*, *Soul Calibur* and *Hydro Thunder*. The lineup hit every target: recognizable characters, sports, beat-'em-ups, racers and more.

➡ And it worked – at first. The Dreamcast

Sonic Adventure's opening set-piece saw an Orca in hot pursuit but, in a sad indicator of where the series would go from here, it was almost entirely on-rails with little player input. Sega's struggles to transition the Sonic games into 3D continue to this day, though *Sonic Adventure* remains the best stab at it.

A BRIEF HISTORY OF VIDEO GAMES

was launched in North America on 9 September 1999, after a huge marketing blitz, and sold more than 225,000 units in its first twenty-four hours on sale. By late November that year it had sold a million. The way it was launched was also new, with a '9/9/99' campaign that encouraged pre-orders and somehow got everywhere – when you see images of people queuing up for their launch PlayStation 4 or Xbox One, this is where it really began.

➲ Sega had completely reorganized its development staff into nine autonomous second-party developers – still dancing to the master's tune, of course, but allowed creative freedom in the hope of an unpredictable hit. Although this never resulted in the commercial smash for which Sega hoped, it meant that Dreamcast saw Sega's developers at their peak, creating brilliant and original titles.

➲ One studio was United Game Artists, headed by Tetsuya Mizuguchi, which focused on bringing audio to the fore. Their first game, *Space Channel 5* (1999), was a Technicolor dream about 'Ulalala's swinging report show' where reporter Ulalala ('Hi Space Cats!') investigates rumours that aliens have captured humans and are forcing them to dance.

➲ *Space Channel 5*'s mechanics were little more than a version of 'Simon Says' – Ulalala automatically walks through locations, then pauses for a dance-off with various enemies who perform moves she then has to repeat (for example, 'right, left, right, left, up, down, chu!' with 'chu' being the action button). But the vibrant setting and funky tunes combined with such simple inputs to create a game where the experience was all about rhythm, the immersion glossing over the core mechanic's simplicity. Later United Game Artists would return to *Space Channel 5* with a semi-remake subtitled *Part 2* (2002),

Space Channel 5's funky
soundtrack, and the winning
interplay between Ulalala
and her boss at the studio,
managed to overshadow
the simplistic mechanics
and make this one of the
Dreamcast's most-loved
titles.

a much-improved version of the original most notable for expanding the role of Space Michael, a cosmic Michael Jackson featuring the voice of the man himself (who was a huge video game fan).

◉ Between these games United Game Artists developed *Rez* (2001), which was based on similar principles but took the idea of synaesthesia even further by combining an on-rails shooter with a player-triggered rhythm and abstract visuals. *Rez* has your craft moving at a constant speed while 'enemies' pop up in the surrounding environment, which can be targeted in groups before releasing any shots – when they're hit, various sound effects appropriate to that stage's backing track play. This means that as you get better at playing *Rez*, the game itself begins to look and sound better, until nothing but a perfect run will do: the reward here is not a high score, but audiovisual feedback that enhances the experience in line with your own sense of the beat and mastery of the levels. *Rez* remains, sadly, something of a singular title with few games following its lead. (However, Mizuguchi later left Sega to form Q Entertainment and developed the outstanding *Rez* 'prequel' *Child of Eden*, released in 2011.)

◉ This wasn't Sega's only experiment with music games, which were popular in Japan thanks to Konami's Bemani games. Sonic Team's *Samba de Amigo* (1999) came with a pair of 'maraca' controllers and, with one or two players, showed patterns on the screen set to a tracklist of classic Latin tunes (a revised version of the game, subtitled *Ver. 2000*, added more contemporary tracks). As a gameplay mechanic there's not really much to say about this, other than it turns out shaking plastic maracas to a crazy-eyed monkey's beat is surprisingly fun.

◉ Another internal studio, Hitmaker, developed driving game *Crazy Taxi* (1999 arcade, 2000 Dreamcast), set in a large city where the player has to pick up and drive customers from location to location. This may sound dull, but the clue's in the title – this city is filled with ramps, curves, onrushing traffic and insane jumps that make each fare a thrill ride, while a strict timer forces the player to drive fast or go home. The most inspired touch in *Crazy Taxi* was the soundtrack by punk-rock bands Bad Religion and The Offspring, which conflated perfectly with the high-octane driving.

→ *Crazy Taxi* saw several sequels, and Hitmaker also developed *Virtua Tennis* (1999), which – with its various sequels – remains the best simulation of the sport available, simple to play in an instant but with mechanical depth that mirrors the real thing's considerations. For example, the most important part of returning the ball is how long your player is in the correct position to do so – being able to 'set' yourself results in

a very powerful return in the desired direction and the type of shot desired (topspin, lobs, etc.), whereas rushing to return gives less control over the shot.

→ The Dreamcast's online connectivity was only fully exploited by a few games, but the most important was Sonic Team's outstanding massively multiplayer online game (MMOG) *Phantasy Star Online* (2000). This catapulted Sega's venerable series into a future of realtime combat, communication across language barriers (thanks to a clever symbol-based system) and lovely loot. The game was inspired by Blizzard's *Diablo* series and focuses on using teamwork to down huge bosses in bitesize worlds, with players levelling up over time and the difficulty increasing in increments up to 'Very Hard' mode (which would be moved further to 'Ultimate' in later releases).

→ Two final games, among many more that could be chosen, show the twin poles

Yah yah yah yah yah! The opening lines to The Offspring's 'All I Want' remain emblematic of the *Crazy Taxi* experience, which demands full-on intensity from the first second to the last. Although the open world is relatively small, *Crazy Taxi*'s strict structure makes it a pleasure to zoom across.

of Sega's ambition and style during this era. Smilebit's *Jet Set Radio* (2001) pioneered the use of cel shading, whereby characters are flat-coloured and surrounded by a thin black outline, giving the visuals a beautiful cartoony quality and rejecting the wider industry's movement towards 'realistic' graphics. *Jet Set Radio* casts the player as various members of the GGs gang in a dystopian future Tokyo, and the object of the game is to rollerskate around its large urban environments and tag walls with graffiti.

➡ *Jet Set Radio* was about both the simple pleasure of momentum and the gradually unfolding complexity of its environments – which could be traversed by 'grinding' along rails, making huge jumps, hanging onto the back of cars or simply speeding along on your skates. An outstanding original sound track by Hideki Naganuma fed into the game's theme ('Jet Set Radio' is a pirate radio station that provides the narrative) and, quite outside

of the game's 'objectives', the pleasure of moving through the stunt-happy architecture of Tokyo-To remains a peerless experience.

➡ Ever since the 1980s Yu Suzuki had been Sega's star designer, the man behind games like *Outrun*, *Space Harrier*, *Virtua Fighter* and many more. The latter had provided inspiration for a Saturn project, tentatively titled 'Virtua Fighter RPG', in which the player would control series protagonist Akira in a 3D world with traditional RPG systems. Progress was slow, but came to a halt with the collapse of the Saturn system.

➡ 'Virtua Fighter RPG' was reborn as *Shenmue* (1999), with Suzuki returning to an initial idea he had originated for a game called 'The Old Man and the Peach Tree'. *Shenmue* would have more of a domestic setting, and focus on evolving the traditional role-playing experience towards something much more immersive and responsive to the player. This would result in one of the most expensive

Yuji Naka's *Phantasy Star Online* had the great idea of putting most of its world-building in the form of optional sidequests, meaning that as players got more interested in the game (and in securing quest loot) the world would also be explained further.

The incredible *Jet Set Radio* had amazing visuals and a world constructed around the abilities of its characters, all brought to life by in-house Sega composer Hideki Naganuma's greatest tunes.

A sequel released for the Xbox, *Jet Set Radio Future*, is equally fabulous. This was Sega at the pinnacle of its creative powers.

Shenmue was so ambitious that it shipped on three GD-ROMs, much of which was down to the quantity of voice-acting recorded for the game. The environmental detail is also, even today, something most other games cannot approach simply because of the labour involved in asset creation.

Shenmue was known as 'Project Berkeley' during development and was used to create tech demos that showed the Dreamcast's capabilities – many of which, in a rare act of frugality, were reused in the final game.

No expense was spared during the production of *Shenmue*. Highly detailed clay models of every character were produced as reference points for animators, while the musical score was performed by a full-size orchestra.

Shenmue II mostly takes place in Wan Chai, a metropolitan area in Hong Kong. Like the first game this is packed with interesting stores and a video arcade containing *Space Harrier* and *Outrun*. It had more of an ensemble cast, and was themed around Ryo growing up away from the safety net of his home town.

games ever made, with a budget of $47 million used to recreate the Tokyo suburb of Yokosuka in a manner that wasn't just visually breathtaking but felt dynamic – NPCs went about their business muttering to themselves, the weather changed as days wore on and the game unfolded over months with main character Ryo going to bed every night.

❯ To describe *Shenmue* Suzuki coined the term 'FREE' – Full Reactive Eyes Entertainment – and the special quality of the game is how much interactive detail is in its world. Yokosuka is small in terms of what one might consider an 'open-world' game, but it is a non-linear environment that the player can explore at leisure, packed with things to find and distractions for the sake of it – such as an arcade featuring many playable versions of Sega classics.

❯ The triumph of *Shenmue* is that, though its plot is a simple revenge narrative, the game itself is more of an ode to mundanity.

This doesn't mean it's dull to play, but rather that the experience captures something of life in a small town – Ryo's days always begin in the same place, the streets become more familiar over time, strangers gradually become friends and working out how to pass time before the next story event becomes a submerged goal. It has moments of drudgery, such as when Ryo gets a job driving a forklift truck, but these have their counterpoint in the rare high-octane action sequences where he gets in a fight or drives his motorbike.

➔ Shenmue's ambition goes far beyond this. The game is not just set in Yokosuka, but set in Yokosuka in November 1986 – so Suzuki's team hunted down weather reports and accurately modelled the virtual world's weather to reflect these. It was the first game where every single NPC was fully voice-acted, and 'stalking' its various inhabitants to learn more about them becomes a minor obsession in its own right.

➔ More than anything, Shenmue's setting and main character encapsulate the ever-present conflict between youth and conservatism – Ryo dresses in stereotypically western garb of jeans and jacket, where his elders wear more traditional Japanese clothes – while focusing on the shared aspects of human experience. The plot centres around Ryo trying to find his dad's killer (a very game-y story) but he never does, instead drifting from job to job and place to place, gently buffeted by passing time. Shenmue is set up as a revenge tale but it is much more a series of vignettes about mourning – Ryo's obsession with feeding a stray cat, his emotional distance from his mother, his demand for simple answers, which are never found.

➔ Shenmue was intended as the first part of a trilogy but, after Dreamcast production was cancelled, its relative commercial failure (apparently each Dreamcast owner would have had to buy Shenmue twice for Sega to

Due to Sega's woes, Microsoft obtained an exclusivity agreement for Shenmue II that – brutally – allowed Sega to release the game on Dreamcast but not to record an English dub. This meant the game was released with subtitles, although an English dub was recorded for the later Xbox release.

break even) meant the third game was never made. This is sad, but the real tragedy of the *Shenmue* series is that it would be Yu Suzuki's last major contribution to the games industry. The two games showcased a new way of creating interactive worlds and giving meaning to characters' personalities, while its 'normal' urban setting remains unique at the big-budget end of the industry.

⊘ In its way *Shenmue* symbolizes Sega's last hurrah as a console manufacturer. You could say it was over-ambitious, blind to market realities and unable to compete with more traditionally favoured ways of making interactive entertainment. This is all true. But it also shows what made Sega special in its originality, quality and visionary recasting of what an interactive world could or should be. No matter how many internet petitions the fans start they will never see *Shenmue III*, but both players and developers must be grateful the original exists at all.

⊘ The question of why the Dreamcast failed, especially after its successful launch, is answered by one word and a number: PlayStation 2. Sony stole Sega's momentum by announcing its upcoming console well before release, making many consumers wait, and the type of games Sega's internal studios were producing may well have been wonderful, but often weren't commercially viable.

⊘ Everything seemed to come together for Sega's last hurrah as a console manufacturer: the launch, the hardware, the software, the brilliant reviews. Yet in the space of nineteen months Sega went from record-breaking comeback to halting production of the Dreamcast and rearranging the company as a third-party software developer. Losing momentum and faced with the huge pockets of Sony and new entrant Microsoft, it simply couldn't compete.

⊘ 'Until the very final moments I was really against Sega leaving the hardware business,' says Yuji Naka. 'In a way I feel that, had that decision not been made, Sega would have gone bankrupt – so maybe it was a good business decision. But at the same time I also feel like, what the hell, we should have given it a go, and we should have taken that risk. But that's just my personal opinion, because I loved the hardware side of things at Sega.'

➲ Sega's final game for the Dreamcast was *Segagaga*, a self-parodying blend of RPG and minigames that put the player in charge of Sega and challenged them to stop the evil 'DOGMA' corporation (i.e. Sony) taking over the games market. Battling Sega employees (to make them work harder), shooting down PlayStation consoles with classic Sega hardware and hiring mechas were just some of the surreal highlights in this Japan-only release. (Director Tez Okano was given a $200 budget to market the game, the majority of which he spent on a lucha libre wrestling mask to use on a 'promotional tour' of Tokyo game stores.)

➲ Sega was out of the hardware business, but clearly its spirit lived on. The late Charles Bellfield, a Sega of America vice president during the Dreamcast's time, said:

We had the content right. We had the marketing right. The product was designed right. The philosophy of networked capabilities was right. The team was right. The partners we had were right. But we didn't have the budget to be able to build the confidence of the brand in the eyes of our competitors that we were going to be around. That, to me, is the Achilles heel of the Dreamcast. The first Xbox console was a far bigger failure than the Dreamcast. But Microsoft has much more money than Sega did. And the Xbox was an ugly motherfucker. [34]

An Ugly Motherfucker

Sega's Dreamcast kickstarted the sixth generation of home consoles, but the world was waiting for PlayStation 2 (PS2). The success of the PlayStation was beyond even Sony's expectations, and the PlayStation 2 was designed to cement this position.

The video games industry is historically fickle, with one company rarely dominating across successive generations of hardware, but Sony had two advantages. The first was the PlayStation brand itself, which had become synonymous with gaming in a manner reminiscent of Nintendo in the 1980s. The second was Sony's genuine drive to maintain the volume of third-party support. Nintendo and Sega had always been somewhat more ambiguous about this because first-party software sales made up a huge part of their balance sheets.

'Ken Kutaragi was very pro third-party,' says Chris Deering, the then-president of Sony Europe. 'He said we should never allow [first-party games] to have more than a third of the software market or we'd drive away other investments, and I believed that.'[35]

This attitude led to Sony budgeting for third-party exclusives, in effect handing over a wodge of cash for certain games to appear on PS2 as system sellers. Such a strategy, where executives would see a work-in-progress and gamble on its eventual success, is by its nature hit-and-miss. Among the exclusives signed up early was the 3D follow-up to a minor PlayStation hit, *Grand Theft Auto*. 'It was remarkably cheap,' Reeves recalls.

The PlayStation 2 was announced (though not shown) on 1 March 1999, earlier than planned, in an attempt to take the wind out of Dreamcast's sails. Just over a year later it would launch in Japan (4 March 2000), but Sony was determined to reduce the traditionally lengthy waiting time between regions: later the same year both

North America (26 October) and Europe (24 November) had the hardware.

➔ PlayStation 2 was wildly anticipated, so much so that despite a weak launch lineup it sold an astonishing 980,000 units on its first day in Japan. The launch price in North America matched the original PlayStation's $299 price point and, in what may have been more of a help to sales than anything else, the PS2 doubled-up as a DVD player – DVD was a new technology and this made PS2 the cheapest player on the market.

➔ The design incorporated several less obvious but important features. Owners of the original PlayStation were delighted that the machine was backwards-compatible, meaning it would play all of their existing games, and a USB port would allow the console, later in its life, to be expanded with a range of peripherals including the PlayStation Eye (a motion-tracking camera), microphones, a trackball, a mouse and so on. This aspect of the console is anything but peripheral – a defining aspect of PS2 is its wide range of non-traditional software, such as the karaoke game *Singstar* or quiz title *Buzz!*, and many depended on the USB port for bespoke controllers.

➔ Successful launches in both North America and Europe saw a brief shortage of units on shelves, and also ensured that PS2 would have the market to itself – in March 2001 Sega discontinued Dreamcast production, while Microsoft and Nintendo were yet to launch their competing hardware. Even when the competition did arrive the PS2 had important counters – Xbox launched in November 2001, but at the same time PS2 received exclusives *Grand Theft Auto III* and *Metal Gear Solid 2*.

➔ In certain respects, it's surprising that Xbox launched at all. The beginnings of the project can be dated precisely – on 30 March 1999 Ted Hase, a Microsoft employee

The original PlayStation 2 (left) and its slimline redesign. Just under 4,000 titles were developed for the console over its lifetime, and over 1.5 billion units of software were sold. (Photo credit: Evan Amos)

working on the company's DirectX technology, sent out a PowerPoint presentation to a small group of Microsoft employees, which advocated that the then-biggest technology company in the world should get involved in gaming. Microsoft already had a games division dedicated to PC but this was a different approach: a home console.

➡ Many key figures at Microsoft thought this was lunacy, a distraction from the company's main business, but a core team of four people – Kevin Bachus, Seamus Blackley, Ted Hase and Otto Berkes – pushed the project hard. They knew that the price and performance of standard PC components had been pushed low enough that Microsoft, with its financial muscle, could build something that would outperform PS2.

➡ 'I remember a meeting with Bill Gates and Steve Ballmer, in a tiny conference room in Redmond,' says Blackley. 'We outlined our pathetic, early, naive business model, and Ballmer started yelling, "You're going to lose a lot of money!" about an inch from my head. We got smart fast, and busted our asses to be sure of all our numbers, and sure enough after that he always supported the project.'[36]

➡ The full story of how the Xbox's final design came together is a book in its own right, but over years and many meetings it was hammered out – most importantly, the team finally got permission to use a Windows-based operating system (OS) rather than Windows itself, crucial to creating a 'console' experience. The importance of out-performing PS2 in a tangible manner meant that Bill Gates himself pushed back the console's launch by a year from 2000 to 2001. Even then, the Microsoft team faced scepticism from the industry itself.

➡ Kevin Bachus says:

We went to meet with Electronic Arts. They said, 'We're very sceptical about

this initiative, because you have a tendency to put your toe in the water and then abandon your partners when things don't go your way. We know that if Nintendo fails, they're done. They have no other products. But if you guys fail you lose a billion dollars; it's a rounding error on your balance sheet and no one even notices.'

For example at the time Robbie Bach wasn't only in charge of Xbox, but also of all Microsoft's printing software and retail initiatives. [EA chairman] Larry Probst said: 'I want to know who gets fired if Xbox fails. I want to know, Robbie, that if Xbox fails you're fired. And we want to see Bill Gates on stage at GDC [Game Developers Conference]. We want to know that this has support all the way up to the top. We want his name associated with it so we know how committed you are.'

Probst got his wish because Bill Gates was thinking along the same lines anyway – at GDC 2000 he took to the stage and announced Microsoft would be launching a console that, in terms of raw power, would blow PS2 out of the water. The Xbox had 65Mb of DRAM to the PS2's 40Mb, and could theoretically show 150 million polygons per second as opposed to PS2's 66 million. Its Intel CPU ran at 733Mhz to the PS2 CPU's 300Mhz while the Nvidia GPU, co-designed by Microsoft, ran at 233 Mhz against the PS2's 150Mhz GPU.

➲ The Xbox name was simply a shortened form of 'DirectX Box', a working title that the team assumed would be replaced by something better from marketing. Marketing hated Xbox, but came up with a truly appalling list of alternatives. During focus-testing 'Xbox' was left on the list to prove that consumers wouldn't like it – and then somehow came out on top. With its resources

Microsoft even hired a company specializing in names to come up with something. Kevin Bachus:

Ultimately they came back and said, 'We've found the name. This is the name. It tests great. We've tested it against Xbox and we think it's fantastic. OK. Here it is: it's the Microsoft 11X. It's not 10. It goes to 11. And "X" is mystery. And it tests great. Everyone loves it.' And I turned to our marketing guy and he turned to me, and we said, 'Well, I guess we'd better go buy Xbox.com.'[37]

> The eventual hardware design of the Xbox was ugly, thanks largely to it using standardized PC components – the internals were much bulkier than its competitors. Thanks to its hard drive (a first), ethernet port and front-loading disk drive the Xbox was enormously large for a console, and came with a pad to match. 'The Fatty' or, as it's more affectionately known, 'The Duke' was a pad the size of a small dinner plate, and when it came to the console's Japanese launch was redesigned to be smaller and sleeker – the 'S' controller. This design proved so popular it was quickly adopted globally and the Duke was put out to pasture.

> The Xbox probably deserved some good fortune after its various travails, and got it with a launch title. Microsoft had purchased developer Bungie outright to secure exclusive rights to the studio's first-person shooter *Halo: Combat Evolved* – which the Xbox team saw as one part of a strong lineup. The Xbox launched on 8 November 2001 in North America, with a dozen games available the same day, among which were some very good titles indeed: *Project Gotham Racing*, a reworked version of the Dreamcast's superb *Metropolis Street Racer* (2000), was a particular highlight. But *Halo* turned out to be a monster.

The Xbox has always been something of a loss-leader for Microsoft, representing a tiny fraction of the company's business but creating a global brand that has found its way into millions of living rooms. But Charles Bellfield was right about one thing. It's ugly. (Photo credit: Evan Amos)

● *Goldeneye 007* had shown consoles could play host to great first-person shooters, and *Halo* was the next evolutionary step. It introduced new ideas to the genre, such as main character Master Chief (I didn't say the writing was great) only being able to carry two weapons at once, and a 'shield' that would absorb damage but regenerate over time (as opposed to a fixed health bar). But what made *Halo* special were its environments and enemies.

● *Halo* has tight corridors and buildings, but mixes these in with sprawling landscapes and vehicles to create a sense of huge scale. The Warthog jeep, found nearly everywhere wide enough to drive it, is hugely satisfying to control: it has a high top speed, feels weighty, boasts a back-mounted cannon (which can be manned by yourself or NPC marines) and can easily plough through groups of enemies. Those marines are a major part of *Halo*'s atmosphere too – the Master Chief is Earth's

Despite the ethernet port built-into the Xbox, the Xbox Live gaming service wasn't ready to go at launch – meaning that *Halo*'s multiplayer mode was local only. *Halo 2* would later become perhaps the most important title in the history of Xbox Live and the first outstanding online console shooter.

last hope, and their joy at seeing him and praise during battle strokes the player's ego.

➡ The Covenant, *Halo*'s bad guys, are sleek and vividly coloured aliens remarkable for the way they work together – the jabbering Grunts fire potshots and cluster around the commanding Elites, who are much more intelligent and will home in on a weakened Master Chief to try and land a killing blow. Take out their captain and groups will panic; fire at them from a distance and they'll take cover; wade right in and you'll take down one or two before being overwhelmed. The best aspect of this is *Halo*'s difficulty levels, which rather than simply increasing enemy damage and health points make them work together even more effectively. Dying in a first-person shooter is not an uncommon experience – but feeling like you've been outsmarted is, and *Halo* delivered.

➡ *Halo* became such a touchstone that future first-person shooters would be referred to as '*Halo* clones' or, if particularly anticipated, '*Halo* killers'. The Xbox had its iconic game from day one, and the launches in Japan (February 2002) and Europe (March 2002) swiftly followed. Only two-and-a-half years since Ted Hase's PowerPoint presentation, Microsoft had built and launched a console globally.

➡ And what of Nintendo? The PlayStation had relegated the once-leader of the industry to a supporting role, with the N64's quality software unable to stop it lagging severely in sales. Nintendo saw this early and Project Dolphin, the codename for the N64's successor, had been initiated in 1997. As always with Nintendo cost was of primary importance, but thanks to its early start in design it managed to produce hardware that arguably outperformed PS2 (or at least was on par) at a much lower price.

➡ Much more importantly, Nintendo realized it had alienated third parties in the past and resolved to make a console that would be easy to develop for – learning a lesson from Sony, Project Dolphin had a simple and clean architecture with a library of technical features that Nintendo's own developers helped shape. It used mini-DVDs, meaning that storage would not be an issue as it had been with N64 cartridges. Deciding to emphasize Nintendo's priorities in the face of Microsoft and Sony's multimedia ambitions, the console was called GameCube.

● The GameCube was a beautiful machine, particularly in comparison to the Xbox – light and compact with a needless but cute 'carrying handle' on the rear. The pad was extraordinarily comfortable, with a gorgeously smooth left analogue stick and giant 'A' button (to reflect the fact that this was the most commonly used button), the only black marks being a somewhat stubby right analogue stick and, alongside its triggers, a strange 'Z' button that few games used.

● The GameCube was launched in Japan on 14 September 2001, with the North American launch just over two months later, and the now traditional lengthy wait for European fans (3 May 2002). The GameCube was the first Nintendo console to launch without a Mario title, which was compensated for by the surprisingly great *Luigi's Mansion* – a strange hybrid of exploring and ghost story, where the less famous brother has to find the kidnapped Mario by hoovering up ghosts hiding in the fixtures and fittings. A reliably great version of *Wave Race*, a jet-ski game with terrific bobbing water physics, and *Super Monkey Ball*[38] rounded out a lean but quality launch lineup.

● The big surprise was the price – where PS2 and Xbox sold at $299, the GameCube was $199. This is much more important than it seems because, where Microsoft haemorrhaged money trying to make the Xbox a success (in an effort to win market share for its successor), and Sega had been mortally wounded by hardware price cuts in the past, Nintendo hung on in its lean years through the blindingly simple tactic of always selling hardware at a profit, no matter how modest.

➔ Faced with a revitalized competitor and a monstrous new entrant, Sony played hardball. In March 2002 the company cut the PS2's North American price from $299 to $199. Now that the PS2 had some great titles, with many more on the way, it began to truly accelerate away from the competition – both GameCube and Xbox had relatively successful launch periods (though the latter flopped in Japan, as would all subsequent Xbox hardware), but the PS2's momentum soon became relentless.

➔ There were roughly 3,900 games developed for PlayStation 2, 1,000 for Xbox and 600 for GameCube: this overview should therefore be taken as just that (see Chapters 21 and 25 for discussion of the *Metal Gear Solid* and *Grand Theft Auto* series). The PlayStation 2 library, in particular, is probably the richest any individual console in history has to offer – its huge installed base supported many niche and original titles alongside the usual hits. Nevertheless there are standouts.

➔ *Ico* (2001) is a minimalist masterpiece, a third-person adventure that takes inspiration from techniques used in Eric Chahi's cinematic platformer *Another World* (1991). The game is about a boy and a girl, Ico and Yorda, trapped in a large castle and trying to escape, with brief snatches of narrative delivered through subtitled cutscenes (though Yorda's made-up language is never translated). In something of a reaction against the ever-present trend of using technology to pile more 'stuff' into a game, every element is as pared-back as possible: there is no head-up display (HUD), e.g. a health bar, to obscure the visuals, there are a limited number of mechanics, and ambient sound effects are favoured over music in almost every section.

➔ You could say that *Ico* is the only great game to be built around an escort mission,[39] and certainly the only example that successfully uses interaction to tell the story of a relationship. Ico finds Yorda trapped in a cage shortly after the game's beginning and, after freeing her, can take her hand while running around the environments. Ico can help Yorda climb and catch her from falling, and Yorda too can help Ico traverse obstacles he couldn't manage on his own – the key part of this is the gorgeously fluid animations, which at once capture the exertion and determination of these children while also emphasizing how they cling to each other in this intimidating place.

➔ In a sense *Ico* is just a game about a boy and girl holding hands. Despite the occasional cutscenes the story and characters are never fleshed out, and yet the game's narrative gathers incredible force because the player lives this experience through controlling Ico. Even more subtle is the way the environments reflect his inner mood – during a sequence when Ico and Yorda are separated, for example, the castle's materials change from stone to metal with a corresponding palette change to muted greys and blacks. The interiors are dimly lit with the occasional shaft of sunlight, but exterior sections use bloom lighting to make the grass and vegetation vivid green.

➔ Japanese designer Fumito Ueda was the director, lead animator, lead designer and art director for *Ico* – he even drew the box art. Clearly Ueda is an enormous part of why *Ico* is the way it is, but the development team (later renamed Team Ico) produced a technological feat: one of the first titles to use bloom lighting, key frame animation, complex cloth dynamics and inverse

Despite a good critical reception *Ico* was not a success on release, though over time its reputation grew to the point where – to coincide with the release of *Shadow of the Colossus* – Sony reissued the game to the larger audience it deserved.

A BRIEF HISTORY OF VIDEO GAMES

What really impresses about the design of *Shadow of the Colossus* is that Team Ico clearly realized it needed more of an action bent to find a wider audience. Yet *Shadow of the Colossus* is an action game like no other, arguably the greatest ever made, and still manages to communicate its themes through the mechanics.

kinematics (which ensure a character's feet are always positioned correctly on steps, for example). *Ico* sadly did not achieve commercial success, although it has subsequently been recognized as one of the most important games of the era.

● Following this Team Ico spent four years working on its next game, *Shadow of the Colossus* (2005). This carried over much of *Ico*'s aesthetic and improved upon many of its technical innovations, but crafts an utterly distinct experience built around a unique idea: what if a game had no 'normal' enemies, but just boss fights? In a way *Shadow of the Colossus* responds to *Ico*'s lack of commercial success by being more action-focused, but this is one of the best and most unusual action games ever made.

● It begins with the player character Wander riding his horse across a long bridge that leads to a temple surrounded by mountains and open plains. Draped across the horse is a dead woman, whom Wander leaves in the temple – after making a deal with its inhabitant, Dormammu, to resurrect her in exchange for destroying sixteen Colossi that inhabit this world.

● *Shadow of the Colossus* is constructed around a simple but highly effective rhythm that alternates between the player riding across a desolate landscape and then fighting a Colossus. The Colossi have an enormous range of sizes and few similarities to each other. Some are found on open ground, some in tight spaces, some fly, some live underwater or underground, some are many hundreds times larger than Wander and some are only slightly taller than him. Most disturbingly, some are instantly hostile to Wander encroaching on their space while others clearly do not want to fight.

● All the Colossi require different tactics and battle is never simple a matter of swinging a sword – Wander needs to climb up and clamber around the larger Colossi to find weak spots, while the giants try to grab or shake him off. This system is brilliantly realized. The player uses a 'grab' button to hold on (which depends upon a 'grip' metre that decreases as Wander exerts himself), with Wander's dynamic animations reflecting precisely the situation.

→ A Colossus found in the desert, for example, is a huge flying beast that occasionally dips its wings in the sand, but moves far too fast for Wander to grab onto. The player needs to ride Wander's horse, Agro, at full speed and correctly judge the angle at which the wings will come low enough, and then jump off onto the wing at the right moment. Wander will then crouch and use all four limbs as he makes his way up the wing's bony ridges. When and if he makes it to the Colossus' body, the beast is aware and will turn itself upside-down in flight, hundreds of metres above the ground – at which point Wander can only dangle from its fur by a single hand. When back 'upright', Wander can slowly inch his way towards the beast's head against the enormous winds that will knock him off in an instant. It's one hell of an experience.

→ You could write about every Colossus like this but equally important to *Shadow of the Colossus*'s brilliance is the horse Agro. In any other game where a character rides a horse, the moment they are in the saddle the player effectively takes control of the horse – for example, Epona in *Ocarina of Time*. In *Shadow of the Colossus* you remain in control of Wander and he is controlling the horse through its reins – meaning that, as you press left and Wander pulls the reins to the left, there is a slight delay to Agro responding. This simple idea is remarkably effective at making Agro feel like an animal with its own personality, a faithful companion and the mute witness to Wander's extraordinary heroism.

Although very different games, *Ico* and *Shadow of the Colossus* are complementary titles. If the first is about companionship and innocence, the latter is about the things to which these may lead. No player of *Shadow of the Colossus* will ever doubt the courage of Wander, but as the game progresses it becomes clear he is paying a toll – Team Ico is too subtle for overt messaging of any kind, but the theme is sacrifice and the consequences thereof. In both games the impact comes not from anything that is made explicit to the player but the experience of the journey.

This principle also applies, though in a somewhat more direct manner, to a genre that bloomed on this generation of hardware – the third-person brawler. The idea of dynamic hand-to-hand combat against groups of enemies was pioneered in *Devil May Cry* (2001) – which had begun as a prototype for a new *Resident Evil* game before becoming its own title. Directed by Hideki Kamiya, *Devil May Cry* introduced combo-heavy brawling that rated players on how stylishly they executed long strings of moves and offered a stiff challenge: the only drawback was that it used a fixed camera in 3D environments, which occasionally didn't give the best view of the action.

This limitation is particularly interesting in the light of Kamiya's next project, a side-scrolling brawler that adapted these mechanics but was built entirely around the camera as concept and mechanic: *Viewtiful Joe* (2003). Kamiya's big break had come in directing *Resident Evil 2* (1998) at a time when Capcom's finest minds were perfecting what swiftly became a niche art – 3D worlds viewed from fixed camera angles.

This is an inevitable result of an industry where art and technology intersect – and what led to *Viewtiful Joe*. Here the camera is fixed on one plane to observe a world that

P.N.03 – 'Never Outgunned' by Dead End Thrills. One of the 'Capcom Five', a collection of titles designed to showcase Capcom's finest designers, *P.N.03* was a third-person shooter directed by Shinji Mikami and built around arcade-style mechanics. (Courtesy of Dead End Thrills)

A BRIEF HISTORY OF VIDEO GAMES

suggests it has many more. When Joe jumps the camera doesn't jump with him, but jerks upwards like an audience member's gaze. When Joe turns corners the camera stays fixed on him, but the environment itself rotates. It is a radical visual style that puts the player in the role of observer as much as participant. Joe's abilities are tied to the camera – moving into slo-mo, speeding up or zooming in, all of which affect the behaviour of enemies and increase the impact of Joe's fists and feet. *Viewtiful Joe* gives the player an enormously flexible moveset and the opportunity to control and simultaneously direct a performance – your own action movie.

▶ The sheer quantity of great third-person brawlers means we have to dash through the rest. *Ninja Gaiden* (2004) stands alone because of its unforgiving enemies and tight patterns of attack/block/counter. Here defence is as important as offence, and the only secret to combat is in fluid and swift

interchange. More so than any game before or since (outside of its remake and first sequel) *Ninja Gaiden* manhandles the player, refusing to compromise its difficulty, and so the reward for eventually mastering it is commensurately greater.

▶ *Devil May Cry 3* (2005) gave lead character Dante five weapons, five sidearms, six fighting styles and challenged the player to build their own way of fighting from the dizzying list of possible combinations. Devil *May Cry 3* doesn't just have a brilliant core system but one that lets the player stretch it to the limits, one where every increase in skill is matched by further possibilities – a game you can never really finish playing.

▶ A direct reaction to this style was *God of War* (2005), which focused on the spectacle of angry man Kratos gradually destroying various Olympian deities in Ancient Greece. Visually stunning, with many bosses simply awe-inspiring to watch in motion, *God of*

Killer 7 – 'Murder Was the Case' by Dead End Thrills. Written and directed by Goichi Suda, aka Suda-51, *Killer 7* was one of the 'Capcom Five' and an on-rails shooter most notable for its stylized art-house visuals. (Courtesy of Dead End Thrills)

War made its combat system basic and kept the difficulty down to open up the genre to players less inclined to spend days mastering combos. This blend has made it the most commercially successful example of the genre, although among its many sequels only *God of War II* (2007) managed to be equally enjoyable. (The third in the series, released for PS3, was something of a disappointment, as well as containing a frankly grotesque sequence where the player depresses both thumbsticks to make Kratos gouge out Poseidon's eyes.)

➔ Finally, there is *God Hand* (2006), directed by Shinji Mikami and the last title from Capcom's outstanding Clover Studio. Unlike the previously mentioned games, *God Hand* is something of an attempt to convert the 2D brawler into 3D, with a system built for one-on-one fighting. Everything is concentrated in Gene, the God Hand himself, and his transitions between cocksure swaying

and one of many brilliantly modelled martial arts styles.

➔ *God Hand* switches up the nature of inputs, allowing you to assign a string of attacks to pressing a single button repeatedly, and pin others to spare face buttons: what this means is that fighting is no longer a question of memorizing button combinations but timing. Dodging attacks is beautifully elegant: head bobs, sidesteps and backflips are all mapped to whips of

The development of *P.N.03* had been rushed by Capcom, and *Resident Evil 4* had been an enormous success. So the company gave Shinji Mikami complete freedom in making *God Hand* – as he would reflect years later, 'perhaps too much freedom'.

Resident Evil 4 arguably still stands as the template for third-person shooters to this day, though few get close to its quality. The game had an unusually troubled development, with at least two substantially complete versions scrapped on the way to the final product.

A BRIEF HISTORY OF VIDEO GAMES

the right analogue stick. Perhaps the most telling aspect of the controls, however, is that there's a button dedicated purely to taunting the enemies.

➜ Among the many innovations of *God Hand* is a dynamic difficulty system, so the game gets harder as you fight better and, if Gene's taking a kicking, cools things down a little. This is a game that focuses on what matters to the exclusion of all else, and gives body to things that were ridiculous in 2D only to emphasize their grotesqueries. Armies of identikit enemies, physically huge bosses, and oversized weapons are the critical vocabulary for an historical tribute as well as a one-off celebration. Whether wrestling giant apes, knocking seven bells out of midget Power Rangers, kicking Elvis in the nuts or spanking a karate-kicking dominatrix, anything goes with *God Hand* – neither entirely old nor new, it's simply the best single-player fighting game in history. (And the funniest too. The

shop between levels where Gene buys new moves is called 'Barely Regal', certain enemies scream Mike Tyson quotes, and here's a typical example of the script: Shannon – 'Looks like this dog can be trained after all!' Gene – 'The only bitch that needs training is you!')

➜ Prior to *God Hand* Mikami had returned to the *Resident Evil* series, which had grown stale by its third instalment and was in need of revitalizing. *Resident Evil 4* (2005) marked a departure from survival horror towards pure survival, emphasizing combat mechanics and introducing an 'over-the-shoulder' third-person perspective that has subsequently become the genre's standard. It abandoned fixed camera angles, fetch-quests and even zombies.

➜ *Resident Evil 4*'s environments were fully 3D but, much more importantly, combat had a greater range of possibilities: location-specific damage, like shooting enemies in the

Leon

knees or the weapon hand, was combined with contextual moves like a roundhouse kick. This ties in to the new enemy types, the semi-intelligent Ganados, who try to mob main character Leon S. Kennedy – making the core combat something akin to crowd control. The Ganados talk to each other, shout at Leon, try to blindside the player by stepping outside of vision and duck when they're lining up a headshot. In a brilliantly game-y touch Leon can counter this by staggering Ganados and executing kicks or throws, which grants a brief second of invulnerability during the move and clears space.

⊙ The game is 'about' saving the president's kidnapped daughter but, in a twist to the standard princess-in-castle formula, Ashley is rescued relatively early in the game and then has to be protected for the game's remainder. As a design element she becomes another variable in combat, a target for the Ganados (who'll try to carry her off) and something

that stops the player simply dashing past enemies or abandoning certain positions.

⊙ The craftsmanship of *Resident Evil 4*'s systems is one thing, but beyond this is a grisly imagination that never stops: Del Lago, a monstrous fish-thing you harpoon from a speedboat, the El Gigantes that batter you into the ground and off walls, a giant statue of a midget that chases you into the waiting arms of the real thing. No single moment astonishes more than the sheer number of them: holding off an angry mob inside a cabin, entering a castle by cannoning down the gate, dodging boulders, riding a minecart, hiding from a half-scorpion mentalist in a cage suspended above a chasm, knife-fighting a madman in his personal labyrinth, freezing unkillable enemies and shattering them like the T-1000, diving through laser traps straight out of *Mission Impossible*, or jet-skiing out on a tidal wave.

⊙ It's not that each individual mechanic of

Resident Evil 4 is so beautifully honed, or that there are so many of them, or even that the enemies are capable of surprises. It's that many elements of this game never needed to be half as good as they are or even present at all, and yet every single part has been sanded off and polished. The inventory system is a puzzle game in disguise. When Leon loses his jacket and is outside in the cold air, his aim shakes a little more than normal. Then you get the Mercenaries, a mode unlocked after the first run through that repurposes campaign environments as wave-based shooter arenas, a 'bonus' mode as good as the main game (so good, in fact, that Capcom made Mercenaries into a standalone title as well as including it in every subsequent *Resident Evil*).

◉ *Resident Evil 4* set a new standard for third-person action games and, though it has subsequently been matched and in some ways improved upon, its influence has never waned – games made today are still working in its long shadow.

◉ This was also one of few third-party highlights for Nintendo, who had *Resident Evil 4* as an exclusive for a period. Yet again the GameCube's software library depended overwhelmingly on first-party and second-party software and, though the overall quality remained high, there were signs that Nintendo was worried.

◉ This is most obviously seen in its two central franchises. *Super Mario Sunshine* (2002) would be by any other lights a great game, but as the successor to *Super Mario 64* it fell short. There are great ideas here: Mario wears a water-spraying device called FLUDD that allows him to hover in the air for a spell, mitigating somewhat the difficulty of judging jumps and distances in 3D, and several of the worlds are as good as anything in its predecessor.

◉ But *Super Mario Sunshine* is strangely

Although much in *Super Mario Sunshine* can be criticized, the water effects are truly outstanding. It also included completely abstract 'hidden' levels, where Mario would have to negotiate 3D shapes without Fludd, which are excellent but also demonstrate why Nintendo felt the need for a 'safety net' mechanic in normal gameplay.

unsatisfying for a Mario game, with minor annoyances that seem worse because of the series' pedigree – such as an early challenge that requires you negotiate a long, thin walkway high above some water, where falling means Mario has to spend several minutes working his way back up for another try. Isle Delfino, the setting, has an uninspired layout next to the uber-hub of Peach's Castle. And then there's the sneaking suspicion, confirmed by some wonderful abstract bonus levels, that FLUDD is something of a gimmick – a great gimmick, but ultimately unnecessary.

➤ *The Legend of Zelda: The Wind Waker* (2002) feels equally unsatisfying, though almost everything can be forgiven for its gorgeous cel-shaded take on the series. The player controls the child Link in this entry, beautifully realized as a cartoon character with big eyes that flick around looking at other people and objects of interest. He's

a stunning creation and worth the price of admission alone, but it gets better: *The Wind Waker* is set on a great ocean that is the deepest blue you'll ever see, dotted with islands, and Link has a boat to sail and can control the direction of the wind.

➤ This setting means that *The Wind Waker* captures more of the spirit of exploration from the original *Zelda* game than any other 3D entry in the series, but a few minor issues bring it down. The game feels unfinished in several respects and the final third, in the absence of dungeons, sends Link on a fetch quest so tedious it's astonishing Nintendo let it out the door. Changing the wind direction, considering how important it is to the game's concept, is an overlong and fussy process that always feels like a chore rather than a fantastic power. These pieces of grit speak to Nintendo's worry that Sony was simply leaving it in the dust, and so development on its prize properties had to be rushed along.

The cel-shaded style of *The Legend of Zelda: The Wind Waker* was met with derision from a vocal element of the series fanbase, which only goes to show that playing video games doesn't mean you have aesthetic taste. Unfortunately this may have influenced the series' subsequent return to a more 'realistic' visual style.

The Wind Waker is a very beautiful game, but the thought of what it could have been is painful.

◉ Nintendo's most surprising GameCube software was *Animal Crossing* (2001), a game originally designed for the N64 – and released for it in Japan – before being ported to the new hardware. *Animal Crossing* is about a town: your town. Moving in at the start of the game, you are immediately put in hock to the house-providing raccoon Tom Nook, and begin to make friends among its inhabitants. These characters are constructed from simple archetypes, the jock boy or the fashion-conscious girl and so on, but many layers are added to their personalities by your ongoing interactions and the shape of the town itself. Over time they become more individualized, with endless little quirks, and soon become favourites.

◉ *Animal Crossing*'s touch of genius is that it works alongside the real world –

seasons pass, holidays are observed (with appropriate in-game celebrations) and the town's inhabitants form their own opinion of you over time. Then there's that bastard Nook, who continually upgrades your house and keeps your debt to him ongoing, while selling desirable furniture from his shop with fresh stock every day. The only thing to do is get involved in fishing, digging up fossils, collecting fruit and sending gifts back and forth.

◉ This is not a traditionally structured game – there's no real end point, although you can eventually pay off your debt to Nook, and the only goals along the way are largely self-assigned. *Animal Crossing*'s appeal lies largely in being a good citizen, in helping people and making friends. This is a world where the mundane is made to somehow feel significant, and where the virtual occupants eventually come to seem something more. Soon the days turn into weeks, the weeks

Animal Crossing's most magical ingredient is the feeling that its residents are responding to your actions on an individual level. It is hard to delineate exactly how they do this, but it has a lot to do with their capacity for remembering your behaviour and reminding you of it at surprising moments – as well as the general charm of its voluminous script.

turn into months, checking in on holidays feels essential, and *Animal Crossing* has you. Like the Hotel California, you can check out – but you can never leave.

→ Almost as surprising, though for entirely different reasons, was *Metroid Prime* (2002). The work of American developer Retro Studios, with Nintendo's guidance, this transplanted the key elements of the 2D side-scroller into a 3D first-person adventure game: there's plenty of shooting too, but this is no first-person shooter. *Metroid Prime* stands out for focusing on puzzle-solving, exploration and navigation in the large open-ended environment of Tallon IV.

→ It is a first-person game where the developers thought about what would specifically suit the game, rather than what everyone else does. Combat is handled through a lock-on that allows Samus to strafe around her enemies and quickly dodge from side-to-side while under attack. A scanning

visor lets the player examine key parts of the environment for clues and information. When needed – such as when using the iconic morph ball power-up – there's no hesitation in temporarily switching to a third-person view. The HUD is designed to resemble the inside of Samus's helmet – and when explosions go off nearby, you can even catch glimpses of her eyes in the glass.

→ *Metroid Prime* adapts and transforms one of the most popular 2D templates into 3D and was so successful that few games have dared follow in its wake – even its own sequels were something of a let-down. Nintendo has always been wary of first-person games but, thanks to the right partner, *Metroid*'s stylistic transition was realized exceptionally well.

→ During this hardware generation Rockstar's *Grand Theft Auto* series was enjoying tremendous success, which gave its various studios the freedom to work on other very different but equally high-quality

Metroid Prime is still a unique style of first-person shooter, with its use of 'lock-on' mechanics in particular never effectively copied. The usually protective Nintendo's decision to outsource development to the American Retro Studios, under supervision, was one of the best the company has made.

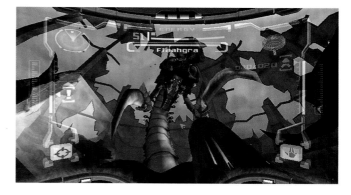

games. Rockstar North's *Manhunt* (2003) is impossible to see as anything but a reaction to the British tabloids' rather brainless coverage of *Grand Theft Auto*'s violence, and is a brutal game too clever by half for those self-same critics.

● *Manhunt* is deliberately nasty. You play a death row inmate given a surprise second chance, 'directed' through levels by a disembodied voice, where the main aim is to hide from and kill gang members. The violence here is truly gratuitous to the extent that this is sometimes difficult to play and you would be hard-pushed to call it enjoyable, but as a straight-faced exploration of the agency, nature and pleasure of video-game violence, *Manhunt* remains unique.

● Rockstar Vancouver's *Bully* (2006), released in Europe as *Canis Canem Edit* ('Dog Eat Dog'), combines an open-world mission structure with a boarding-school setting. Casting the player as Jimmy Hopkins, a bolshy young tough brand new to Bullworth Academy, the game revolves around a day/night cycle where you have to attend lessons (which are played out through puzzles and minigames), negotiate around the various gangs in the school and kiss the occasional girl (or boy). Although its highly polished mechanics were nothing revolutionary, the bitesized open world and mix of activities suited *Bully*'s setting perfectly and, in concert with one of Rockstar's better scripts, make it a gem.

● Other noteworthy titles include Free Radical Design's smooth-as-silk multiplayer-focused first-person shooter *Timesplitters* (2000), which *Timesplitters 2* (2002) improved upon in nearly every aspect. This is the last hurrah of the local multiplayer shooter, with hundreds of characters and modes, sixty frames-per-second and a cartoony aesthetic that holds up to this day. Free Radical would also go on to develop *Second Sight* (2004), a

Rockstar North's *Manhunt* positively revels in the violence it displays, with increasingly creative and distressing ways to kill people as it progresses. The genius touch here, however, is in how the enemies call out to the player as they hunt you, which is both intimidating and something of a motivation.

psychic-themed stealth game that was ahead of the curve but sadly made little commercial impact: cover-based shooting with destructible elements, physics manipulation, rag-doll animations, and a smart central twist that meshes the mechanics and narrative in a manner few games match.

➤ Bungie's *Halo 2* (2004) finally delivered on the promise of Xbox Live, adding online functionality alongside a slightly undercooked single-player campaign – but the former was all that mattered. *Halo*'s mechanics are a perfect fit for competitive online gaming and, alongside Bungie's outstanding map designs (in particular Lockout, an all-time classic), saw this dominate Xbox Live from its release until many years later – in fact, when the servers were closed down, it was still being played by tens of thousands of people. *Halo* introduced the Master Chief, but *Halo 2* online is where he really started to show his chops.

➤ The greatest aesthetic achievement in this period is Clover Studios' *Okami* (2006) for PS2, directed by Hideki Kamiya. Drawing on a combination of the ancient religion of Shinto and traditional Japanese watercolour art, *Okami*'s cel-shaded visuals are filtered through a parchment effect to create the overall impression of a moving painting.

➤ Such a stylistic triumph would have been enough for other games, but *Okami* also ties this into its core mechanic: at any point during play you can 'freeze' the scene, which becomes a piece of sepia-tinted parchment. Then objects can be drawn using 'The Celestial Brush', which, when the scene is unfrozen, will spring into existence – players can create lily pads on the water, sprout bamboo cages to trap enemies, slice trees in half and encircle parched wasteland to bring it blooming back to life.

➤ Amaterasu, the main character, is capable of such feats because she's a Shinto sun goddess who takes the form of a white wolf

Okami's 'parchment' effect can be clearly seen in the sky here. Rest assured that however good it looks in still images, in motion this is a transcendent visual achievement.

A BRIEF HISTORY OF VIDEO GAMES

– and also mute, which means most of the amusing script is delivered by an inch-tall artist called Issun living in her fur. Issun himself is clearly a kind of Kamiya-proxy, prone to both flights of inspiration and rather perverse digressions on the glory of bosoms, but this touch of companionship lets the loftier themes of *Okami* swirl around his feet of clay.

● It is no small feat to recast the tale of a traditional goddess as a *Zelda*-style action RPG, never mind make it an exciting and original game in its own right. *Okami* is a long and involved journey, and what makes it so remarkable is that the visual invention never lets up, the beautifully realized aesthetic the starting point for endless flourishes rather than a self-satisfied whole.

● The PlayStation 2 era saw games begin to find a broader audience, and become broader in their choice of subject-matter and style as a result – an evolution that is almost entirely down to Sony's success in how it sold and supported its console. Games became both more sophisticated and simpler. There isn't much to say about *Singstar* (2004), for example, because it's a karaoke game where you sing along to on-screen lyrics, but in the right setting it's fantastic fun to play. It's all the more surprising, in this context, that Sony wouldn't be the company to capitalize on this expanded audience.

● The most telling statistic, alongside the sales figures, is that the GameCube ceased production in 2007 and the Xbox ceased production in 2008. When the dust settled the former had sold 21.74 million units worldwide and the latter just over 24 million. The PS2 continued selling well into the next generation of consoles, and production finally stopped in 2013 with over 155 million units sold. Sony hadn't just cemented its position at the top with PlayStation 2. It had created the most successful console in history and left its rivals fighting over scraps.

Since the industry's earliest days the idea of handheld gaming has been an irresistible allure for developers and players. It's not hard to see why. Video-game consoles are often bulky things trailing wires everywhere that need a television (which may well be the only one in the house), whereas a handheld system is portable, self-contained and need never inconvenience the rest of the family. These characteristics eventually led to a unique style of software, where the principle of short play sessions was applied to everything from text adventures to universe-spanning epics.

The first handhelds were made by American toy company Mattel, which over 1976–8 released a series of calculator-like devices that played a single game: from sports titles like *Football*, *Baseball* and *Basketball* to *Missile Attack* (the first released), *Computer Chess* and even a licensed version of *Dallas*. Needless to say these are extremely simple LED-based machines with tiny displays, and have aged badly, but they were there first.

A conceptual leap forward was Milton Bradley's Microvision (1979), the first handheld to resemble a console in that it used interchangeable cartridges. Unfortunately its LCD screen displayed only 16 x 16 pixels (hence the name) and this was one of many technical problems: static would permanently ruin the cartridges and the buttons were easily damaged through general use. Needless to say the Microvision was quickly discontinued. Epoch's Game Pocket Computer (1984) was released only in Japan and also used interchangeable cartridges – though this was rendered somewhat pointless by the machine only ever having five games.

Despite these commercial failures, Nintendo's Game & Watch series (running from 1980 to 1991) showed there was a large potential market for handheld gaming, and creator Gunpei Yokoi would invent the first great portable console: the Game Boy (1989). This hardware is the purest distillation of Yokoi's design philosophy of 'lateral thinking with withered technology'. The Game Boy had a green monochromatic display (derisively referred to by competitors as 'pea soup'), an 8-bit CPU, a mere 8 KB of RAM and a single tinny speaker (though it could output stereo sound through headphones).

➡ The Game Boy was released in April 1989 in Japan, July 1989 in North America and September 1990 in Europe. In October 1989 its first serious competitor, the Atari Lynx, arrived on the scene, and by October 1990 there was Sega's Game Gear (based on the Master System). Both of the competing consoles offered backlit colour screens, larger than that of the Game Boy, and were designed to be held in a landscape format – superficially, at least, they were much more attractive hardware.

➡ But the Game Boy had been designed with purpose: Yokoi's team had intuited that the most important thing with a portable games console was not grunt, but more practical issues such as battery life. The Game Boy could be played for upwards of fifteen hours on 4 x AA batteries: but thanks to those backlit LCD colour screens, the Game Gear and Lynx each needed 6 x AA batteries that would last three to five hours. In addition, the Game Boy was significantly cheaper and smaller than both.

➡ Despite the competition's superficial advantages and aggressive marketing, the Game Boy absolutely massacred Game Gear and Lynx. While its clever design played an important role, the real weapon Nintendo had (as ever) was outstanding software, and its pack-in title for the North American release is an all-time classic: *Tetris*.

➡ *Tetris* (1984, Game Boy version 1989) was designed by Alexey Pajitnov, an AI researcher working at the Soviet Academy of Sciences in

The Game Boy single-handedly created the handheld market as it exists today and put Nintendo at the very top – a position from which the company has never shifted. (Photo credit: William Warby)

A BRIEF HISTORY OF VIDEO GAMES

Moscow. Pajitnov's job involved testing new hardware, which he had a habit of doing by designing simple games, and when he was given an Elektronika 60 in June 1984 – a clone of the US-made LSI-11 CPU – this time didn't seem any different.

➔ Based on physical puzzles he had played as a child, Pajitnov thought about making a game using pentonimoes – shapes formed from five blocks. But there are twelve variations of pentonimoes, which he considered too many, and so he settled for tetronimoes (seven variations). The Elektronika 60's display was text-only, so the shapes were formed out of letters and Pajitnov created a program that had the player stacking them neatly as they fell from the top of the screen.

➔ In this form the playing field quickly filled up, so in a Eureka moment Pajitnov decided to make 'completed' horizontal columns disappear – the key mechanic behind *Tetris*

(the name combines 'Tetronimo' and 'Tennis'). Pajitnov showed the game to his colleagues, who quickly became addicted, and two of them ported it to the IBM PC where its popularity increased. Soon *Tetris* could be found all over Russia and Eastern Europe. A British software developer, Andromeda, fudged a deal – securing the rights to make a PC version, but no more. Despite this Andromeda sold on other rights it didn't own, such as console and arcade rights, resulting in technically unlicensed versions appearing in the USA and Europe.

➔ This did not go unnoticed by the Soviet Union's bureaucracy and, fearing repercussions, Pajitnov ceded the rights to Elorg (the Soviet Ministry of Software and Hardware Export) for ten years. Andromeda continued to negotiate with third parties over rights it didn't own, while at the same time trying to renegotiate with Elorg for those same licenses, to the extent that by

Many attempts have been made to 'improve' on the design of *Tetris* over the years, with almost all of them merely showing the level of perfection the original attained. One possible exception is the addition of the ability to store a tetronimo for later recall, though this arguably taints the element of random chance that makes the 'pure' form so delicious.

1989 half-a-dozen publishers were 'licensees'. There is much more detail to this mess, but it came to an end when Henk Rogers, who had a close relationship with Nintendo, saw the game and persuaded NoA chief Minoru Arakawa that *Tetris* could be the upcoming Game Boy's killer title.

➤ Such an unusual situation meant that, despite *Tetris* existing since 1984 and being ported to many platforms, it was really the Game Boy that brought the title to prominence – and *Tetris* itself was the greatest demonstration of the machine's capabilities that could be wished for. It is simply a perfect puzzle game, with mechanics that couldn't be recreated in the real world, and one where not a single element could be changed or removed.

➤ *Tetris* works in layers. It is easy to play: the abstract shapes and fixed 'bucket' of the playing field are visually clear, and the simple controls are instantly comprehensible. But

as you build the shapes together and make lines disappear it speeds up, and the random element of which shape comes next means that – inevitably – mistakes will follow. The fact that it is the player making them is key, as is the minor frisson of freeing up a previously covered space and correcting earlier errors. As the game gets faster and faster it is almost as if instinct takes over, with learned configurations coming to the fore, but the end is always the same: a flat parp as a block overlaps the top of the screen, the display filling up and your score displayed. *Tetris* is ideally suited to bitesize sessions and thus portable play, but it also proved the worth of the Game Boy's technological approach: if the machine could host games as good as this, the pack-in title, then who needs a backlit LCD screen?

➤ The Game Boy also played to Nintendo's traditional strengths with *Super Mario Land* (1989), versions of hits like *Donkey Kong*, and as time went on increasingly sophisticated adaptations of classic franchises. Among these *The Legend of Zelda: Link's Awakening* (1993) is exceptional, somehow squeezing a huge action-RPG every bit as good as its console brethren onto a tiny Game Boy cartridge.

→ Against this the Game Gear offered titles like *Sonic Chaos* (1993), the excellent action-RPG *Ax Battler: A Legend of Golden Axe* (1991) and several *Shining Force* games. Lynx tended towards arcade ports like *Ms. Pac-Man*, *California Games*, *Paperboy*, *Rampart* and *Qix*. Both handhelds had good games, but simply couldn't compete with the quality and quantity of Game Boy software – especially when the latter's sales figures increasingly attracted third parties.

→ The Lynx would see a hardware revision that addressed some of the issues with the original, and Sega would release the Nomad in 1995 – a portable Mega Drive that didn't

have its own games library, but played that console's titles. Neither made a significant impact, and the Game Boy's momentum was about to become unstoppable thanks to a game inspired by collecting bugs.

→ *Pocket Monsters: Red* and *Pocket Monsters: Green* were released in Japan in February 1996, but would take over two years to reach America (September 1998) and three to reach Europe (1999), by which time they were known as *Pokémon Red* and *Pokémon Blue*. When a child, creator Satoshi Tajiri was known among his friends as 'Dr Bug' for his obsession with collecting insects – he grew up in a suburb of Tokyo and, as the city became increasingly urban, was saddened by the decline in the number and types of insects he saw. Tajiri was also obsessed with video games, enough so he set up a fanzine called *Game Freak*, and, later in life when he saw the Game Boy's link cable, had a vision of insects travelling across the thin wire.

The Game Gear's similarity to the Master System hardware meant that Sega could easily port versions of its biggest hits across, but Nintendo's much more successful strategy was based around bespoke software.

◆ *Pokémon*'s structure has remained essentially unchanged over countless iterations: a major part of the game is a top-down RPG where the player moves between towns and wilderness, chatting to NPCs and getting into battles. But here it diverges. *Pokémon* is constructed around its titular monsters, found everywhere in the world, and players can capture and train them. *Red* and *Blue* had 151 monsters to collect and, though they were essentially the same game, the distinction was in a few monsters exclusive to each version, which Tajiri thought children would enjoy trading with each other.

◆ The pacing of *Pokémon* and the way its worlds gradually unfold, as the Pokémon themselves become more unusual and evolve into new forms, is beautifully balanced between adventuring, exploration and discovery. The turn-based battling, where trainers face off against each other using up to six Pokémon, looks simple but has enormous tactical depth thanks to the rock-paper-scissors interplay of the monsters. A fire-type monster, for example, will be super effective against a leafy grass-type monster – but will come unstuck when faced with the dousing power of a water type.

◆ *Pokémon* is fundamentally designed to delight children, and its monster designs and twee script reflect this, but the appeal is universal – tempting the part of our minds that likes to collect things, to obsess over the few monsters we don't yet have and to wonder about what might lie in unexplored regions of the map. I was no boy naturalist, unlike Tajiri, yet vividly remember catching my first tadpole in a crisp packet, then cradling this sloppy pouch all the way home. When you know Tajiri wanted to make a game to communicate his enjoyment of catching insects as a boy, and look at *Pokémon*, it is impossible not to feel how powerfully it succeeds. Whatever else *Pokémon* does, and

At the start of *Pokémon* the player is given the choice of a grass-type, fire-type or water-type Pokémon, each of which has the capacity to develop into a fearsome member of their team. This pattern is followed throughout the subsequent games, and the series is extraordinarily careful about innovating on even minor parts of its original formula.

A BRIEF HISTORY OF VIDEO GAMES

it does much more, it zeroes in on the feelings of that child and catches them all.

● These games, and the subsequent sequels, became a marketing phenomenon for Nintendo (as of 2014 the *Pokémon* games had sold over 250 million copies) to the extent that it established the Pokémon Company to focus on this one series – and of course the lunchboxes, cartoon series and trading cards soon followed. Pokemon single-handedly turned the Game Boy, which was arguably outdated even at the time of its release, into a must-have just under a decade later. Nintendo would continue producing the handheld, with hardware revisions, until March 2003. By this time it had sold roughly 120 million units.

● Not only did such success mitigate Nintendo's difficulty with its post-SNES home consoles, but it enabled it to dominate the handheld market. There were missteps, such as Gunpei Yokoi's Virtual Boy, a 3D-capable successor that was rushed to market and was simply too unusual for commercial success. But the Game Boy ruled all and 2001's Game Boy Advance only cemented Nintendo's position.

● The Game Boy Advance's capabilities were comparable to the SNES, and the machine had both a colour screen and a landscape format. It competed with several other handhelds that found it impossible to gain any kind of a foothold: the Neo-Geo Pocket Colour (1999) was nice hardware that never sold, while Bandai's Wonderswan[40] at one point had an 8 per cent market share in Japan but ran out of steam.

● Nintendo began to leverage its past with the Game Boy Advance in a big way, meaning the platform saw many ports of SNES classics such as *Super Mario Advance 3: Yoshi's Island* (2002), remakes such as *Metroid: Zero Mission* (2004), as well at bespoke entries in its most-storied series: *Mario Kart: Super Circuit* (2001),

Metroid Fusion (2002), *Fire Emblem* (2003), *Pokémon Ruby/Sapphire* (2003), *Mario Golf* (2004) and *The Legend of Zelda: The Minish Cap* (2005).

➡ There were more unusual offshoots, too. *Mario & Luigi: Superstar Saga* (2003) cast the brothers in an action-RPG that combined the series' traditional mechanics with turn-based battling and an extremely funny script. *Advance Wars* (2001) was the first of the outstanding *Famicom Wars* series to make it to the west – a turn-based strategy game where players command entire armies, and much deeper than it looks.

➡ The most original and downright fun Game Boy Advance game was *Wario Ware: Twisted!* (2004). This series had began with *Wario Ware: Mega Microgames*, a madcap collection of ten-second minigames that changed the interactions every time, but *Twisted!*'s cartridge took this further by incorporating a gyroscopic sensor – that is, tilt controls.

The player has to tilt the Game Boy Advance to guide hang-gliders, move an arm to catch fruit, dodge falling poo, create fire with sticks, lift a giant's legs to let characters walk under, dodge crocodiles while swinging, shake up soda, play table hockey, inch a caterpillar towards an apple, dance with the console held aloft and so much more.

➡ If the Game Boy Advance's library could be accused of playing it a little too safe (though not of lacking great games), *Twisted!* is the exception that allowed Nintendo's designers a new kind of creative freedom – and a hint of the innovative approach to control systems that, shortly afterwards, would prove crucial to Nintendo's future.

➡ Nintendo had dominated the handheld market since 1989, but had surrendered pole position to Sony in the home, and at E3 2003 Sony announced the development of the PlayStation Portable (PSP). The PSP was the antithesis of Nintendo's technological

The PSP was a powerful machine with a beautiful screen, both of which elements Sony emphasized in the head-to-head marketing war with the Nintendo DS. The PSP concept of delivering handheld experiences akin to home games seems misjudged with hindsight, though over its lifetime the console acquired a very respectable software library. (Photo credit: Evan Amos)

approach: an extremely powerful handheld console comparable to the PS2, featuring robust multimedia capabilities, games on optical discs (more storage), an analogue stick and online functions.

● But Nintendo hadn't been standing still either, leading to one of the most fascinating hardware face-offs in gaming history. As Hiroshi Yamauchi stepped down as chairman of Nintendo in 2002 and handed the reins to Satoru Iwata, he had made a suggestion about the company's next handheld: 'You ought to do one with two screens.'

● This in itself was something of a puzzle to Iwata and Shigeru Miyamoto, who were concerned that relying on traditional ways of playing would see the company's audience gradually shrink. Wouldn't two screens lead to a more complex device and games for hardcore players? At a lunch in the spring of 2003, Miyamoto solved the problem. 'It would be neat if one of the screens were

a touch display, wouldn't it?'

● The design process for the Nintendo DS ('dual-screen') began in earnest. One of the machine's screens would be used as a display, and the other for intuitive touch controls, allowing not just traditional styles of play but entirely new breeds of game that could appeal to a much wider demographic. Where Sony was chasing processing power, Nintendo began to move in a completely new direction.

● When revealed, the DS was greeted with a mixture of cynicism, confusion and some small amount of optimism – in the light of the PSP, few thought Nintendo's comparatively underpowered hardware would stand a chance. It was hard to avoid comparing the two handhelds: the DS launched in North America in November 2004 (the PSP in March 2005), and both launched in Japan in December 2004 (the DS would reach Europe relatively early in March 2005, while stock shortages meant the PSP didn't

An original 'fat' model Nintendo DS in electric blue. The console was widely derided when announced, not least thanks to its form factor, but of course Nintendo had the last laugh. (Photo credit: Evan Amos)

release in the territory until September 2005).

➡ But they were diametrically opposed machines, equally good at what they set out to achieve. The DS was marketed worldwide under slogans involving the word 'touch', and a later series of software titles were sold under the banner of 'Touch Generation'. Nintendo's instincts about reaching a broader market with this interface were absolutely right, with the key piece of software being *Dr Kawashima's Brain Training* (2005, retitled *Brain Age* in North America).

➡ *Brain Training* is essentially a collection of puzzles, ranging from maths to memory tests to Sudoku, loosely based on and inspired by Dr Kawashima's work in neuroscience. The game is designed to be played for a short time every day, and after a series of exercises gives the player their 'brain age' – improving this over time is the goal. There is some dispute over whether *Brain Training* is anything more than pseudoscience, although

Nintendo was careful to make no false claims for the product, but its success among older players is undeniable – since release it has sold nineteen million copies, seen many sequels and become something of a cultural touchstone.

➡ Equally unusual was *Nintendogs* (2005), a 'pet simulation' where the player uses the DS microphone and touchscreen to care for and groom one of many breeds of dog. Again this is software designed to be played regularly in short bursts (perfect for a portable console), and makes clever use of the system's internal clock and calendar in the dog's behaviour – for example, if you don't play for a while then, upon returning, the dog will be both hungry and dirty.

➡ *Nintendogs* was met with widespread derision from Nintendo's traditional demographic but this was foolish snobbery. It is not a game in the traditional sense of having a 'win state' or indeed many explicit

Dr Kawashima's Brain Training appeared to an audience outside of the traditional gamer demographic, and also made doing daily maths puzzles surprisingly compulsive.

Nintendogs was inspired by the pleasure Shigeru Miyamoto found in taking care of a new dog with his family, and the game focused on the fun of interacting with and caring for a virtual pet.

A BRIEF HISTORY OF VIDEO GAMES

goals at all, but the simple act of looking after a virtual dog is fun and rewarding in itself. *Nintendogs* attracted new demographics to the DS, among them female gamers, and by 2008 had become the single bestselling DS game published by Nintendo.

❯ In its drive to produce new kinds of software Nintendo sought collaborations from beyond the industry, and the best result of this was artist Toshio Iwai's *Electroplankton* (2005). This is a series of music-creation tools themed around plankton, with ten modes setting up an interactive system with which the player can then mess to create different tunes. It also contains an Audience mode to watch and listen to what is possible, and no save function whatsoever – the developers felt that, if compositions could be made permanent, it would remove the spontaneity and fun from experimenting and playing with the title.

❯ Classic series were also reimagined for

an audience that was not familiar with Nintendo's history. *New Super Mario Bros.* (2006) introduced a new visual style and slightly slower pacing to that series, and proved enormously popular, while *The Legend of Zelda: The Phantom Hourglass* (2007) had a more traditional structure but was controlled entirely through the touch-screen interface – a bravura performance by Nintendo's development team that proved a complex and tactically demanding game could be made simple to control. *Animal Crossing: Wild World* (2005) allowed players to travel to other cities via wi-fi, and the game's design was already perfect for the 'play every day' principle Nintendo was pursuing.

❯ The DS has the greatest library of any handheld to date and it's impossible to accurately convey its sheer range. Beat-matching games like *Rhythm Heaven* (2009) stand alongside uber-JRPG *Dragon Quest IX* (2009); the incredible puzzler *Picross* (2009)

Electroplankton has the simple quality of a child's toy but the infinite variations of a sequencer. A huge part of its pleasure is in how the sounds you create start simple and layer into complex performances.

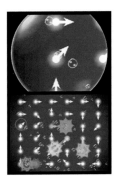

rubs shoulders with *Grand Theft Auto: Chinatown Wars* (2009); courtroom drama *Phoenix Wright: Ace Attorney* (2005) has players scouring crime scenes and putting together the case in front of a judge; *The World Ends With You* (2008) is Square-Enix's most original RPG in recent history; and the instalments of series like *Castlevania*, *Pokémon* and *Mario Kart* take them to new heights.

➲ In contrast to this the PSP offers a more familiar gaming experience, with its best titles appealing to the hardcore enthusiast. Much of its popularity in Japan is down to Capcom's *Monster Hunter Freedom* (2005), an extremely deep multiplayer game centring on groups of players meeting up to go and hunt down giant monsters – which, if defeated, can be carved up and made into pretty costumes and awesome weapons. The combat system in *Monster Hunter* is a top-of-the-class example of system design, built around learning enemy attack patterns but also each weapon's

capabilities – there's no surer way to be knocked out than by over-extending yourself.

➲ Tetsuya Mizuguchi's Q Entertainment developed puzzler *Lumines* (2004), which winningly blends its mechanics to a techno beat, and semi-shooter *Every Extend Extra* (2006), where the player detonates bombs amidst swarms of enemies, trying to chain together explosions to take out as many as possible. *Half-Minute Hero* (2009) distils the traditionally lengthy JRPG formula into unhinged thirty-second bursts of action where efficiency and speed are the order of the day. Sony Japan Studio's *Patapon* (2007) asks the player to beat a pattern, to which tiny warriors on-screen will respond, guiding them past obstacles and against giant monsters, while colourful platformer *Loco Roco* (2006) luxuriates on the PSP's gorgeous screen and squeezes all the fun it can from simple two-button tilt controls.

➲ The PSP also played host to popular

New Super Mario Bros. reimagined the 2D Mario games with a much gentler learning curve and certain power-ups that focused more on fun – such as turning Mario into a giant that can bash through the levels in a frenzied run.

versions of 'big screen' games such as *Grand Theft Auto: Tales from Liberty City* (2005), but this title stands for many of them in being a disappointing experience – not because it's badly made but because the style of play doesn't lend itself well to portable gaming. The exception to this rule, and perhaps the PSP's finest moment, is *Metal Gear Solid: Peace Walker* (2010).

→ *Peace Walker* takes a series that is built around large continuous environments and an ongoing narrative, then chops it into bitesize missions – which shouldn't really work, except it's all tied together by the idea of 'Mother Base'. This hub, to which the player returns between missions, is an ever-present entertainment and ongoing project, with actions in the 'main' game (for example kidnapping soldiers) directly impacting what is going on at Mother Base. It is an absolutely stunning achievement, and incidentally one of the few games to go out of its way to use

nearly every one of the PSP hardware's more recherché features.

→ The PSP was discontinued in 2014, having shifted around eighty million units over its decade on sale. This is an impressive achievement, of course, yet Nintendo's strategy was proved right. The DS is still being produced and currently stands at over 155 million units sold.

→ In this light it is strange that Sony continued to pursue the same kind of strategy with the PSP's successor, the PlayStation Vita. Released in 2011 in Japan, and February 2012 in North America and Europe, the PS Vita is once again an absolute powerhouse with a cosmically beautiful and crisp OLED screen, and among many minor improvements to the PSP's structural design adds a second analogue stick. The major change, and maybe the single concession, is a back-mounted touchpad (which is used in several games but is not nearly as central to

Kojima Productions's *Metal Gear Solid: Peace Walker* included, among its many charms, a camera for players to take photographs of the game world – which came in particularly handy on co-op missions.

functionality as the DS touchscreen).

➲ The Vita hosts new versions of some of the PSP's strongest titles, such as *Lumines: Electronic Symphony* (2012), but from the start has offered a much stronger lineup. Particular highlights are *Persona 4 Golden* (2011), a definitive and significantly improved version of a classic RPG; lightspeed shooter *Velocity 2X Ultra* (2014); the ragtag aesthetic of Media Molecule's Tearaway (2013); and original puzzler *Escape Plan* (2011), the latter in particular making excellent use of the touchscreen. Perhaps Vita's biggest strength, however, is a much-improved digital store that picks the cream of PC indie titles and presents them anew on that OLED screen: *Spelunky* (2013), *Rogue Legacy* (2014) and *Guacamalee* (2014) to name but a few.

➲ Yet since release Vita has struggled, selling an estimated eight million worldwide (Sony is reticent about exact figures, rarely a good sign). This may be to do with the rise of mobile gaming over the same period, yet Nintendo's successor to the DS, the 3DS, has sold around forty-five million units over a roughly similar timeframe.

➲ The 3DS is less radical than it first appears, the headline feature being a screen capable of projecting a stereoscopic 3D image without the use of 3D glasses. This is an impressive effect, to be sure, though the novelty quickly wears off and many of its players claim never to use it (it is no accident that Nintendo has subsequently released the 2DS, a cheaper and more robust version of the hardware intended for children). The machine is a natural successor to the DS, offering more power and improved online features, as well as backwards compatibility with the enormous DS software library.

➲ Naturally it has its own growing list of essentials including *Fire Emblem: Awakening* (2013), the best in that particular series, while the fun *Kid Icarus: Uprising* (2012) offers

The PlayStation Vita had a shaky launch but its software library has quickly become superb, thanks mainly to a clever strategy of signing up popular PC indie titles. It also features a 'remote play' capability when linked to a PlayStation 4, allowing you to play the latter's games in bed. (Photo credit: Tokyoship)

Jeff Minter's TxK is a fabulous reworking of *Tempest* that incorporates mechanics from the same designer's *Space Giraffe*. Undoubtedly the PlayStation Vita's best-kept secret, it is also the best tube shooter ever made.

A BRIEF HISTORY OF VIDEO GAMES

an experience that actually is better in 3D. Nintendo also cheekily secured the rights to *Monster Hunter 3 Ultimate* (2013), the latest instalment in the PSP's biggest-selling series, which is as great as ever, while coming up with unexpected sequels like *Luigi's Mansion: Dark Moon* (2013), a brilliant ghost-hunting jaunt. Classics like *Starfox 64* and *Ocarina of Time* have received 3D makeovers, while the incredible *Super Mario 3D Land* (2011) saw the company's mascot outdo himself once again. As with PS Vita, the 3DS also benefits from a vastly improved digital download service, with quirky titles like *Pullblox* (2011) as good as anything you'll find in a box.

❯ It is clear that the history of handheld games consoles is in a sense a history of Nintendo handhelds. Ever since the Game Boy's debut the company has faced competitors and yet, over roughly twenty-five years, only the PSP could reasonably be called a success – and even then, one that took place in the shadow of Nintendo's greatest triumph, the DS. The rising importance of mobile gaming presents more of a challenge to Nintendo's handheld future than any other traditional games company – at least in theory. As things stand, and despite all the tablets and smartphones in the world, the 3DS and its many wonderful games just keep on selling.

Nintendo has been experimenting with stereoscopic 3D since the N64 era, with GameCube launch title *Luigi's Mansion* built to support 3D visuals. The 3DS marked the key point where 3D could be delivered without glasses, though whether consumers want 3D visuals is another matter. (Photo credit: Evan Amos)

Super Mario 3D Land is one of the few 3DS titles that goes beyond the headline gimmick to make 3D an essential part of how many of its levels work, resulting in some delightful puzzles and visual effects alongside the scintillating creativity that 3D *Mario* titles deliver as standard.

Mobile Gaming

19

→ Throughout the history of video games there are figures like Clive Sinclair and Jack Tramiel trying to bring computers to the masses, Trojan Horses for interactive entertainment and successful in their way. But the most widespread way to play video games turned out to be nothing to do with consoles, PCs or dedicated handhelds.

→ The Pew Internet Project's research shows that, as of 2013, 91 per cent of American adults own a mobile phone with 50 per cent of that number using it to download apps.[41] Further to this, 43 per cent own a tablet computer or an e-reader (which have their own app stores). These devices are now the most popular gaming platforms around, almost by accident, with Google's Android and Apple's iOS the major players.

→ The first game to be released on mobiles was a variant of *Tetris*, ported to run on 1994's Hagenuk MT-2000, an early phone with an LCD screen. But the most iconic starting point has to be *Snake*. It is perhaps more correct to call *Snake* a minor genre of games rather than one specific title; the idea originated with the 1976 arcade game *Blockade*, which was ported to the Atari VCS as *Surround* and over the years found its way to many other platforms.

→ The game is simplicity itself: you control the 'head' of a short line that can move in four directions, in an enclosed space filled with blocks. By guiding the head over blocks the line gets bigger, and the only objective is to get as big as possible without running into your own tail. Such a concept was a perfect fit for the lowly processors of early mobile phones and Nokia, one of the biggest phone manufacturers around, pre-installed Snake on all of its devices from 1997. Extremely easy to play, perfect for filling in a boring five minutes and running on something most people carry around anyway – such things are unquantifiable, but *Snake* must be one of the most well-known and popular games in history.

Simple games were available on mobile phones in the late 1990s and early 2000s, but the devices were too basic to run much more than puzzle games and (particularly in Japan) pet simulators, and number pads simply were not a good control method. Added to this there was often no centralized marketplace from which to purchase and download titles.

Everything changed with the advent of smartphones and, in particular, the launch of the App Store in 2008. The iPhone was a powerful device with a full-colour display doubling up as a touchscreen, and its centralized marketplace offered developers a clear route to a huge installed base with a simple licensing agreement. Google's Android operating system lagged slightly behind iOS at first, but now offers a similar ecosystem across an even wider range of devices.

The mobile video-games market is stratified in a manner that you don't see with more traditional platforms, simply because of the lower costs involved and the huge potential audience. For example, an early iOS success story is *Paper Toss* (2009), a game where you 'flick' the screen to send a wad of crumpled paper towards a bin. That's all there is to *Paper Toss*, but it's fun enough and has just the right amount of depth to its controls to make it a hit. This game could never have existed on a traditional platform for many reasons: the control method; the ad-supported business model that makes it free to download; the fact that mobile

In Konami's *Tomena Sanner* you control a salaryman racing through various surreal stages by rhythmically tapping as he meets obstacles – and at the end of stages you get to dance in celebration.

Angry Birds combines simplicity with a devilish three-star structure – that is, to complete any of its levels isn't particularly hard, but to do so while being awarded three stars is awfully tricky. This is how it hooks players.

players don't mind, if you'll excuse the pun, a throwaway experience.

⊙ The first genuine phenomenon was Finnish studio Rovio's *Angry Birds* (2009). Here the player has to pull back a catapult's elastic to aim a rotund bird at various physics-enabled structures housing a collection of snorting pigs. The aim of each short stage is to destroy all the pigs by either hitting them directly with the bird or causing the level's structures to collapse atop them.

⊙ *Angry Birds* had a winning visual style, backed up by amusing sound effects like the pigs laughing at an especially bad shot. But it is a brilliant mobile design because the game is easy to understand, each level lasts around a minute or less, and the physics-enabled structures and nuance of aiming the catapult give its simple objectives depth – there are hundreds of levels in *Angry Birds*, with the game continuing to be updated for years after release, and the later levels test even the

most dedicated of players. It's a mobile game that can be played in short bursts, but with an overarching structure that keeps it interesting over much longer periods.

⊙ The structure of games is one thing, but these mobile marketplaces have also precipitated an enormous rise in popularity for the free-to-play (F2P) business model. This originated in Asia with MMOGs, but has found a natural home on platforms where consumers are constantly browsing storefronts and unwilling to commit large amounts of money upfront – even 'paid-for' games tend to hover between 69p and £2.49, with very few premium experiences daring to go above these levels.

⊙ Free-to-play is both a blessing and a curse for game design. Its greatest asset is unquestionably that it opens the gates to an enormous player base willing to take a chance on something that doesn't cost any money. The downside is that developers need

EA's F2P version of *Dungeon Keeper* is a particularly egregious example of constructing a Skinner box (by which the player is psychologically conditioned to expect reward and becomes addicted to playing) around a beloved licence. Thankfully games such as this are becoming less frequent as consumers wise up to common tactics.

to make money somehow, and so F2P games have a reputation for either locking away large chunks of content behind 'paywalls' or using the dreaded mechanic of timers. Among the biggest successes with this model is developer Supercell's *Clash of Clans* (2012), a simple strategy game where progress can be speeded-up through purchasable gems, which along with the company's other F2P title *Hay Day*, resulted in 2013 revenues of $892 million.

→ Supercell's successor to *Clash of Clans* is interesting for being a more refined take on F2P that retains the same core mechanics while mitigating the aspects players often find frustrating. *Boom Beach* (2014) has the player slowly constructing an island base of defences while sending out troop boats to attack other players' bases. Each defensive structure on the island can be upgraded, to a maximum level of 20, with each level taking incrementally more resources and time: for example, taking a sniper tower from level 1 to

2 takes five minutes, level 10 to 11 takes five hours, while level 19 to 20 takes thirty hours.

→ The number of structures to upgrade, and the increasing time it takes to do so, creates endless minor objectives for the player but has the added bonus (for Supercell) of slightly frustrating those who want to progress faster. This then ties into the realtime strategy side of the game, invading other players' bases, because this is a key way of obtaining resources. On top of this are layered other goals: an armoury to upgrade troops; creating statues that can boost certain aspects of your base or army; the accumulation of 'Victory Points' for rewards; a submarine that can go diving for treasure, and so on.

→ There is a large element of busywork in designs like this, creating a nearly inexhaustible list of stuff for players to do so that the game doesn't feel 'finished' for a long time, and also encouraging the spending

Boom Beach is designed to reward players constantly, the thinking being that the longer a player spends time with and enjoys the game, the more likely they are to spend money. At heart it is still a F2P game, however, and so there are carefully designed bottlenecks on progress to encourage spending.

A BRIEF HISTORY OF VIDEO GAMES

of a 'premium currency' to speed things up. In the case of *Boom Beach* these are gems, sold in a manner that encourages bulk-buying.

➲ It is only fair to say that Boom Beach is much more generous to players than this model has traditionally been, suggesting that the audience is becoming more savvy about F2P in general – gems are given frequently as rewards, and bottlenecks that encourage spending them are few and far between. Other titles are more generous still: Blizzard's brilliant card-battler *Hearthstone* (2013) is free-to-play and, though players can buy further packs of cards to improve their collection, can be enjoyed to its fullest without ever making a purchase. The more exploitative examples of F2P tend, unfortunately, to be aimed at a younger audience, though regulatory bodies are currently examining the business model's excesses. This shouldn't overshadow the fact, however, that F2P is an increasingly popular way to get games into the hands of players and the majority of titles offer a lot of value for no upfront cost.

➲ The difficulty with Android and the App Store is the scale. The App Store, for example, had 1.25 million apps available for download in June 2014, with around 60,000 new apps being added every month – note that these are apps and not video games, but the latter are responsible for roughly 80 per cent of App Store revenue (there's no way of breaking the numbers down further).

➲ The great side to such range is that almost every genre is represented on mobile, from text adventures to searingly original hits and even ports of major console releases (for example *Bioshock*). The bad side is that games can sink without a trace, and successful titles are almost instantly cloned by unscrupulous developers who copy the basics and give their app a very similar title (most recently seen with the success of Dony

Popular series are increasingly finding their way to mobile. Games like Capcom's *Monster Hunter: Dynamic Hunting* straddle between what makes the original appealing and the simplicity demanded by touch screen controls.

Nguyen's *Flappy Bird* which, at the height of its popularity, was seeing sixty clones a day released on the App Store).

➡ In the early years of the App Store and Android many publishers were guilty of simply porting games without considering the controls or form factor of their new host platforms, leading in the worst cases to on-screen 'joypads' that never really work. But independent developers have tended to be more creative with inputs, leading to a new wave of twitch-type games like Terry Cavanagh's *Super Hexagon* (2012) – a demanding action experience where the player rotates a small triangle inside layers of collapsing hexagons, desperately trying, to a pulsating techno beat, to be in the right position to pass through the missing side of each hexagon.

➡ Although the major financial successes get the headlines, an equally important aspect of these platforms is that the audience is large enough to support individual creators. Michael Brough's games have bespoke aesthetics which, though beautiful, are about as non-commercial as it gets, and offer extraordinarily deep systems at – for the mobile market – premium price points. *868-HACK* (2013) is a turn-based roguelike themed around invading a computer system, with lo-fi visuals and an inventive set of core 'programs' that, in their sheer variety of applications, force every playthrough into a particular style.

➡ Simogo's *Year Walk* (2013) is an adventure game that mixes puzzles with a dark, piecemeal narrative that depends on the player putting everything together – the exact opposite of the 'bitesize' playing experiences that have been considered traditionally suitable for mobile. By mixing a lot of clever tricks and depending on the player's knowledge of how a smartphone is typically used, however, *Year Walk* subverts expectations and presents a rich experience

Terry Cavanagh's *Super Hexagon* is a creation of genius, with its simple controls and objective married to a frenetic pace and pulse-pounding techno soundtrack.

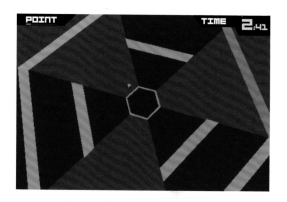

that simply wouldn't suit another format. The same developer's surreal *Device 6* (2013) offers a completely different aesthetic but shows a similar desire for blending genres, messing around with the possible uses of the device you're playing it on, and a willingness to push the player's mental limits.

● There are so many more. *Bad Hotel* (2012) manages to revitalise the overplayed tower defence genre by having you protect an awful establishment from rats, yetis and various other miscreants – but, in a beautiful flourish, syncs the soundtrack to how you go about doing it. Developer Toca Boca's range of children's apps are simply outstanding, emphasizing freeform play over rigid structure and resulting in the likes of *Toca Band* (2012) – where you can play one super-funky song in hundreds of different ways. Vlambeer's *Ridiculous Fishing* (2013) has you hauling multiple denizens of the deep into midair then blasting them away

with a minigun and spending the proceeds on further destructive powers, while *Threes* (2013) is an elegant puzzle game so simple you won't believe it has just swallowed four hours.

● The increasing power and reach of mobile devices means that this may well be the single largest audience video games will have in the immediate future. Although the various marketplaces are in their infancy the breadth and depth of content offered already is astonishing, and every month sees new top-quality games (albeit often surrounded by dross). This is to say nothing of the future potential for educational apps that incorporate video-game mechanics and structures, companion apps that work alongside 'larger' releases like movies or books, and the increasing involvement of the world's biggest publishers. Pocket-sized it may be, but that just means mobile gaming is everywhere.

The ethics of games made for children on mobile devices are sometimes questionable, particularly when the F2P model is involved. Toca Boca is easily the best children's developer around, its toy-like games simply a delight to fiddle with and featuring no in-app purchases.

eSports

● eSports has nothing to do with sports games. From the very first multiplayer video game organised competition has been inevitable, though it is only in recent times that competitive gaming has come to mainstream prominence: this is the white-hot virtual arena where mentality, skill and tactics separate winners from losers.

● Although eSports as a concept could be traced back to early *Spacewar!* competitions, the Atari-sponsored Space Invaders Championship in 1980 (which attracted 10,000 entrants), or Twin Galaxies' record-keeping of arcade high scores, it wasn't until around the millennium that international tournaments and leagues setting players against each other on a regular basis were established. The Deutsche Clanliga was founded in 1997 but became the Electronic Sports League (ESL) in 2000, the most venerable in this young industry, the same year the first World Cyber Games tournament was held in Seoul, South Korea, and 2002 saw the founding of Major League Gaming (MLG).

● Outside of South Korea, to which we will come, eSports was never considered an attractive prospect for television – and this is one of the reasons its rise in the later 2000s was so meteoric. The truly dedicated could always find grainy footage or results, but the advent of sites like YouTube and Twitch saw eSports find a much wider audience.

● Twitch in particular is crucial for allowing spectators to watch tournaments live, and the growth of this gaming-dedicated network is exponential: in 2013 it had forty-five million unique viewers per month (from twenty million in 2012), and six million broadcasts per month (doubled from 2012). 2013's League of Legends world championship final was watched live by 8.5 million people, while over thirty-two million watched it after the event. If all this smells like eSports is beginning to attract serious money, you'd be right: Amazon acquired Twitch in 2014 for just under a billion dollars.

➡ There are many games with competitive modes, but not all become eSports. The first to become a phenomenon was *Starcraft*, Blizzard's 1997 realtime strategy title, and though it has aged the sheer scale of the industry it created in South Korea is still the benchmark (the expansion pack *Brood War* later became the standard for competitive play, but in the name of simplicity this chapter will just refer to the game as *Starcraft*). Of the 9.5 million copies Blizzard sold, 4.5 million were in South Korea (population: fifty million), and in many ways the nation was a perfect cradle for an eSport. At the time it had the most advanced broadband infrastructure on the planet, with nineteen out of twenty houses across the country connected with blistering 20 MB/second download speeds, but *Starcraft* also hit at a time of mass youth unemployment

caused by 1998's Asian financial crisis. One of the most popular and cheap pastimes was to hang out at a PC *baang* (net café) to play games and, in a culture obsessed with crazes, *Starcraft* simply became the next craze.

➡ That doesn't quite cover it, though. Crazes can die down as quickly as they appear, and with *Starcraft*'s popularity there was no shortage of competing RTS games rushed to market – many with more appealing visuals or gimmicks. But no one remembers them now.

➡ *Starcraft* remains a competitive draw for players and spectators because it balances three asymmetric races, tests a wide range of skills and has an enormously high skill ceiling. Professionals will execute between 300 and 400 actions-per-minute (i.e. mouse clicks or keys pressed) with as little redundancy as possible – and be competing against someone doing exactly the same thing.

➡ To fully explain *Starcraft*'s interplay would take a book in itself, but the general principles

Competitive matches of *Starcraft 2*, along with many other games, are now streamed live to audiences across the globe. An average audience will be in the tens of thousands, but for major tournaments featuring the likes of *League of Legends* and *Dota 2* the audience will hit millions.

underlying a match are simple to understand. Most players specialize in one of the three races (some crowd-pleasers play 'random' every game), and at the start of the match will spawn with a central base structure and some workers. They will immediately start the workers collecting minerals, construct more workers from the central base and shortly afterwards start building structures: a player controlling Terran, the humanoid race, will build a barracks to train marines; a player controlling Zerg, the insectoid alien race, will build a spawning pool so they can hatch dog-like zerglings.

➡ From this point each race in *Starcraft* can follow one of various 'tech trees', each of which will result in a different kind of army, and players will be trying to tailor this to counter their opponent's army composition. The match has barely begun, but already a professional is juggling their economy (workers) and their production (army), and is scouting the map to find their opponent. Neither can see what the other is doing unless a unit has vision on that part of the map – so mind games often come into it, with players hiding important buildings in unlikely places or taking extra care to head off scouts.

➡ After the opening five minutes or so of a match each player will have a humming base that requires constant management, the beginnings of an army that will need to be micro-managed in the field, and scouts roaming the map for information. Letting any one of these elements slide by even a tiny amount is the surest way to lose a game – Korean professionals practise up to sixty hours a week, placing special emphasis on execution in the belief that mind games only go so far. That is, you can't always predict what your opponent is doing, but if you out-produce him then the bigger army will nearly always win.

➡ This is why *Starcraft* is such a great

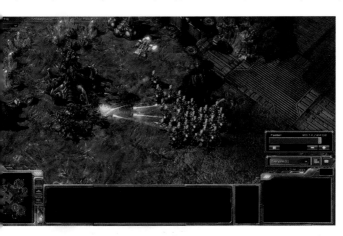

The essence of *Starcraft 2* is in the grand vision required to execute an overall gameplan and the minute attention to detail required in every engagement. Here we see a brave Terran force destroying a filthy Zerg hatchery.

spectator sport. These players have superhuman capabilities and are trying to not just out-perform an opponent with skill but out-think them at the same time. They are Rommel overseeing the battlefield, but also managing the munitions factories and fighting in the front lines all at once – multitasking doesn't even begin to cover it. The most popular players became genuine celebrities in Korean society – Lim Yo-Hwan, who played under the name SlayerS_BoxeR and was nicknamed 'The Emperor', earned hundreds of thousands of dollars a year and had a fan club with half a million members.

→ A particularly interesting aspect of *Starcraft* with regard to eSports is that the original game was designed simply to be a good game – but its success led to *Starcraft II* (2010) which, given the original, was designed from the start to be an eSport. Thus it comes with a vast range of options for spectators and a visual style that, while pretty, is all

about clarity – you can tell at a glance what a unit is and it is easily distinguished from the environments. Huge effort was put into seemingly minor details like relative unit size, death animations, terrain textures, impact SFX and the voice samples for various characters. At the time of writing Korea has a professional league dedicated to *Starcraft II*, it is played at every major eSports event and its future seems secure.

→ Strategy games are only one part of eSports. An ever-popular genre is the first-person shooter, and among these games the premiere title is *Counter-Strike*. This was initially a *Half-Life* mod designed by Minh Le and Jess Cliffe in 1999, before Valve hired both and acquired the rights – since which point the game has been remade three times, always retaining the core elements, with each version constantly balanced and updated. The current incarnation, and tournament favourite, is *Counter-Strike: Global Offensive* (2012).

Over time Blizzard has improved the spectator features of *Starcraft 2* enormously, which helps both tournaments and YouTubers to show the game at its finely detailed best.

➜ *Counter-Strike* pits two teams of five against each other, playing as either Terrorists or Counter-Terrorists and switching sides after fifteen rounds – a match has thirty rounds total, so the first team to sixteen wins. The teams have access to slightly different equipment, and the maps are asymmetrical locations – the latter going against the vast majority of other first-person shooters, which value symmetry above all in the false belief this automatically equates to balance.

➜ In each round the Terrorists win by planting a bomb at one of two potential sites, which then starts a countdown, and the Counter-Terrorists can win by defusing the bomb before it goes off – if either team kills all five of the others, that's an automatic win unless the bomb's been planted, in which case it can still go off for a Terrorist victory.

➜ *Counter-Strike* is a precision shooter, where each gun has a distinct recoil to it, firing while moving is incredibly inaccurate

and a headshot with most weapons is an instant kill. What gives it a rhythm over the course of a match, rather than being a series of disconnected rounds, is that each team is awarded money at the end of a round based on kills and whether they won or lost – so teams can be forced into 'economy' rounds with just a basic pistol and no Kevlar, or have to buy less-than-ideal weapons when they're desperate to get back on track.

➜ This creates a metagame over and above the second-to-second headshots, an intersection between theory and execution. And with a map like Dust II, professionals know not just where everything is but also how players will move through it – where and when they'll enter areas during the first thirty seconds, likely hiding places, the best routes to take when rushing to another site. *Counter-Strike* is fun to watch not just because these players are amazing at the game, but because it's also a mental battle around a location that all ten know incredibly well, matched to an unforgiving test of skill.

→ The most recent eSports sensation are Multiplayer Online Battle Arena games, always referred to as MOBAs, pre-eminent among which are *League of Legends* (2009) and *Dota 2* (2013). The numbers for *League of Legends* can make your head spin. In January 2014 developer Riot Games disclosed the game had sixty-five million unique players per month, with around twenty-seven million of those playing per day, and during peak times

7.5 million people playing concurrently. That's roughly 1.5 times the population of Scotland.

→ Both *League of Legends* and *Dota 2* are based on a genre invented by the original Dota – a mod called *Defense of the Ancients* (the game soon became known as *Dota*, used as the full name rather than an acronym) for Blizzard's RTS *Warcraft III* (2002). First released in 2003 by mapmaker Eul (who remains anonymous), *Dota* was so popular it inspired countless variants of its own, the most successful being modder Steve Feak's *Dota Allstars*, which was subsequently taken over and further developed by anonymous modder IceFrog. The importance of this is that *Dota* is not and never has been a fixed game – ever since its first release it has been balanced and refined, a template that its contemporary successors follow.

→ The gameplay of a MOBA sets two teams of five champions (called 'heroes' in *Dota 2*) against each other, all controlled by players,

League of Legends is an enormous success story, and two of the original four developers were key members of the community that had grown around the original *Defense of the Ancients* mod. Developer Riot Games now employs over 1,000 people.

on a large map bisected with three lanes between each team's home base. Both teams have a small army of AI monsters, called 'creeps', who will push forwards, and a series of defensive towers on their half of the lane. The goal is to destroy the enemy team's base, but the game is to level up your champion as fast as possible by landing the killing blow on enemy creeps and, if possible, enemy champions – which grants experience and gold.

● MOBAs are infinitely complex games because of the sheer number of champions from which to choose, the range of items they can buy in-game, and thus the in-depth and unexpected strategies that a team of five can bring to bear. *League of Legends* offers 120 champions from which to choose and *Dota 2* has 108 – each with their own levelling arc, which often forks, and particular specialization. To give an idea of this range in *League of Legends* a player could choose

Fiddlesticks, a mage that can make enemies weak to magic and then apply magic damage – Fiddlesticks can also 'Terrify' enemies, forcing them to run away, or stop other champions using magic for a short spell. There's Nidalee, a mix of assassin and hunter that can move at double speed through the map's jungles, lay traps, 'mark' enemies and transform into a cougar to deal huge melee damage. Or there's Warwick, a giant wolf-thing that just wants to get close to enemy champions and rip them apart with bare claws, and is healed by doing so.

● The skill required to execute in *Dota 2* and *League of Legends* is enormous, with the range of attacks and the capabilities of enemy heroes absolutely essential to bear in mind – which often results in games of footsie, where opposing players dance around in front of each other just out of range, picking off creeps and waiting for the other to make a mistake. The range of possibilities with all of these different champions is also the mental side of things, encapsulated in the 'draft' process before a competitive game begins, where teams alternate between choosing one hero themselves and banning one choice for the other team.

⮕ If all this sounds very complex you would be right – it is impossible to enjoy watching a game of *League of Legends* or *Dota 2* without having considerable experience of the game, and some knowledge of what is happening. For an outsider it is a confusing and seemingly messy spectacle. Concurrently this is exactly the reason for its appeal to the initiated, who have the time to pour into

Developer Valve employed the creator of the original *Defense of the Ancients* mod, *Icefrog*, to work on *Dota 2*. After many years of development the game was released for free, with money made from micro-transactions.

learning about the game, love the fact that there is always something new to learn, and greatly enjoy watching highly skilled players execute new and surprising strategies.

⮕ It is interesting to note that this goes against the principles of eSports design originally followed by Blizzard in creating *Starcraft 2*, but despite that game's success it is currently outranked in popularity by *League of Legends* and *Dota 2*. The fact is that these games have such enormous audiences that they don't need to appeal to a more general type of player, and the popularity of MOBAs is such that Blizzard is just one of many major publishers in the process of developing their own.

⮕ By some measures *League of Legends* is the most popular PC game on the planet, with one estimate claiming that 2012 saw over 1.3 billion hours of playtime.[42] *League of Legends* currently supports its own European league, the Championship Series, where games regularly attract over 200,000 viewers, and has

The International 2014, an annual *Dota 2* competition, was held in the KeyArena Center in Seattle, Washington, and featured a grand prize of over $5 million from a prize pool of just under $11 million – making it the largest eSports event to date. (Photo credit: Jakob Wells)

an annual World Championship – in 2014 the prize pool for this was over $2 million, with $1 million going to the winners. Valve runs *Dota 2*'s equivalent, The International, and in 2014, thanks to in-game sales contributing, the prize pool hit $10.9 million.

→ Both fans and players used to consider that eSports could have 'made it' if competitive gaming was shown on television. The simple fact is that, with the advent of streaming and on-demand video, eSports no longer needs television – it broadcasts straight to enormous audiences, offers multimillion prize pools, and can attract serious sponsors like Coca-Cola and Intel.

→ There remains some snobbery about the idea of watching other people play games, but this will fade with time. In Asia the most important *Starcraft* and *Dota 2* games are already held in huge stadiums, with crowds in the tens of thousands. Before too long you'll see the same at Wembley.

Blizzard's *Hearthstone: Heroes of Warcraft* is a competitive card battler that has shown there is a considerable audience for almost any type of competitive play, providing it is presented well enough.

Metal . . . Gear?

21

Metal Gear Solid is one of video gaming's longest-running, most critically acclaimed and commercially successful series. Hailed by fans as the greatest games ever, scorned by detractors for narrative indulgences and leaving many in the middle baffled either way, Metal Gear Solid is also notable for its indelible link to creator/director Hideo Kojima. The auteur theory is always dodgy ground with modern big-budget video games, which are made by teams of hundreds, but in this case the stamp of one man's personality is all-pervasive and impossible to ignore.

➔ The series would come to prominence with Sony's PlayStation but Metal Gear was first released on 7 July 1987 for the MSX2 computer, a popular platform in its native Japan. Hideo Kojima's debut as a lead designer begins with special-ops soldier Solid Snake swimming to a dock entrance at a military base: over a decade later, so would Metal Gear Solid. The game looked like a top-down 2D shooter, but the way you played had been a pet idea of Kojima for several years – a military game about avoiding confrontation. Although the game can't quite maintain this focus for its entire duration (the second half is more traditional gunplay) this mixture of systems created the stealth genre.

➔ Guards in Metal Gear follow set patrol routes and only react to Snake if they see him. The game's main building has been lavished with attention to this end, most obviously in the way that guard patrols change depending on the side of the screen from which you enter. Metal Gear paid great attention to seemingly trivial details: Snake begins with a packet of cigarettes, which can be smoked but will reduce his health, while he has a radio with which to call a support team for advice. At one point he gets deliberately captured and stages a MacGyver-esque escape. Trucks move around the base, and sneaking onto the back of one can net you a free ride.

Metal Gear Solid toyed with its players in various ways, and a dry sense of humour shone through in many of its interactions. Unfortunately on modern platforms the codec frequency has to be placed in a digital instruction manual, and Psycho Mantis can no longer read memory cards, but that's the price of progress.

➡ Near the end of the game Big Boss, Snake's commander, gets agitated and radios through:

**This is Big Boss.
Solid Snake!
Stop the Operation
Switch off your MSX
At once.**

➡ The *Metal Gear Solid* series is obsessed with talking at and to its players, and the fourth wall is something of an obsession for Kojima. This was the first time he stabbed at it.

➡ *Metal Gear* did well enough to be ported to several platforms, and gain a quick Kojima-less sequel, but after this the series disappeared. Nevertheless the original has embryonic ideas that make *Metal Gear*, if not a classic, the prototype for one. It would take another eleven years for technology to catch up with Kojima's vision, and make it *Solid*.

● *Metal Gear Solid* is one of the most important games ever made. Released in 1998 for the PlayStation, from the start it demonstrates sky-high production values: the opening shows Snake approaching a base through the water, the camera angles changing as his commander delivers a mission briefing and actor/developer credits overlay the screen.

● The game is played in third person from an angled top-down view and, as the opening ends and play begins, the credits continue to roll as the player explores a loading bay. This is like a microcosm of what's to come: patrolling guards have 'vision cones' and can hear as well as see, puddles splash and cause Snake's feet to leave traces for a few steps, and crawlspaces change the camera to a first-person perspective.

● One of the key aspects of Sony's PlayStation was the use of CD-ROM media, which allowed *Metal Gear Solid* to have full voice acting and orchestral backdrops. The original game's radio returns as the Codec, through which Snake's comrades give instructions and, by calling them up in almost any location, advice on the current situation. It's not quite that simple though: Kojima's interests are extraordinarily wide, and the Codec reflects this. Your companions discourse on *Godzilla*, local flora and fauna, cold-war paranoia, trends in military hardware, the nature of war, and above all else on the interwoven thread of fate and genetics.

● A heady brew, to be sure, if fundamentally a non-interactive way of creating narrative and world texture. But what makes *Metal Gear Solid* stick in the mind is its imagination and variety in the situations players face: sneaking past guards and security cameras leads to challenges that test every limit of the game's mechanics. A boss battle with Vulcan

Raven, a huge chaingun-wielding mercenary, revolves around Snake avoiding detection and leading him into traps (or guided missiles), while the fight against Sniper Wolf is a pure test of sniping skills (where Snake's hands tremble and taking a shot knocks the first-person camera severely off-kilter).

➔ Kojima's tricksy nature comes to the fore when the Colonel, Snake's boss, tells him to contact fellow operative Meryl by using the Codec frequency on the back of the CD case. There is no CD case in the game, but of course *Metal Gear Solid* is packaged in a real-world CD case – players who check the back find a screenshot showing Meryl's frequency. In a later sequence Snake is captured and tortured by antagonist Revolver Ocelot, told there are no continues and that to survive he has to mash a controller button. Ocelot: 'Don't dare use autofire [a function on most third-party controllers], or I'll know.' And he does!

➔ The boss character Psycho Mantis exemplifies *Metal Gear Solid*, beginning the fight by reading Snake's 'mind': if the player has a memory card containing saves from Konami games like *Castlevania* or *International Superstar Soccer*, Mantis comments on their tastes. He talks about your playstyle, based on how many soldiers Snake's killed and alerts he's triggered so far ('You are reckless'). Mantis tells the player to put their controller on the floor, then uses the rumble feature to make it 'move' as the screen flashes between different angles. He switches the TV display to a recreation of a standard 'VIDEO' mode, except in this case spelled 'HIDEO'.

➔ When the fight begins Mantis flies around boasting that he can 'read your mind' and avoiding every attack. The only way to get around this is to unplug your controller from the PlayStation and reinsert it in controller slot 2. Even when you figure this out, Mantis's final trick is controlling Meryl and trying to make her shoot herself (Snake has to put away his guns and knock her out to avoid this). The fight with Psycho Mantis showcases Kojima's fourth-wall infatuation, but the number and quality of ideas used in this short spell make it a bravura performance rather than a mere novelty – as well as driving home how few other games try to confuse and toy with their players.

→ *Metal Gear Solid* was a phenomenal success and raised the bar for the presentation of narrative in games. Its intricate take on the military-industrial complex, which was at bottom about the role genetics play in fate and free will (Snake is a clone of America's greatest soldier: so is he fated to follow in the footsteps of his 'father'?), makes the average video-game plot seem like *Teletubbies*. Despite moments of over-indulgence ('Can love ever bloom on the battlefield?') it was a quantum leap for action games.

→ What makes the *Metal Gear Solid* series unique is what happened next. The video-game industry at the big-budget end is largely based around sequels, in a manner quite unlike that of Hollywood. Where movie sequels tend to diminish the original (with exceptions) and by the third or fourth entry have played out the concept, video games have different circumstances. Most obvious is the fact that technology is constantly improving in concrete ways: this is why *Metal Gear* plays like a prototype for *Metal Gear Solid* – 3D gave the original ideas a new form and function.

→ This doesn't mean that every video-game sequel improves on the original, but some do so by pruning, refining and improving upon an established set of core mechanics. In contemporary times the major third-party publishers have reliable 'sequels' as the bedrock of their business: Ubisoft's *Assassin's Creed* series is a juggernaut of samey third-person action that changes the setting but sticks rigidly to formula; Activision are masters at releasing annual entries in the huge *Call of Duty* series; and EA's sports titles are perhaps the ultimate case-study of incremental improvement.

◉ *Metal Gear Solid* has lasted much longer than most series and continued to push interactive entertainment forward in a singular manner. *Metal Gear Solid 2* (2001) was a game designed to upset player expectations in several ways, and is relatively open about how ambiguous Kojima feels about making a sequel at all.

◉ The main tool is lead character, Raiden, who was omitted from the game's promotional materials in favour of the first game's hero Solid Snake. *Metal Gear Solid 2* begins with a short mission featuring Snake (on which all pre-release reports were based) and so players naturally expected he was the sequel's lead: the prominence of Raiden

caused an enormous fan backlash post-release.

◉ This is the point. Raiden, it is eventually revealed, is a child soldier raised on virtual reality missions to emulate his hero Solid Snake. Throughout the game he is constantly one step behind Snake, makes rookie mistakes and has to follow similar objectives. He is a parallel to the player. This point is driven home when Raiden later reads a dog tag he's wearing and finds it imprinted with personal information the player had supplied much earlier in the game – in a symbolic moment he tosses it away.

◉ Near the end *Metal Gear Solid 2*'s world begins to crumble. Raiden is naked after being tortured, and looking for his clothes, when the Colonel starts to lose the plot: he calls on the Codec with a distorted voice, his profile flickers into a skull, and becomes more incoherent as the calls go on. He tells Raiden to 'switch off the game console now' and

Many subsequent video-game sequels have tried to follow *Metal Gear Solid 2*'s lead in questioning the nature of what a sequel is, though none have done it quite so comprehensively, explicitly or successfully. Hideo Kojima seems to have got over his doubts and it's a masterpiece.

Why not? This is a type of role-playing game.

starts repeating lines from *Metal Gear Solid*. The game itself seems to end as the 'Mission Failed' screen appears – except misspelled 'Fission Mailed' and with play continuing in the top-right corner.

➡ The big reveal is that Raiden is the ultimate example of the US government's control, genetically engineered and taught through virtual reality systems, and that this mission has deliberately paralleled *Metal Gear Solid* in order to create a soldier on par with Solid Snake. Raiden has 'played' both *Metal Gear Solid*'s Shadow Moses incident and *Metal Gear Solid 2*'s opening as his hero, and the Big Shell's challenges are designed to mimic everything Snake has overcome.

➡ At the game's climax Raiden has to fight Solidus, an ex-President of the United States who is also his adopted father and leader of the game's antagonists. By this point Raiden has learned that the Big Shell setting of *Metal Gear Solid 2* houses an internet-controlling

AI program, designed to maintain America's military and cultural dominance through censorship, and that Solidus's true goal is to expose this program. Killing the final boss will thus protect the totalitarian project of the 'real' bad guys.[43]

➡ The point is obvious: in video games players have to follow a path that has been designed for them by the developers. Any illusion of choice is exactly that. The US government's aim to control information and, through this, personalities via the internet parallels this. Just before the fight with Solidus Raiden receives a Codec call where his lack of choice is emphasized and he's told to 'finish the game'. The final boss fight against Solidus ends with Raiden slicing him in half. Good soldier.

➡ *Metal Gear Solid 2* is a sequel about the problems of making a sequel: whether to make the same game again or offer something different, or whether it needs

to exist at all. Raiden is a poor man's Solid Snake, the Big Shell is revealed as an intentional rearrangement of *Metal Gear Solid*'s challenges, and the game's events turn out to have been a 'mere' computer program. The limitations of a player's agency are exposed and then the game forces Raiden to kill Solidus when we know that's not the right thing to do: this may strike some as frustrating, but of course that's the point, and allowing an option to 'spare' Solidus would have cheapened the message that players are not in control.

➔ Although *Metal Gear Solid 2*'s plot is a good subject for chin-scratchers and critics everywhere, it also alienated those who felt the ending was convoluted and dominated by non-interactive cutscenes. There is some validity to these claims, even if part of the point is the removal of agency.

➔ As an examination of free will *Metal Gear Solid 2* goes deeper than most other games,

but the darkness of its tone suggests one more thing. The themes imply Kojima didn't know how to follow up the first game and didn't necessarily want to anyway. The fact is that he did. So at the core of *Metal Gear Solid 2* is the message that, though you may have free will, this doesn't mean that you can change or deny reality.

➔ Kojima had clearly reconciled himself to the art of sequels by the time of *Metal Gear Solid 3: Snake Eater*, a prequel that changed up the series' mechanics to further emphasize stealth and stripped back the more out-there plot elements. Again the main character is new, Naked Snake, but this time more deliberately echoes the first game's Solid Snake in appearance.

➔ *Metal Gear Solid 3* is a prequel set in the early 1960s during the cold war, and moves from the slightly angular and enclosed settings of the earlier games to the jungle. It is by no means an open-world game but

Metal Gear Solid 3 arguably tried to introduce too many new mechanics to the series, with the camo index, for example, being a great idea that is a bit of a faff in practice. Kojima and his team clearly realized this because the 'Octocamo' suit in *Metal Gear Solid 4* is basically a smarter implementation of the same principle.

it is a more spacious and alive environment, populated by all manner of animals as well as soldiers, that rewards use of appropriate camouflage and slow movement. The original release suffered from a cramped fixed camera angle, thankfully changed in the Subsistence director's cut to a free camera, and when Snake is in tall grass it switches to first person.

◉ The idea of Snake having to make his way to the enemy base, rather than starting at its front door, is novel in video games and allows *Metal Gear Solid 3* to use the mechanics people would expect but freshen them up in a different context. The earlier games had limited the abilities of guards, most notably in their short vision cones, to keep the stealth aspect manageable for the average player – this also mitigated the occasional issue with the top-down camera position. In *Metal Gear Solid 3* their eyesight and intelligence has improved considerably such that, even though Naked Snake is incredibly capable at both

long- and short-range, avoiding attention is more of a priority than ever.

◉ Snake survives in the jungle by catching and eating animals (tranquilizing them will keep the meat fresh for longer), changing his outfit to blend into the background, using period-themed gadgets and performing basic surgeries when injured such as removing bullets from wounds. The game is also stuffed with detail: Snake's eyes will gradually adjust in darkened caves, killing a young Ocelot will result in a 'Time Paradox' (he features heavily in *Metal Gear Solid*'s subsequent history), and when Snake later loses an eye the right side of the screen in first-person view is dimmed at the edges.

◉ This kind of attention to detail is why *Metal Gear Solid* appeals to many players, and another is Kojima's consistent creativity with boss battles. In *Metal Gear Solid 3* Naked Snake battles The End, an ancient sniper who is fought in a gigantic open arena that

has to be divided into four zones so that the PlayStation 2 can handle it. Most boss fights are short, bloody affairs but this is designed to be played over hours as a more 'realistic' sniper battle and succeeds brilliantly in not just creating a unique experience, but one that feeds off and into the core mechanics.[44]

➲ A contradictory aspect of *Metal Gear Solid* is that, as it has progressed and become a more prominent piece of video-game culture, so too it has become more explicitly anti- the military-industrial complex and war itself. Whereas Solid Snake and Raiden were marked down at the post-game results screen for the number of enemy soldiers killed, Naked Snake has to battle The Sorrow.

➲ This ghost floats around a waist-deep river as Snake wades forwards, and the ghosts of all the soldiers the player has killed walk towards and try to grab him: so the more bloodthirsty a player is, the more they must face. The Sorrow has no health bar, cannot

be harmed in any conventional manner and, if you manage to twist the camera to catch a glimpse of his face, it's a distorted image of Hideo Kojima. The only way to escape is for Snake to die himself and use his revival pill.

➲ The game ends with another question about agency. Naked Snake eventually confronts his mentor the Boss and, at her forcing, they battle to the death – the final scene has Naked Snake standing over her with his pistol drawn, and the player has to pull the trigger to complete the game. After this Naked Snake would go on to be better-known as Big Boss, the antagonist of the original *Metal Gear*, and so his position as the game's hero becomes much more interesting.

➲ Where *Metal Gear Solid 2* mocked the idea of player agency, *3* is more concerned with the idea of human agency at all, and so its conclusion produces one of the series' great antagonists. Big Boss is a man who refuses to accept soldiers should die for governments

Metal Gear Solid 4 balances on a very thin line between farce and tragedy, and overall the player gets the sense that Kojima Productions perhaps had too much ambition and money, and not enough editorial control. That said, the more obsessive fans of the series adore this entry and arguably that was the target audience.

A BRIEF HISTORY OF VIDEO GAMES

and, soured by the great trauma he undergoes in *Metal Gear Solid 3*, becomes a rogue actor – a terrorist. It is to *Metal Gear Solid 3*'s credit that it's hard to see the character in such simple terms or even as an antihero.

→ *Metal Gear Solid 3* is all about environment. Where the first two in the series focused on the individual's ability to change their fate, *Metal Gear Solid 3* is much more sanguine about the idea of freedom. The central point is that people are defined by the circumstances and times in which they live, such that a pupil might have to kill his teacher simply because the events taking place are larger than both of them.

→ *Metal Gear Solid 4* is an attempt to escape what the series has become. What many criticize as fanservice is in fact an overbearing amount of loose ends being tied up and favourite characters being wheeled out to say goodbye. The game was made for the PlayStation 3 and this is behind its greatest strengths and weaknesses: the visual detail and effects are outright incredible, but the sheer volume of non-interactive sections detracts enormously from it as a video game.

→ This is *Metal Gear Solid*'s Achilles heel – despite its enormously creative and deep mechanical systems, the series has always walked a narrative tightrope. *Metal Gear Solid 4* falls off by dividing itself into discrete chapters, each of which begins with a long cutscene that often tops the half-hour mark, and then interrupting the player throughout missions for more overlong non-interactive segments of questionable value.

→ This is a great pity because the central premise of *Metal Gear Solid 4*, which is that series hero Solid Snake is prematurely aging and on his last mission, allows for some great links to players themselves – in particular those who played the first *Metal Gear Solid* a decade ago. In the fourth chapter Snake returns to Shadow Moses, the setting of

the first game, and on the journey there daydreams about the original – a perfectly emulated sequence in which the player controls 'young' Snake.

➡ After he wakes and the player creeps into Shadow Moses, rebuilt two generations of technology later, it is impossible for a player who's grown up with the series not to reflect on what has happened in the intervening years. To further tug those heartstrings the music used at key moments in *Metal Gear Solid* begins playing, and exploring certain locations reminds Snake of Codec conversations from years ago.

➡This would be impressive enough if all you were going for was nostalgia, but then *Metal Gear Solid 4*'s biggest gut punch hits. Shadow Moses is now an empty ruin, with no soldiers patrolling those familiar paths. Snake sees a rusty security camera on the wall and has a flashback, but as he's looking it drops to the floor. As people age we become more likely to

romanticize the past and often want to revisit those places that made us. But when you do they're never the same: it's impossible to truly go back.

➡ It's a pity the rest of *Metal Gear Solid 4* isn't so elegant in the way it makes its points, but at least the overarching series theme of identity is woven into the player's own response to the game. Where previous entries explored identity in terms of science (*Metal Gear Solid*), psychological control (*2*) and politics (*3*), the focus here is more fatalistic: a particular person's memories and perception of the world, their way of looking at life, and how this indefinable outlook is lost forever when they die.

➡ In this way *Metal Gear Solid* has taken its players in something of a circle. In contrast to most other games, the characters are always pawns, even if they might not seem so while blowing up a Hind and dismantling special forces units. There is a theatrical side to

Metal Gear Solid V: Ground Zeroes hints at a more directly political direction for the series, which has hitherto commented on geopolitics largely as a series of 'what ifs' and nightmare futures. In paralleling Guantanamo Bay and Abu Ghraib so clearly, Kojima Productions has changed the tone significantly.

A BRIEF HISTORY OF VIDEO GAMES

the games too, not least in Kojima's fourth-wall breaking, that constantly conflates player/avatar and reinforces the idea of a performance.

➡ The *Metal Gear Solid* series is unique in how it has handled the nature of the modern video-game sequel. Rather than a dilution or a repetition it has been able to renew itself with each instalment, crafting new ways to use its mechanics and refining common elements. It is also one of very few video games to offer any kind of perspective on world affairs such as privatized militaries, the war industry and the place of human combatants on a modern battlefield.

➡ This is one of the contradictions that makes *Metal Gear Solid* such an interesting series: war is an evil that creates more monsters than it ever destroys, so here you are as a soldier killing some enemies with fetishized military hardware. The prequel to *Metal Gear Solid V: Ground Zeroes* (2014), has

a title alluding to the Twin Towers after 9/11 and is set in an imitation of Guantanamo Bay – the full game, *The Phantom Pain*, takes place in Afghanistan.

➡ Hideo Kojima's genius lies in blurring the lines between player and character, then introducing ideas that make the latter question their actions and role. Put so baldly this may sound like a simple trick but the fact is that very few games can approach *Metal Gear Solid*'s core mechanics and production values, never mind blend the two with a meta-narrative about the nature of the individual – and carry this theme across different games, giving it a twist each time. *Metal Gear Solid* is impressive as a sustained performance if nothing else. And the beauty is that, if you just want to play a great stealth game without all these high-falutin' ideas, *Metal Gear Solid* works on that level too.

Here Comes Everybody

➤ Massively multiplayer online games (MMOGs) are virtual worlds that can play host to tens of thousands of players at a time – the most popular have subscriber numbers in the millions, though they can't all play together at once. MMOGs are quite simply alternative universes, places with their own sets of rules, social mores, problems and opportunities. And it all began in Essex.

➤ Roy Trubshaw was a student at Essex University in 1978 and a fan of *DUNGEN* (a port of text adventure *Zork*). Will Crowther's *Adventure* and its successors had inspired a generation of programmers to try their own hands at developing games, but while most simply copied the formula Trubshaw saw the potential for something more – an *Adventure* where people could play together.

➤ Naming the project *Multi-User Dungeon (MUD)* in tribute to his inspiration, Trubshaw started figuring out how to make a game world that multiple players could connect to and communicate through. He wasn't fussed with a traditional structure, a great dragon to slay at the end or objectives for players to fulfil, so much as the idea of players interacting in a world that wasn't the real world. By 1980 Trubshaw had made some progress on the network side but, needing to concentrate on his degree, turned to his friend and fellow student Richard Bartle for help in creating a world that could actually use it.

➤ Bartle realized that while Trubshaw's concept of an open world with no rules or goals was attractive, it was also more or less impossible: players had to have something to do. So he focused on giving *MUD* structure by adding things like puzzles, a levelling system, treasure and chains of minor objectives that would lead to larger objectives. This was intended as a foundation for the true goal of social interaction.

➤ This version of *MUD* went live on the Essex University servers in 1980 and, though it wasn't the first networked multiplayer game, it was the first where socializing was a central part of the experience. Players would get into arguments and fall out, then demand to know what Bartle was going to do about it. 'Griefers' would harass new players – 'newbies' – while kinder souls would teach them how *MUD* worked. It was a learning experience for everyone, not least Bartle himself, and one that by its nature is now mostly lost to time.

→ 'How can you recapture what a *MUD* was like? All you can do is look at the evidence of the time, the archaeology,' says Bartle. 'In essence you're undertaking some kind of anthropological research. People reminisce about things that happen in games, describing what was going on – but it's like saying what was life like in the 1980s? When confronted with a film or video of the 1980s you say "look at the hair! The clothes! The cars! Were we really like that?"

You remember things selectively.'

→ Nevertheless *MUD*'s influence on early MMOGs was enormous, largely because it was never seen by its creators as a commercial product – Bartle would happily distribute copies of the game, while other programmers freely ported and adapted *MUD* to other systems with new rules, new emphases and new structures. Even as some moved far away from the freedom that was at the heart of Trubshaw's initial concept, that core of social interaction remained constant, the glue binding these disparate experiences together.

→ 'There are things in *World of Warcraft* today which are only there because I put them in *MUD*,' says Bartle. 'Even terminology like mob: that comes from mobiles, which were mobile objects. The reason it was mobiles was because I couldn't use two words! Straight from *MUD*. I get called a noob and think "good god, you're calling me by a term I introduced!"'

The obvious progression from *MUD* was to represent such a world visually, and LucasArts developed *Habitat* in the mid-1980s with exactly this intention. *Habitat*'s most striking design choice, as suggested in the name, was to move away from fantasy archetypes towards a more suburban setting – something closer to real life. Players had third-person avatars and a broad range of possible interactions with other avatars: from simply communicating to bartering for goods to robbing and even killing each other.

Although this was an intentional part of the design LucasArts hadn't quite bargained for how bloodthirsty players could be. *Habitat*'s beta test saw a range of problems, with 'criminal' gangs roaming its world and murdering other players, ransacking unguarded areas and generally being a nuisance. In response the victimized players formed their own groups, with one electing a police chief and demanding LucasArts grant that player's avatar special in-game powers to deal with trouble.

Unfortunately *Habitat*'s beta test proved too popular for Quantum Link, the pre-internet online service it was intended to use, with the companies involved realizing a full launch could crash the entire network. Thus it never saw release in the west, though a heavily stripped-down version was released as *Club Caribe* in 1989 and a visually reworked version was released in Japan in 1990 as *Fujitsu Habitat*.

By the mid-1990s the internet had made MMOGs an inevitability, and the first to gain traction was *Meridian 59* (1996). This had a fantasy setting where players teamed up to fight against monsters, or each other, and introduced staples like guild halls, in-game bulletin boards and mail, and player-run guilds with voting systems. Perhaps its most important influence, however, was in establishing both a subscription model of

$9.95 a month (previously players had paid by the hour or in some cases by the minute) and regular content expansions.

➔ The game that changed perceptions was *Ultima Online* (1997). Designed more or less from scratch to be as freeform as possible, *Ultima Online* changed drastically throughout development and immediately after release in response to player behaviour. The most famous incident involves Richard Garriott, the creator of the *Ultima* series, touring the world at the end of the beta period for the game – at which point the servers would be shut down, progress would be lost and the game would be released shortly afterwards.

➔ Garriott was playing *Ultima Online* as his alter-ego, Lord British, and during one stopover a rogueish type in the crowd tossed a Firefield spell at the battlement where he and fellow designer Starr Long were standing. Naturally, as designers and major characters within the world, neither's avatar could be killed. 'My first reaction because it was a fire was to step out, however, then I thought I don't have to worry, my character's immortal,' says Garriott. 'So I just walked back into the fire and then fell over dead.'[45]

➔ Garriott had forgotten to turn his invincibility on and a random player had killed Lord British – one of the most central characters in *Ultima*'s world. His avatar's corpse was immediately surrounded by game masters, players who are basically the police of MMOGs, and Starr Long (playing as Lord Blackthorn) started summoning demons and monsters into the crowd in a virtual rage. They were far more powerful than the human avatars in the town square and ripped everything apart in minutes.

➔ But more important than this, Richard Garriott had just been killed in his own game. If you're inclined to look for symbolism, this is the moment where the dynamic between players and developers shifts. To

put it in simple terms, MMOGs are not like single-player games where a team makes a game, puts it in a box and moves onto the next thing. MMOGs require an ongoing relationship, and one where what the players want to do often doesn't coincide with what the game's creators want.

→ With its *Meridian*-inspired subscription model *Ultima Online* showed the financial viability of a big-budget MMOG, being the first to attract over 100,000 subscribers and peaking in 2003 at 250,000 – and to this day the game is live (unsuccessful MMOGs are quickly shut down because of the running costs).

→ The next step was *EverQuest* (1999), another fantasy-themed MMOG where players could choose from sixteen races and explore the world of Norrath while fighting enemies and finding loot. EverQuest's most important innovations were structural, giving players a range of quests to undertake that

Ultima Online's initial ambitions were for a working ecosystem, where animals would hunt each other and their populations would have to be carefully husbanded by the players. Of course, in the very first tests players simply killed everything so that idea had to go.

encouraged cooperation and the formation of guilds, while limiting player vs player (PvP) battles to designated zones.

> *EverQuest* was in some ways more limited than *Ultima Online* in terms of what players could choose to do in the world, but this also made it a slightly more accessible experience and led to it becoming more popular – four years after launch it had 430,000 subscribers. But, by that time, the biggest MMOG in history was about to launch.

> Blizzard is a company that specializes in perfecting genres. While it didn't invent the RTS or the dungeon-crawler it had made some of the finest examples of each (*Warcraft*, *Starcraft* and *Diablo II*), simply by refining and polishing existing designs to an extraordinary degree. *World of Warcraft* was designed to do exactly the same for the MMOG, primarily through making it an experience that a solo player could enjoy from the very start – without all the hassle

of working out where to go or being killed by stronger players.

> *World of Warcraft* also divided its servers into 'realms' that allowed players to select the kind of MMOG experience they wanted – a 'Normal' realm is player vs environment (PvE) focused, so emphasizing cooperation, and PvP fights must be consensual; PvP realms are anything-goes; and both of these variants are available in role-playing flavours too, where players are expected to act and communicate 'in character' while playing.

> The emphasis in Blizzard's design, and the genius of it, was in letting players play the game. Where previous MMOGs tended to have levelling curves that took huge amounts of playtime to see, *World of Warcraft*'s characters levelled faster and tie into a comprehensive quest list that leads the player onwards – so you always know where to go. Where death in previous MMOGs had been a very big deal indeed, and often

EverQuest is still running to this day and its world now consists of over 500 zones. The combat design of *EverQuest* is a model for other MMOGs, with its emphasis on asymmetrical classes heavily encouraging player cooperation.

A BRIEF HISTORY OF VIDEO GAMES

costly to the player, in *World of Warcraft* your avatar quickly recovers and can return to battle. When a player has been away from the game for a while, upon their return the game applies a 'rested bonus', meaning they get more experience points for a short time to help catch up with any friends that have continued levelling.

It has been said that, thanks to its comprehensive quest structure, *World of Warcraft* feels like a single-player game – which would of course be to ignore the hundreds of other people you see and pass on every trip to Azeroth. But this structure is the heart of *World of Warcraft*, and why it is so accessible – it takes an extremely intimidating concept, and crafts an experience that almost anyone can play and enjoy. At higher levels 'Raids', which often require coordinated action and tactics from groups of up to forty players, offer an experience every bit as challenging as the game's predecessors

The most impressive aspect of *World of Warcraft*'s design is how Blizzard has continually freshened and maintained Azeroth for the existing audience, while continuing to work on making it accessible for new players. It is also an eminently scalable game, capable of running on almost any hardware but truly beautiful on a powerful PC.

– but *World of Warcraft*'s genius is that this aspect is only there if you want it. Such design saw *World of Warcraft* become the most popular MMOG in history and, thanks to its subscription model, the highest-grossing game as well – at its peak in October 2012 the game had twelve million subscribers, and in 2014 Blizzard announced that over 100 million accounts had been created.

➲ *World of Warcraft* establishes a definite fork in the road for the MMOG, one that offers the ultimate structure for such an experience. The freeform style of play that had originally inspired the creation of *MUD* is somewhat lost, though you could argue that the sheer quantity of material in *World of Warcraft* is a worthy substitute. Instead, that lineage continues in the remarkable *EVE Online* (2003).

➲ Developed by Iceland's CCP games, *EVE Online* is a player-driven MMOG set in space where everything takes place in a single universe. This in itself is unusual, as nearly every other MMOG splits its player base between identical server 'shards' – that is, *World of Warcraft* may have millions of players, but you'll only ever be playing with a few thousand of them at any one time. EVE's Tranquility server hosts everyone (except players in China, which has its own server, Serenity), and its space system is inhabited by between 30,000 and 60,000 people at any time.

➲ Nearly every object in *EVE* can be constructed by players. Some players will spend their time mining asteroids or gas fields and then sell these raw materials at a space station to a dealer. The dealer will take these raw materials in great rabbit-runs to a central trading hub, where they will be sold in bulk at a mark-up. These raw materials will be bought by individuals or player-owned corporations and used to construct ships, fittings, space stations and any number of

other items. Players will go out in their ships and get into fights, with the wrecks leaving salvage that is hoovered up by drones or other players, and the cycle continues.

➲ The great genius of *EVE* is that players can choose the part of its universe in which they want to participate. They could be a shipwright, able to build the most complex spaceships in the game and hired for this expertise at great expense. They can be a fighter pilot working for a corporation, a mercenary available for hire or a pirate looking for easy prey. They can run a corporation, keeping its players in line and focused on long-term goals, or they can be a spy in an enemy corporation. But the roles only go part of the way to explaining what makes EVE special.

➲ While its universe operates on the mechanics and rules created by CCP when it comes to combat or travel, there are no developer-ordained goals or a traditional

CCP's magnificent *EVE Online*. Every ship in these screens is piloted by a player. Quite apart from the game itself an enormous part of the attraction of *EVE* is knowing that every single player is in the same universe as you are – which, of course, is also why the 'metagame' of social politics is so important and unique to *EVE*.

'endgame' like *World of Warcraft*'s epic raids. Instead, players band together to create their own goals, annex their own little corner of the universe, form alliances and foster animosities with other groups. This is referred to by *EVE* players as the metagame and it is a point of pride for certain high-profile individuals to say that they don't play *EVE* at all but control it through their networks.

➲ Two very different examples show this in action. In 2009 one of the largest alliances in the game was Band of Brothers (BoB) – an alliance being a group of corporations that work under the same banner. Another alliance, known as Goonswarm, was contacted by a high-level defector from BoB called Haargoth Agamar. Goonswarm CEO, The Mittani, groomed this defector and guided them through the process of using their position to dismantle BoB's assets and structure from within.

➲ On 5 February 2009 the defecting player stole material assets and an enormous amount of in-game currency, and used their administrative privileges to disband the BoB alliance – booting every corporation out. They then joined Goonswarm. In a few hours one of the biggest power blocs in the *EVE* galaxy had been dismantled by a single player, leaving its thousands of other members in the cold with no way of re-establishing its former position. BoB has never recovered.

➲ Then there are the big-game hunters. The dream for many *EVE* players is to fly a Titan, the largest and most expensive ship in the game – enormous death machines that can take six months of real-world time just to build. If you have a Titan, you play *EVE* a lot. And some players specialize in hunting them.

➲ One Titan pilot called FomkA decided to take a break from playing, but to do this he had to move his Titan to a safe location – where, just before he logged off, it was spotted by a member of the Sniggerdly group. These pilots are big-game hunters. The spotter noted FomkA's name, tracked down some other info about him and kept him on a watchlist. But FomkA wasn't coming back. Months passed, then a year.

❯ At some point FomkA decided to return to *EVE* and sell his Titan. The Sniggerdly group was ready – and when he logged back in after twenty months, they pounced. These players had waited over a year-and-a-half to bag this prey, and all the while he never knew a thing about it. Do not misunderstand this as meaning that Sniggerdly had been waiting twenty months just for FomkA, but rather they had passively kept tabs on him using in-game tools – nevertheless, it shows the lengths that players go to when the goals are self-created.[46]

❯ 'To us it's a challenge,' says Quickload, one of the hunters involved. 'It's a mindgame. It's part of the greater game itself. It's not the greatest *EVE* story, it's just an example of what can happen. A Titan's the biggest ship of all, it's the ultimate ship.'

❯ The future of MMOGs is unclear because they do not have lifespans like traditional games – both *World of Warcraft* and *EVE* receive constant updates, have had their visual styles overhauled to stay current, add mechanics and attract new players all the time. They represent the two current poles of MMOG design: *World of Warcraft* offers the ultimate structure, while *EVE* is ultimate freedom.

❯ Both have strengths. But in allowing players to shape its universe and ultimately construct a meaningful virtual identity, EVE perhaps contains the seed for a future revolution in interactive entertainment. Humans are social creatures. How long, one wonders, before we are offered a game that is better than life?

Revolution

➔ Since the SNES days, Nintendo's home consoles had suffered a commercial battering at the hands of Sony, and even the original Xbox had outsold GameCube. Hiroshi Yamauchi had stepped down from his position as chairman after overseeing this console's production, and new president Satoru Iwata felt that continuing Nintendo's previous strategy was doomed to failure – it needed to stop competing at the bleeding edge of technology and come up with something new.

➔ During the N64 and GameCube eras Nintendo had maintained profitability through its enormously successful handheld consoles, and the release of the DS in 2004 had not only continued this but found a new audience that was termed the 'Touch Generation'. These were players who wouldn't consider buying a 'traditional' gaming machine, but found lifestyle software such as *Brain Training* attractive. (Naturally the DS also had a wide range of more familiar software, including Nintendo staples such as *Mario*, *Pokémon* and *Zelda*.)

➔ In June 2004, a month after the announcement of DS at E3, Iwata briefed Nintendo's shareholders on the direction of the next home console. 'What's important isn't next-generation technology, but next-generation experiences,' said Iwata. 'Computing power isn't that big of a deal. At this year's E3 we announced the DS, with a design unlike anything that's come before it. With our next home console we'll be doing the same thing, and you'll see it at the next E3. Inside the company it has been code-named Revolution.'

➔ Iwata had instructed Genyo Takeda, the head of Nintendo's hardware division, to 'get off the technology roadmap' and consider instead the purpose and nature of the new hardware. The concept was simple – a console that, in Iwata's words, 'Mom wouldn't hate'.[47] Where Microsoft and Sony's next-generation machines were focused on delivering more power, the priority with Revolution was reducing power consumption and making the machine as small and unobtrusive as possible. It was designed around an improved and smaller version of the GameCube's CPU, with great emphasis given to durability and noise control, and the difference would be the interface.

➤ Nintendo had been experimenting with motion controls since the development of the GameCube, and this was the defining aspect of Revolution's design. Controllers were intimidating to non-gamers, great hunks of plastic with buttons everywhere, and so Revolution's controller had to be simple and intuitive. Iwata thought that a TV remote control was a good place from which to start because most people would be familiar with its form factor and function.

➤ The teams under Shigeru Miyamoto and Takeda worked together for six months to design the new controller, going through prototypes like the 'cheddar cheese' – a large disc coloured orange – before Takeda's team found inspiration. They used an imaging sensor, of the kind found in any video camera, to track two light sources placed near the television. It could feed its position to the console 200 times a second and, because it had to be pointed at the light sources, it was held vertically like a TV remote too. Iwata's desired form factor quickly followed, and the addition of cheap accelerometers and a tinny speaker allowed the controller to detect tilting and produce additional sound effects. On Iwata's insistence it became the first video-game controller to be called a 'remote'.

➤ The work didn't stop here. Iwata assembled twenty-five of Nintendo's top talents into the 'Console Functions Team' charged with making the experience of using the Revolution fun and surprising – quite apart from the games themselves.

Nintendo's first president from outside the Yamauchi family, Satoru Iwata is the only man in charge of a platform holder whose background is in game design. (Photo: courtesy of Nintendo)

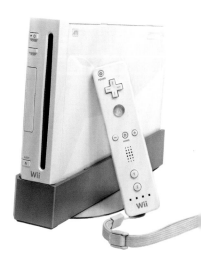

The console would be online, but where its competitors focused on multiplayer shooters and the like, Takeda came up with the idea of 'something new every day' – the home menu would be filled with weather reports, news tickers, a photo channel, a fun arena where players could answer quiz questions and see what others said, and even oddities like an astrology channel. (Although the console wouldn't launch with all of these ideas, the 'Everybody Votes' channel and many more would be released post-launch.) The home screen's look came from a member of the team walking past an electronics store with rows of televisions in the window, and so the Console Functions Team designed a grid-like pattern of small displays that each showed a different piece of software. In line with the remote, these were dubbed 'channels'.

➡ At E3 in May 2006 the Revolution was shown under its final name of 'Wii' – as in 'we' – which tied into Nintendo's cute new 'Mii' avatars. Every member of the family would have a Mii, not just giving Wii a personal touch but allowing it to distinguish who was playing and track saves and statistics individually. The killer touch, however, was the game that was packed-in with every system: *Wii Sports* (2006).

➡ *Wii Sports* may be the best and is definitely the most important piece of launch software in video-game history. A collection of five sports games – baseball, bowling, boxing, golf and tennis – that were simplified to their basic interactions and controlled through the Wii remote's motions, it encapsulated the most important technology advance since 3D visuals. Wii Sports's controls had depth and subtlety, but much more importantly anyone could pick it up and play: the link between flicking the remote and hitting a tennis ball or sweeping it underarm to launch a bowling ball is exactly the kind of intuitive interface for which Nintendo had

Everything about the Wii was designed to be non-intimidating and quiet – in stark contrast to the brash and noisy powerboxes that Nintendo's competitors were pushing. It was also designed to be able to withstand an average person's weight, in the knowledge it would probably be stood on at some point. (Photo credit: Evan Amos)

Wii Sports rarely gets credit for its enormous depth because the genius of the game is in getting almost anyone to pick up the remote and have a go. The direct link it creates between physical motion and on-screen action has not been bettered since.

aimed. Naturally the games were multiplayer and used Miis, further cementing its family-favourite status, and anecdotes about granny bowling at Christmas soon swept not just the industry but the mainstream.

➡ Microsoft's Xbox 360 had been launched on 22 November 2005, almost exactly a year before the Wii hit shelves. This was a more traditionally designed console intended to capitalize on the Xbox's strengths with greatly improved HD visuals and online multiplayer services. The Wii, by comparison, didn't offer HD visuals and had been roundly mocked for this, with many in the industry believing it would be the misstep that finally brought Nintendo down.

➡ Wii launched worldwide from late November (North America) to early December 2006 (Europe and Japan), with its technology allowing a significantly cheaper price than the competing PS3 and Xbox 360. It quickly sold out everywhere. Nintendo sold over 600,000

units at $249 in its first week in North America, and in the UK stock couldn't keep up with demand – it was the fastest-selling console in that territory's history.

➡ Nintendo's success caught Microsoft and Sony completely flat-footed. Sony had pursued a 'luxury' angle with PS3, believing that its brand was strong enough to support an extremely high-powered and expensive HD console that (with shades of the PS2's pioneering use of DVD) used Blu-ray as a storage medium. The PS3 used a complicated custom chip design, called the 'Cell' CPU, that left many developers baffled, and launched at a premium price point of $499/$599 in North America (depending on the model) and £425 in the UK.

➡ In the first half of 2007 Wii sold more units than the PS3 and Xbox 360 combined, and less than a year after launch had overhauled the lead that Xbox 360's earlier launch had built. Nintendo

The Xbox 360 hardware was rushed to market in an effort to steal a march on Sony. This initially worked wonders but soon enough revealed a huge hidden cost in the infamous Red Ring of Death. Later hardware revisions fixed this but the damage to Microsoft's bottom line was done. (Photo credit: Evan Amos)

was manufacturing just under two million consoles a month during this period and yet still couldn't keep up with demand, and by 2008 was producing 2.4 million a month and selling them all.

● After fourteen months on sale, Wii had sold more units than the GameCube had managed in its lifetime. In January 2010 Wii became Nintendo's most successful home console ever with over sixty-seven million sold, surpassing the NES. As of June 2014, 101.15 million Wii consoles had been sold. It is worth remembering, in this context, that unlike its competitors Nintendo sells hardware at a profit. (It has been estimated that, despite the high price, each PS3 launch unit cost Sony over $200. This was eventually improved through hardware revisions.)

● *Wii Sports* was one of many innovative titles that broadened Wii's appeal. *Wii Play* (2006), a collection of minigames that came packaged with an additional Wii remote,

introduced more traditional game designs but simplified them as much as possible (leading to many negative reviews that rather missed the point). *Warioware: Smooth Moves* (2006) went loco with the possibilities of motion-sensing, offering a brilliant mix of totally original ideas and reworked traditional styles, and ending with a funky dance-off.

● The twin poles of this strategy are *Wii Fit* (2007) and *Wii Music* (2008). *Wii Fit* was packaged with the Balance Board peripheral, which the player stands on while performing exercises, and tracks a player's 'fitness' over time – very gradually moving from gentle exercises to more demanding workouts. It is hazy as to whether *Wii Fit* could really be considered a video game, which speaks volumes about Nintendo's innovation during this era, but it was a sales sensation that appealed broadly and particularly to more mature gamers – it has subsequently been used for physiotherapy, in health clubs and in

The PlayStation 3 followed its predecessors by championing a new storage medium – the Blu-ray disc. In retaliation Microsoft adopted the HD-DVD format and released an add-on for the Xbox 360 to support it, but eventually Blu-ray won out. (Photo credit: Evan Amos)

old people's homes as a fun and gentle way to encourage exercise.

➡ *Wii Music* is a pet project of Shigeru Miyamoto, and swims against the tide of music games such as *Guitar Hero* and *Rock Band* (which ask players to press buttons in time with a song) by creating a freeform way of 'playing' music. The game is constructed around a broad selection of musical instruments (sixty-six in total) and plays an existing tune that the player can then improvise upon by moving the Wii remote in an instrument-specific fashion.

➡ Sadly *Wii Music* was panned on release and sold extremely poorly (for a Nintendo first-party game), perhaps because its style of play – with no scoring system and no fail states – was too distinct from the rhythm games of its time. But it is a product of depth and imagination, as well as enormous fun, and despite its poor reception established a system that has much more connection to the experience of playing an instrument than other games in the genre.

➡ Despite this focus on new ways of playing, Wii also saw a spectacular return to form for the 3D *Mario* games in *Super Mario Galaxy* (2007) and *Super Mario Galaxy 2* (2010).[48] The 3D platformer had seen little innovation since *Super Mario 64* but Galaxy introduced a new concept – most levels were constructed from spherical planetoids with their own centre of gravity. At certain points the player could make Mario jump such distances that he would seem to be going into space but the gravity effect would 'catch' him and pull the arc of his jump around the planetoid's surface, an experience that feels every bit as brilliant as it looks.

➡ The *Galaxy* games also have such a cavalcade of ideas that it simply leaves a player open-mouthed: planets aren't just round, but can be long or short, fat or thin, shaped like spikes or wraparound lozenges.

Wii Fit may be even more important to Nintendo's future than is currently known – based on its success the company has established a division devoted solely to lifestyle products. An early example, the 'Wii Vitality Sensor', never made it to market, but Nintendo's ambition in this area is considerable.

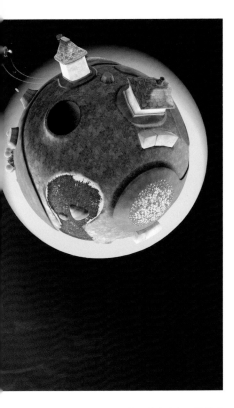

There are planets constructed entirely from water, planets with giant holes in the middle to send Mario careening through, and wide stretches of space to float across while hanging onto a flower stem. As the game progresses the level design begins to become equal parts surreal and impossible, and in the sequel Nintendo's designers begin to pull the entire idea of a platformer apart in front of the player's eyes – moving towards abstraction, tying your eyes and fingers in knots, and displaying the kind of fertile creativity no other developer can match.

➔ The Achilles heel of the Wii, as ever with Nintendo, was third-party software. Although the console's sales meant that the biggest third-party publishers supported it wholeheartedly at first, the only software that sold in any great quantities was first party. Among the rare exceptions was Ubisoft's *Just Dance* (2009), which combined simple on-screen avatars performing dance

Super Mario Galaxy – 'Orbital' by Dead End Thrills. Nintendo had been experimenting with a gravity-based *Mario* game since completing development on *Super Mario 64*, and this long gestation bore fruit in the stunning imagination of *Galaxy*. (Courtesy of Dead End Thrills)

moves with a poppy licensed soundtrack, and *Carnival Games* (2007), a cutesy minigame collection that appealed to families with young children.

➡ The rest was a train wreck with extremely high-quality titles like *Boom Blox* (2008), a collaboration between EA and Steven Spielberg, failing at retail. Grasshopper Manufacture's *No More Heroes* (2007), a witty third-person brawler designed to appeal to the traditional young male demographic was another high-profile failure, and countless other examples (along with the increasing sales of PS3 and 360) saw third parties more or less give up on Wii – near the end of its life, sales of the console slowed dramatically, though it still ended up selling more overall than the competition.

➡ While the Wii offered a new way of playing, the PS3 and 360 concentrated on perfecting existing genres – not least because the transition to high definition (HD) resulted

in a spike in development costs, making innovation much more risky. This also meant that exclusive third-party titles were slowly becoming a thing of the past, though among the exceptions are many of each platform's standout titles.

➡ One of these was the 360's earliest system-seller, developer Epic's *Gears of War* (2006), a third-person shooter that perfected the cover mechanic and showcased the potential of HD visuals with incredible textures (though it has about as much aesthetic style as a dead fish). *Gears* offered fantastic shooting alongside one of the first great multiplayer offerings of the generation, ensuring it was a top seller, and spawned several more-or-less identical sequels.

➡ The Microsoft-owned Lionhead Studios developed *Fable II* (2008), the sequel to an uninspiring Xbox original, and through the clever idea of removing death crafted a memorable and funny action RPG. The *Fable*

games were always marketed as responding to the player's actions, though this is wild exaggeration, but *Fable II*'s 'actions' wheel was a particular highlight – when approaching any NPC your character can perform tricks, the funniest being a fart which, if the button is held too long, noisily follows through. This mix of toilet humour and 'ye olde Britain' vibe added up to a world in which it is a genuine joy to spend time.

◉ Bungie continued Xbox's flagship series with *Halo 3* (2007), which offered an excellent single-player campaign alongside a truly comprehensive suite of multiplayer options and additional features – players could record playthroughs, construct their own layouts atop pre-existing levels, take screenshots and share everything online. This led to experiences like 'Halo Kart', levels rebuilt as racetracks with the players spawning next to Mongoose quad bikes, and 'Grifball' which is basically rugby with plasma swords and hammers (every bit as brilliant as it sounds).

◉ User-generated content is not a new idea for gaming but this hardware brought it to the living room in a manner like never before, most notably with Media Molecule's PS3 exclusive *LittleBigPlanet* (2008). The foundations of *LittleBigPlanet* are a 2D platformer with three planes that main character Sackboy can jump between. Sackboy can also push and grab onto things – but after completing a brief tutorial section the player can begin constructing their own levels from *LittleBigPlanet*'s vast selection of materials and objects.

◉ An enormous part of *LittleBigPlanet*'s success, and the rapturous critical reception, is the peerless aesthetic that meshes with the creation theme by channelling arts and crafts – Sackboy is seemingly constructed from sackcloth, while objects are textured to resemble plasticine, wool and various fabrics with elements like buttons and stickers mixed

Gears of War 3 – 'Quad Damage' by Dead End Thrills. Although the aesthetics of Epic's *Gears* series aren't to everyone's taste, the games are a superb showcase for the company's middleware, and there is the visceral pleasure of squishing an enemy Locust's head with a size-fifteen jackboot. (Courtesy of Dead End Thrills)

in. The 'creation' mode also has a simple interface that makes it easy to construct new levels, and this ties in beautifully with the ease of uploading your own levels and downloading those made by others.

➲ *LittleBigPlanet 2* (2011) improved on this already impressive base in almost every way, adding many more objects and allowing players to change fundamental aspects of how the game operates. *LittleBigPlanet 2* adds the option to make puzzle, racing and RPG games among others, as well as allowing creators to customize the HUD, assign buttons to specific actions, manipulate the camera and create cutscenes for levels. There's even a fully featured music sequencer.

➲ Together the games have seen over eight million levels created, and while these are obviously of wildly varying quality there can be no disputing that this is by a distance the most successful UGC-focused game that consoles have seen (for PC owners this is all

old hat). The only downside to *LittleBigPlanet* is that the fundamental platforming mechanics leave a lot to be desired, making many of its user-created levels feel more like sightseeing tours than great gaming. This is best shown by the most infamous *LittleBigPlanet* creation: a level that, through an amazingly complex system of pulleys, operates as a fully-working calculator. Nevertheless, *LittleBigPlanet* is a singular achievement.

➲ Sony acquired *Crash Bandicoot* developers Naughty Dog in 2001, and the PS3 saw its greatest work yet: *Indiana J . . .* sorry, *Uncharted: Drake's Fortune* (2007). A third-person adventure heavily inspired by the Spielberg movies and *Tomb Raider, Uncharted* casts the player as Nathan Drake in a series of awe-inspiring tropical locations on the trail of El Dorado, the lost city of gold. *Uncharted* is not innovative but it is super-polished and a pleasure to play, the only pity being

LittleBigPlanet's emphasis on creativity found a willing partner in its interconnected player base. Although the concept wasn't wholly original, *LittleBigPlanet* arrived at a time when hardware allowed users to easily share creations – and they did, in their millions.

Naughty Dog's over-reliance on cutscenes to tell the story.

➤ This weakness persists through *Uncharted 2: Among Thieves* (2009) and *Uncharted 3: Drake's Deception* (2011), though the strength of the writing is uncommonly good. This type of narrative design is a dead end for an interactive medium, but Naughty Dog is among the foremost practitioners of it and created the best example in this style with *The Last of Us* (2013). Although again a third-person shooter, *The Last of Us* is set in a post-apocalypse scenario where main character Joel has to alternate between stealth and gunplay on a journey with young compatriot Ellie.

➤ Although *The Last of Us* is an enormously satisfying game to play, Naughty Dog's aim was clearly to try and build a relationship between Joel (i.e. the player) and Ellie. The cutscenes are as great as ever and manage this feat admirably, but unfortunately Ellie's AI is an unmitigated failure – so much so that the game's enemies have been programmed to ignore her presence. While Joel has to sneak around for fear of alerting deadly foes, Ellie (and other companions) will merrily walk right in front of and occasionally bump into these creatures, constantly shattering the immersion. Despite this, *The Last of Us*'s art direction, weighty combat and script are excellent, and if you can ignore the fault line running throughout it is one of the best adventures gaming has to offer.

➤ Among third-party titles Ubisoft's *Assassin's Creed* (2007) kickstarted this generation's most successful new series, though it was an abominable game. *Assassin's Creed* recreates the Holy Land in 1191 with quite astonishing visual fidelity, but unfortunately it is also largely empty and lacking anything interesting to do. This was much improved upon by *Assassin's Creed II* (2009), which changed the setting to Renaissance Italy and introduced the

Devil May Cry – 'Bad to the Bones' by Dead End Thrills. Capcom's third-person brawler was rebooted by UK-based studio Ninja Theory, and this Dante was as hardcore as ever. (Courtesy of Dead End Thrills)

rogueish Ezio as the main character. More importantly, it filled the world with treasures to find, improved combat, and used famous Renaissance figures such as Leonardo da Vinci, Niccolo Machiavelli and Rodrigo Borgia as characters in an entertaining ahistorical narrative.

⮞ Infinity Ward's *Call of Duty: Modern Warfare* (2007) brought a historically-themed first-person shooter blazing into the modern day with a new level of sophistication in camera technology and beautiful controls. The game's shock factor is undeniable: in the first scene you control a Middle Eastern president and can only turn his head as rebels take him to a square, stick a gun in his face and pull the trigger. Later sequences include an outstanding sniper mission set in Chernobyl and a cinematic eye for setpieces that has been imitated relentlessly.

⮞ *Modern Warfare* was an enormous success thanks mainly to its multiplayer, which features a wide range of modes and a brilliant 'levelling' system that allows the player to customize their multiplayer characters over time – unlocking new weapons and 'perks' consistently. Publisher Activision, on the strength of this title, turned *Call of Duty* into an annual juggernaut and it is the most commercially successful AAA game to this day.

⮞ Irrational Games's *Bioshock* (2007) has the greatest setting video games have so far produced: Rapture, a city at the bottom of the ocean created by uber-capitalist Andrew Ryan as an escape from the 'petty moralities' of surface-dwellers. Rapture is simply gorgeous, a series of skyscrapers enclosed in glass and joined by curving tunnels, its blazing neon illuminating the surrounding ocean. Your first glimpse of it, at the climax of an Andrew Ryan speech, is spine-tingling. Here is a world where the scientist is free to pursue his research, freed of ethical constraints; here is a place where the artist need not cater to popular taste; here is a place where a man can choose his own destiny.

→ *Bioshock* is an extremely good shooter but its ambitions are more grandiose and its greatest achievement is also its undoing: it questions the nature of player control and our unquestioning acceptance of narrative conventions. Three words encapsulate it: 'would you kindly'. As you move through Rapture, guided by unknown benefactor Atlas and hounded by Ryan, these words unobtrusively creep into the script in a manner that first-time players rarely notice. By the time you reach Andrew Ryan, around halfway through the game, he's worked it out and explains in a sequence of extraordinary power.

→ Disregarding the opening and ending, this sequence is *Bioshock*'s only cutscene – and with good reason. 'Would you kindly' is a conditioning mechanism. You were one of Rapture's experiments, Ryan's secret lovechild spirited away and raised to act normally until those words are used. The centre of Ryan's philosophy is the single sentence: 'A man chooses, a slave obeys.'

→ As a final gift from father to son, he demonstrates your pitiful condition in a series of commands prefaced by 'would you kindly': Sit . . . Stand . . . Run . . . Stop . . . Turn . . . Such instructions are the typical actions a player performs while playing an first-person shooter. Powerless, the player watches each command followed. The final instruction is to 'Kill'. As you hit an unresisting Ryan, he pulls the screen towards his bloodied face and screams 'Obey!'

→ As Ryan's lifeless corpse drops to the floor, so does the illusion of agency. All that players ever do in first-person shooters is follow commands, whether they be from an SAS commander or simply on-screen text, and this moment shows what kind of control the audience has in such worlds. A game chooses, and the player obeys.

It is a great tragedy that, following this climactic moment, *Bioshock* can't take it home with a second half that delivers – or even suggests – some kind of alternative. Instead, the game plays itself out in typically objective-led fashion, expecting players to somehow forget that the wool has just been removed from our eyes. One of *Bioshock*'s themes is how Ryan's rigid ideology led himself and Rapture to a sad and eventually inevitable end. It is a great pity that, in this respect, the game mirrors him.

Bioshock Infinite (2013) offered another visually outstanding setting: the floating city of Columbia, seceded from the United States in 1901 and run by religious zealot Zachary Comstock, who is worshipped by most of the city as 'the prophet'.

Where *System Shock* and *Bioshock* are cramped, scary places, *Bioshock Infinite* glories in sunshine and blue skies. Although this world is nowhere near as open as it appears, your first sight of its giant floating islands, suspended by fans and unknown engineering magic, is simply jaw-dropping. So too is the thrill of hooking onto one of the 'skylines' that connect the land and zooming round their length like a rollercoaster.

Sadly *Bioshock Infinite* was, despite a rapturous critical reception, a step back for the series. The combat remains dependent on plasmids (called 'vigors') and enemies are simply bullet sponges with little variety. *Infinite*'s best moments are when you're allowed to simply explore its crazy world, while its frequent low points are the attritional engagements. Indeed, where Bioshock questioned the nature of the shooter, *Infinite* makes you wonder why it's a shooter at all.

Mirror's Edge (2008) by Swedish studio Dice offered an original take on the first-person perspective, casting you as a 'runner' who had to parkour their way through

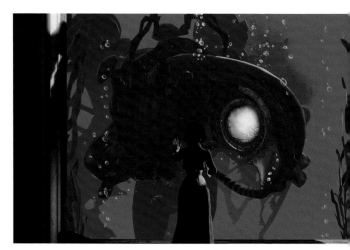

Bioshock Infinite was arguably a step too far for the formula it was using – the incredible visuals and setting were weighed down enormously by its frequent combat sequences and the last third in particular plays like a slog.

A BRIEF HISTORY OF VIDEO GAMES

a gorgeously realized future city, but unfortunately the game design didn't live up to the idea – resulting in a popular and much-heralded but ultimately disappointing experience. Rockstar's *Red Dead Redemption* (2010) combined the company's open-world expertise with a love letter to the spaghetti western, creating the most awesome sunsets in gaming alongside an affecting tale of former outlaw John Marston trying to escape his past. *Red Dead*'s pacing was the real triumph, mixing up the inevitable high-noon shootouts with a great deal of travelling by horseback, in a setting that rewarded exploration and was content to let players be rather than prodding them through the story.

➔ Although Harmonix's *Guitar Hero* (2005) had made its debut on PlayStation 2, it was in this generation that its sequels began to achieve huge success. *Guitar Hero* is a game where you play a silly-looking plastic instrument in time to a song by following

Mirror's Edge – 'Tunnel Deep' by Dead End Thrills. Developed by Swedish studio Dice, *Mirror's Edge* was a first-person game about parkouring through a gleaming futuristic metropolis. Although the game is compromised by needless combat sections, its visual style remains breathtaking. (Courtesy of Dead End Thrills)

on-screen prompts, and it feels just fantastic. After the superb *Guitar Hero II* (2006) Harmonix moved onto *Rock Band* (2007), which broadened out the experience to allow up to four 'band members' at once – which made it even better. For a time these music games were something of a craze, though publisher Activision quickly drove the market into the ground by releasing new *Guitar Hero* games multiple times a year.

❯ First-person RPGs took a major step forward with Bethesda's *The Elder Scrolls IV: Oblivion* (2006), *Fallout 3* (2008) and *Skyrim* (2011). These games are constructed around worlds where there is simply so much to do – and the character's abilities offer the ability to specialize in whatever style of play you prefer – that they're really many games in one. Although there are shonky aspects to their construction, the sheer scale of possible activities (and the gorgeous landscapes) is remarkable, and on PC in particular the games are favourite targets for modders.

❯ Third-person RPGs, too, were particularly well-served by BioWare's *Mass Effect* trilogy, three games that tell the universe-spanning story of Captain Shepard. *Mass Effect 2* (2010) enormously improved the combat at the game's core and, by allowing the player to make choices at key moments during its story the trilogy fostered an effective illusion of narrative control – so much so that the story's canonical and unavoidable ending saw a furious reaction from series fans, who felt cheated at the implication that their actions had been for naught.

❯ Fine as Bethesda and BioWare's work is, the best games of this generation are the action-RPGs *Demon's Souls* (2009) and *Dark Souls* (2011), the former exclusive to PS3. Directed by Hidetaka Miyazaki and developed by Japan's From Software, the *Souls* games introduced a new style of play built around challenging combat with a high skill ceiling,

Alan Wake – 'Kingdom Come' by Dead End Thrills. Finnish studio Remedy's *Alan Wake* tells the story of a novelist, clearly inspired by Steven King, who finds himself afflicted first by writer's block and then by what appears to be a plot straight out of his own novel. (Courtesy of Dead End Thrills)

Fallout 3 – 'The Quiet Carriage' by Dead End Thrills. *Fallout 3* didn't quite have the grim edge of its 1990s predecessors but it brought Bethesda's strengths to bear in creating a huge and fascinating open world to explore. (Courtesy of Dead End Thrills)

extremely threatening enemies, and elaborately constructed 3D environments that twist and warp around themselves to connect in unexpected ways.

⊘ Among the *Souls* games' innovations are the inability to pause (because this breaks immersion) and the ability to 'invade' the world of other players as a dark spirit – or be invaded. Almost every other multiplayer game in history depends on consent – that is, you click the option to go into competition. Here, it happens whether you like it or not and the effect in an already-scary game is simply terrifying – it is not uncommon to successfully invade a player's world and then immediately be removed because they have turned off the console (the only way to 'escape').

⊘ In many ways the most notable achievement of the *Souls* games is how narratively sophisticated they are. There is little explicit story in either game,

but through talking to the rare NPCs and collecting items the player acquires fragments of some great jigsaw for which they have the vague outlines. But the game rarely provides definitive answers. It means that the *Souls* games combine environmental, oral and textual narrative fragments to create a complex and fascinating backstory to their worlds, but fundamentally remain something of a puzzle for the player's imagination.

⊘ Finally, a word for the little guys. Each console in this generation offered the ability to download smaller titles (the original Xbox had featured the Xbox Live Arcade, but this came near the end of its life and saw only twenty-seven titles released) – which often showed more originality than their bigger brothers. The first hit was Bizarre's *Geometry Wars: Retro Evolved* (2005), a game that had originally been included as an extra in the same studio's *Project Gotham Racing*, but was updated and re-released on Xbox 360.

Mass Effect 2 – 'Son of Man' by Dead End Thrills. BioWare's science-fiction trilogy took players across the universe and back again, though it wasn't until the second entry that the game lived up to the visuals. (Courtesy of Dead End Thrills)

➲ *Geometry Wars* popularized and is the best example of the twinstick shooter, whereby the player controls their craft with the left analogue stick and the direction of fire with the right. The playing field is a rectangle of fixed size and the objective is simple: survive. Abstract enemies constantly spawn and home in on your craft, with different types having different behaviours, and as the intensity ratchets up the only way to stay alive is to keep moving and clear a forward path. *Geometry Wars* also featured one of the first creative uses of the Xbox 360's new 'Achievements' system, which rewards players with 'gamerscore' for performing certain in-game feats, most notably 'Pacifism' for surviving the first sixty seconds without dying. Pacifism was such a good idea, in fact, that it became a distinct mode in the excellent *Geometry Wars 2* (2008).

➲ The key aspect of this distribution method is that it allowed small teams and in some cases individuals to reach a home-console audience, which had previously been a remote possibility. Developer Jonathan Blow's *Braid* (2008) is one of the titles that best encapsulates the fruits of this approach, a unique platformer that uses time-manipulation as its core mechanic and wrings out every drop of potential.

➲ A particularly brilliant element of *Braid* is how the final stage in the game brings together the idea of rewinding time and a traditional platformer objective to twist the player's understanding of its piecemeal narrative. Its twin themes are obsession and regret, which at certain (hidden) points are directly related to the Manhattan Project, and it seems that much of the game may take place in the lead character Tim's muddled brain. Is he a scientist remorseful for his part in the creation of the atom bomb or is that just another metaphor? Are the jigsaw pieces the player collects forming repressed

Most games are extraordinarily ham-fisted in the manner in which they deliver narrative, but the system used in the *Dark Souls* games – which depends on puzzle solving and reading comprehension above all else – is considerably more effective when used well.

memories? Is it, at bottom, all about regretting breaking up with an ex-girlfriend? *Braid* gives plenty of clues but ultimately remains ambiguous, and what that says about how we construct our own identities is its final and finest revelation.

➜ There are many more downloadable classics from this generation. Toru Iwatani returned to his iconic creation with *Pac-Man: Championship Edition* (2007) and, by making it faster-paced and adding a time-limit, revitalized the core run-then-chase mechanic. Team Meat's *Super Meat Boy* (2010) is a precision platformer with beautifully tuned controls, bags of content and a wicked sense of humour in how its challenges are constructed. There are great side-scrolling brawlers (*Castle Crashers*, 2010), re-released classics (*Outrun Online Arcade*, 2009), richly atmospheric isometric adventures (*Bastion*, 2011), monochrome minimalist platformers (*Limbo*, 2010), physics-based motorbikes (*Trials Evolution*, 2012) and that's not the half of it.

➜ Despite sales falling off badly, Nintendo's Wii, with 101 million, still ended up outselling both PS3 and 360 overall, with the latter pair sitting at around eighty million units shipped. Although Wii ceased production in 2013 following the arrival of its successor, Wii U, Sony are committed to supporting PS3 until 2015 and Microsoft are supporting 360 until 2016, despite both releasing new hardware.

➜ These consoles have shown an uncommon longevity due to a number of factors: constant software updates, delivered online, have completely changed the experience of using a 360 from launch day to now, while developers continue to squeeze genuinely impressive performance from that 'difficult' PS3 hardware. But the biggest reason is simple: video games are getting better, increasingly sophisticated and are serving a larger audience than ever before.

Steam and Valve

24

● There is no single way to describe Valve Corporation, co-founded by Gabe Newell and Mike Harrington in 1996 to make *Half-Life*. Thanks to its distribution service Steam and an unmatchable lineup of top-class titles, the company is now at every front of PC gaming: part-developer, part-publisher, part-distributor, part-toolmaker, part-sponsor and part-haberdasher (we'll come to this).

● Before Steam, Valve was merely a fantastic developer. Steam grew out of the company's frustration with patching its games, which at the turn of the millennium involved players having to first find out a patch was available, go to the correct site to download it and then run it. This problem first came to light with *Counter-Strike*, a competitive game that regularly needed exploits and bugs fixed, and where Valve noticed that, post-patch, the player base would drop off significantly.

● Steam was concepted as a way to

The reception area of Valve's Seattle office contains a *Team Fortress 2* Sentry Gun made by special effects workshop WETA that tracks visitors. Nearby there's an entire hall – which could be filled several times over – covered in awards the company has received.

distribute and update games automatically, and then, through this constant connection to players, also help Valve deal with constant problems like cheaters and piracy. The service went into beta with *Counter-Strike* in January 2003 and was officially released for Windows PCs on 12 September 2003. But it wasn't until the release of Valve's highly anticipated *Half-Life 2* – where Steam installation was mandatory even with a copy bought in stores – that it began to gather serious numbers of users.

➡ The first non-Valve game to be released on Steam was *Rag Doll Kung Fu* in October 2005, and the service's features and user base soon saw this turn into a flood of third-party PC releases. Every year it gets larger. Some numbers: in 2011 Steam had forty-four million users and saw 323 games released; in 2012 it had fifty-two million users and 382 new games; in 2013 this was seventy-five million users and 636 new games. That figure

of seventy-five million active users was up ten million from October 2013, a 15 per cent rise in four months and, though Valve haven't released more figures since, one can only assume such growth continues.

➡ No one is exactly sure how much of the PC games market goes through Steam, but estimates range from 70 to 80 per cent. This creates its own problems, such as usability and visibility of newly released and indie games that don't have huge marketing budgets. Valve's solution is *the* Valve solution: community. Steam is at the time of writing evolving its social features to make peer-recommendation a central part of the network, with users able to 'curate' selections of games – with the theory being that the community will find their own good sifters.

➡ Steam's position looks unassailable, but equally has led to various attempts to compete with it. Impulse was launched in 2008 by developer Stardock, and bought by

Counter-Strike: Global Offensive is the current iteration of a series that began as a mod and has grown into the ultimate competitive first-person shooter. It is notable that, though *Counter-Strike* is frequently updated, the basics have remained almost unchanged over more than a decade.

American retailer Gamestop, but discontinued in 2008. Both EA and Ubisoft have launched their own platforms, but both are much inferior to Steam in the range of games offered – and the thing is that the vast majority of players and developers don't want an alternative.

➔ This is because Valve is an unusual company, highly responsive to feedback and particularly driven by what the data says. Since release it has continued to add features to Steam: 2007 saw the launch of Steam Community, a suite of user-focused additions like chat, a web browser, various lists and an overlay that can be brought up in-game to access any of them. 2008 saw Steamworks, an application programming interface that in plain English is a bunch of developer-focused tools that lets games hook into all of Steam's features (e.g. achievements, cloud saves, networking, Valve's proprietary anti-cheat software). By 2013 Steam was available on

Windows, Mac, Linux and, in limited forms, on PS3, iOS and Android.

➔ Steam's dominance is not welcomed by all PC gamers because it allows Valve unprecedented access to customer data and habits, and also gives the company the right to revoke ownership of a user's content. That is, if you own games on Steam they are only 'your' games until either Steam disappears forever or Valve decides to cancel your Steam account. The chances of either of these happening is extraordinarily slim, of course, but the principle remains.

➔ Regardless, the future of PC gaming looks very much like Steam, and this will only be reinforced by Valve's 'Steam Boxes' – essentially custom PCs designed to plug into a television, launched in late 2014. Although these are currently too expensive to be considered as serious competition to home consoles, the cost will only go down over time and they have one huge advantage – instant

access to thousands upon thousands of Steam-compatible games.

➲ It is almost incidental that Valve develops some of the best PC games around and is run in a manner quite unlike any other company. There are no job titles at Valve, its developers are free to move from project to project as they see fit, and marketing director Doug Lombardi estimates more than half of the company's employees come from the community. The team that made *Portal* were hired after presenting a student demo; the *Team Fortress 2* designers were contracted after making the original mod, before being employed outright.

➲ The company's obsession with data has increasingly come to inform its design decisions. says Josh Weier, a lead developer on *Portal 2*.

We take an idea and test it. The biggest thing in our process is that from day one if there's a map, even if it's in a rough state, then you start throwing people at it, seeing how they react to it, then tweak it, throw more people at it. By the end of it anything you play has had 50 or 60 people playing through and we make revisions based on that. That's pretty core to how we work.

➲ Steam's 'launch title' *Half-Life 2* (2004) was probably too early in Valve's evolution to feel the full benefit of this approach, so it merely demonstrates that the company has some of the finest developers in the world. *Half-Life 2* moved beyond the original in every regard, creating a world where the characters are more believable, the environments tell half of the story and the overall tone is darker.

➲ The game puts the player once more in the shoes of Gordon Freeman, but where the original was confined to the Black Mesa lab, here we travel through City 17 –

a dystopian vision that shocks by association. The buildings seem like those in any Eastern European city, for example, so the armed checkpoints and fences around tenements are more dissonant. The Combine's fascistic technology frames almost every sight without ever obscuring what this place once was, allowing you to see a familiar-looking past underneath the cripplingly ordered present. Headcrabs and zombies are still a part of this universe, but the real horror in *Half-Life 2* is what's becoming of humanity.

➲ This would all be for naught if *Half-Life 2* wasn't also a great shooter, capable of moving from relatively peaceful contemplation to panicked conflagration in a heartbeat. The Gestapo-like Combine soldiers bark instructions as they hunt Freeman down, zombies wail in agony at the parasites locked into their brains, headcrabs chitter in unseen corners, and Valve knows exactly where they're most effectively placed. Freeman's armoury is most notable for its incorporation of the gravity gun – a weapon that allows him to pick up objects in order to solve puzzles, construct new routes or smash something into an enemy face.

➲ Finally there is Alyx, an AI companion that in certain respects is still *the* AI companion – simply because she's capable and brings a sorely needed sense of humour to the grim setting. She is not alone in being believable as a person, with *Half-Life 2*'s story told almost entirely through non-cutscene dialogue by characters in the world – talking to Gordon face-to-face or, in the case of Dr Breen, from City 17's various screens. Breen is a good example himself: no comedy villain, he may be the man saying that humanity should work with the Combine but he is also constantly trying to reason with Freeman, to cajole and persuade him that this is the right choice to make. Such a cast, in an environment so rich in stories itself, creates a world in which we can believe.

Half-Life 2 – 'Knock Three Times' by Dead End Thrills. The opening sequence of *Half-Life 2* emphasizes how far humanity has gone down the wrong path since the events of the first game, with Gestapo-like police searching through apartments trying to find Freeman. (Courtesy of Dead End Thrills)

After *Half-Life 2* came *The Orange Box* (2007) and *Left 4 Dead* (2008), showing just how wide-ranging the company's development talents had become. *The Orange Box* included both of *Half-Life 2*'s additional episodes, three- to four-hour long continuations that were every bit as good, first-person mind-bender *Portal* and multiplayer shooter *Team Fortress 2*. Three games for the price of one because Valve believed that it represented a good deal for its customers.

Portal casts the player as Chell, a lab rat in an antiseptic future lab where the only voice is a computerized instructor. The game's central mechanic is the portal gun, which can spit out a blue portal and an orange portal that connect – allowing you to walk into a wall on one side of the room and come out on the other. Or why not put one on the floor, one right above it, jump in to create an infinite loop, then fire off another at max velocity to send yourself shooting across the environment?

As this suggests, the portals are fun simply to toy with, but the puzzles Valve manages to craft from them are outstanding and guide the player gently from the most basic links to brain-twisting solutions. One later level presents a series of ascending platforms, like giant steps, with a pit at the bottom. It's hard to see how to get up to the first, never mind all of them. But if you put a portal on the floor and one at the bottom of the pit, then jump into the latter, Chell shoots straight up out of the floor – and you can see the top of the first platform and place a portal there. Do so and she'll fall back into the portal from which she's just been shot and then shoot up from the one you have just placed. Repeating this trick multiple times will get you up.

What made *Portal* truly special was the computerized voice, which belongs to the

Half-Life 2 – 'A Watchful Eye' by Dead End Thrills. The mysterious G-Man is spoken to at various points throughout the *Half-Life* games, and in a brilliant piece of world-building can also be spotted on rare occasions in places he shouldn't be. (Courtesy of Dead End Thrills)

lab-controlling GLaDOS. As you progress it becomes clear that GLaDOS is demented, and you're not the first test subject she's had – not by a long shot. Chell finds scattered hints of previous 'testers' while GLaDOS frequently refers to her inevitable death, and as you get further and further the experiment begins to take on a frantic and funnier aspect.

◉ *Portal* was such a hit it spawned a follow-up that encapsulates why Valve is a special developer – the company had noted that *Portal* was a popular game to play with friends. So where the original was a small but perfectly formed solo trek, *Portal 2* (2011) is a sprawling comedy co-op game. The first game's Aperture Science lab expands into an overgrown complex halfway between collapsing and eating itself, a dying machine.

◉ There's a consistently funny single-player adventure, but *Portal 2* really gets going with a friend. It is a game that understands the pleasure of playing with others is in communicating, laughing together and the kind of mishaps that see you put a portal in the wrong place and send your buddy flying into a wall at 100 mph. There are no restarts for dying, though: why punish players for having fun?

◉ That brilliant central mechanic is even better with friends: it's a glorious spectacle to watch one player backflipping through a spike chamber, while the other casually pops out mid-leap to grab a cube from them. It is amazing how much Valve wrings out of the portals, and the sequel enhances them with gels that add momentum and bounce to these elaborate rabbit runs, resulting in some of the most dizzying, thrilling motion the first-person perspective has achieved. Valve looked at people enjoying the original together and built a sequel that's a conduit for a joint performance, one that puts most comedies to shame.

◉ At the other end of the co-op spectrum is

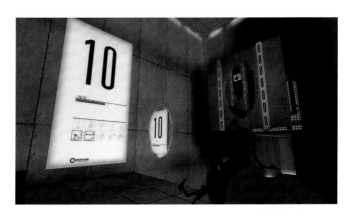

The most Valve-like aspect of *Portal* is that the game's creators presented the prototype, 'Narbacular Drop', to Valve while still at university, and were swiftly hired and given the resources to turn it into a full game. *Portal* was an instant classic, which suggests Valve may be on to something..

Left 4 Dead, co-developed by Valve and Turtle Rock Studios, an intense four-player shooter set in the zombie apocalypse. The most notable aspect of this and its near-instant sequel *Left 4 Dead 2* (2009) is how it makes itself replayable. Both games come with four levels each, though they have subsequently received many more through free updates, but the placement of enemies in *Left 4 Dead* isn't down to the developers (as in almost any other shooter). Instead it has an AI dubbed the Director.

➡ This means that every time you play a level in *Left 4 Dead* the experience will be different. You might walk through an alleyway one time and nothing happens. A couple of weeks later you'll go back and be ambushed from above by a Hunter, while endless waves of zombies pour in and trap your group in a corner. Sometimes you'll waltz through sections without a scratch, and others you'll be ripped to shreds in a minute. Every game

in which Valve is involved is different like this: there's always something special, some feature that elevates it well above standard fare.

➡ *Team Fortress 2* (2007) was so long in development that it was considered vapourware. Now there isn't one game called *Team Fortress 2*, but hundreds. More so than any Valve game (at least prior to *Dota 2*, covered in Chapter 20: eSports), the development of *Team Fortress 2* goes on and on: new weapons, new levels, new gametypes, new accessories, new achievements, new features and . . . new hats. All updates are free. And in 2011, the game itself became free.

➡ This kind of long-term development means that *Team Fortress 2* remains as fresh as its day of release, and the content therein has expanded so much that the sheer quantity is bewildering. Since release there have been over 200 updates for the game,

Team Fortress 2's visual style was developed around the idea that each class should have an instantly distinguishable silhouette – a goal that, despite the accumulation of hats over the years, is achieved with style.

twenty-nine new maps and numerous new pieces of equipment across the nine classes. And that's just the stuff Valve has made. The game's community has added much more, all easily accessible through Steam, and the best creators can make serious money through players buying 'stamps' to support them.

➲ It is almost incidental that *Team Fortress 2* is the best team-based multiplayer shooter around, one where every class suits a particular playstyle and changes the experience of playing to suit the individual. A lot of stuff ubiquitous to other shooters – grenades, assault rifles, recharging health, the straight deathmatch mode – just isn't here. *Team Fortress 2* doesn't use the genre's crutches, but absorbs and transforms the best of its inspirations: the original *Team Fortress* was a *Quake* mod, and the Scout and the Soldier are simply aspects of *Quake* turned into classes.

➲ *Team Fortress 2* is the purest embodiment of Valve's philosophy: listening to its audience, forever updating, always over-delivering. From the perspective of a gamer it's also the single best argument for Steam as a platform: it has averaged one update a fortnight over seven years, expanded and changed so much, yet remains at its core the same brilliant game.

➲ Valve provides endless sources of interest. To name a few: co-founder Gabe Newell is an inspiring speaker, whose genuinely benevolent instincts have somehow made his company one of the richest in gaming; its practice of hiring modders and community creators, rather than posh graduates; the sheer quality of every product it releases, and the satisfaction that comes with knowing it will be supported for a long time.

➲ Calling Valve the world's greatest games company would be pointless, of course, because such labels are meaningless. But they may well be in the top one.

Go Anywhere, Do Anything:
Grand Theft Auto

➔ A man stands on the corner of a bustling city. The passers-by ignore him, curving their walks around his position while traffic shifts in neat patterns and vendors hawk the day's papers. Suddenly the guy runs towards a slow-moving vehicle, yanks open the door and hurls its elderly occupant to the ground before taking off at high speed. 'Personal Jesus' by Depeche Mode booms from the speakers as the car careens into pedestrians, immediately attracting the attention of some nearby cops who give chase.

➔ The driving gets wilder, shots blow out tyres, and soon half the city's police force is boxing this maniac into a final showdown. A SWAT van rams the vehicle to a standstill, countless squad cars pull up, and before he can pull a gun the thief is blown away. The screen goes black and a few seconds later he walks out of hospital, ready to do it all over again. Welcome to the world of *Grand Theft Auto*.

The *Grand Theft Auto* series made its debut on the original PlayStation with four top-down 2D games. They were fun enough, and laid the foundations for what was to come, but no more than that. For *Grand Theft Auto* the change to a 3D setting was absolutely profound: it was always an open-world game, but giving that world a third dimension was the most important part of the equation.

➔ DMA Design's *Grand Theft Auto III* launched on the PlayStation 2 in October 2001 and did no less than create a new type of gaming experience. Here was a heaving city in 3D where you could drive from one side of the map to the other, with bustling sidewalks, busy roads and strangely familiar landmarks. It was an astonishing technical achievement, a visual marvel, but much more importantly it felt alive. Simply walking around you would overhear arguments, witness car crashes and bump into walls because you were so busy looking at something else.

The game had a structure and a story, told through cutscenes with better acting than most TV shows, but the missions weren't really the point. The attraction was that you could get into a car – any car – and simply drive where you wanted and see what you could see. While driving there's a selection of radio stations playing classic songs, a thread of pop culture that's impossible to disentangle from the tapestry of this virtual world and gives it an irresistible edge of realism.

Certain elements of *Grand Theft Auto III* leave something to be desired – the shooting controls, the occasional dull texture, and the inherent contradiction between its mission structure and the freeform play it encouraged. But to focus on this is to miss the wood for the trees because *Grand Theft Auto III* created an illusion of freedom that only its successors have managed to recreate, a sense that here was a place where you were the lead actor and the next scene was whatever you wished it to be. A car chase better than anything in the movies? Easy. The odd psychopathic rampage? Why not. And then sometimes you'd just drive out to the beach slowly, park up and stand there, taking it all in. The silent lead may have been your avatar, but this remarkable setting was the character you would return to again and again.

In one of the most impressive development feats of the modern era *Grand Theft Auto: Vice City* was released one year

Grand Theft Auto III, seen here in its PC incarnation, had a relatively conventional mission structure but that was the only thing conventional about its incredible open world. To this day no one has proved as adept as Rockstar North at pushing this genre of the medium forward.

A BRIEF HISTORY OF VIDEO GAMES

later, in October 2002. Rather than a straight sequel this transplanted the game from the murky Liberty City (New York) to the Miami of the 1980s – a world of pastel suits, scarlet Testarossas and neon lights.

→ *Vice City* is a kind of period parody piece, heavily inspired by *Miami Vice* and sending up the coke-fuelled excesses of that era in a blaze of disco tunes and palm trees. The casting of Ray Liotta as main character Tommy Vercetti gave the atmosphere a permanent tinge of the mafia, but the tone throughout is of profligate excess – speedboats, fast cars, and beautiful women – where crime is almost incidental to the fun. It is almost more 1980s than the 1980s, with the references piling up and the tunes as brilliantly selected as ever, and achieves the impossible by making *Grand Theft Auto III* feel dull by comparison.

→ *Grand Theft Auto: San Andreas* was released in October 2004 and the most impressive part about these games is that success, rather than making the developers complacent, drove them to even greater heights. Where the two previous entries had been set in cities, *San Andreas* was an entire state. Set in the early 1990s and loosely themed around the Los Angeles of that era, *San Andreas* traded organized crime for gangbangers and disco tunes for rap music.

→ *San Andreas* introduced light RPG elements to the series, with lead character

Grand Theft Auto: Vice City was all sun, sex and drugs, and where *Grand Theft Auto III* was happy to imitate a real city this sequel wanted to capture a specific time and place – which it did with enormous style. The ability to hire in A-list voice talent like Ray Liotta didn't hurt either.

CJ's body gradually changing to reflect the player's behaviour over time – if you were always eating fast food and drove everywhere, he'd put on weight, whereas running around and choosing the salad would keep him muscular and trim.

➔ What astonished about *San Andreas* was the sheer scale of the thing and the amount there was to do. There are more vehicles than ever: cars, buses, bikes, boats, planes, helicopters, motorbikes, trains and tanks can all be stolen. There are more side-jobs than ever: drive a cab or an ambulance, be a firefighter or a delivery man, burgle houses or become a pimp, or even steal a police car and take down crooks as a vigilante. CJ could swim and climb walls, making the environment more negotiable, and even elements like stealth were incorporated.

➔ There is nothing like *San Andreas*. It is a game where you can get in a vehicle and just drive for hours and hours, leaving the cities behind to hit the sticks and cruise. Its map is so big that it feels impossible to see everything, and makes it feel like the ultimate embodiment of *Grand Theft Auto*'s free-roaming design.

➔ *San Andreas* was somewhat overshadowed by one element removed from the final game. The fact that the *Grand Theft Auto* games allow players to break the law, drive over innocent bystanders and even shoot police officers means that ever since the originals there has been controversy. Such tabloid outrages, of course, ignore the fact that it would never occur to the vast majority of human beings to link virtual acts to their real-world equivalents, never mind be encouraged by a video game to go and jack a car.

➔ During development of *San Andreas* the ability to have sex with other characters was added as a minigame called 'Hot Coffee'. This was removed from the final product, but enterprising hackers discovered the

remaining code and released a patch that allowed players to access it on every platform – causing a major controversy that led to the game being temporarily withdrawn from sale and re-rated by the ESRB, and also led to a series of lawsuits against Rockstar and the game's publisher, Take-Two Interactive.

➡ Given that Hot Coffee is inaccessible without unauthorized modification of the game files this seems ludicrous, but the consequences for Rockstar were serious indeed and included a federal investigation. It is a great pity that the achievements of *San Andreas* will forever be twinned with this, though it does say something interesting about American cultural attitudes towards video games. Violence is fine, for the most part, but if you represent sex between consenting adults then a line has been crossed.

➡ The increase in power between the PS2 and PS3 generation of consoles was a mixed blessing for *Grand Theft Auto IV* (2008).

Grand Theft Auto: San Andreas focused on gangbangers, and with that came the series' finest villain to date in the vicious Officer Tenpenny, played by Samuel L. Jackson. Although nobody really plays a *Grand Theft Auto* game for the story, it is an area where the series has improved consistently over time.

This was in many ways a more stunning technical achievement than ever, particularly its incorporation of Euphoria physics, which means that characters in the world react in a bespoke way to every collision – drive up to someone slowly and they'll put their hands on the car bonnet; throw a bunch of people downstairs and each fall will look different.

➡ *Grand Theft Auto IV* returns to *Grand Theft Auto III*'s Liberty City, and the increase in graphical fidelity means this is a place of unparalleled detail and atmosphere. It also means that *Grand Theft Auto IV*'s aesthetic is much more tonally dark than the previous games – as the visuals move closer to realism, the cartoony excess of the PS2 era's more angular characters is lost. This tallied with the game's narrative, which concentrates on Eastern European immigrant Niko Bellic trying to start afresh and being dragged into the underworld, and adds up to a markedly more mature atmosphere than the previous titles.

Grand Theft Auto IV – 'Faux York' by Dead End Thrills. The jump in hardware allowed a level of visual fidelity far beyond the *Grand Theft Auto* trilogy, and Rockstar North took advantage better than any of the competition. (Courtesy of Dead End Thrills)

➔ It is also even more of an incredible soundscape, with many more ambient noises everywhere: pedestrians shouting, cars honking, waves lapping, train tracks rattling and engines humming. Almost every mechanical aspect of the game is improved, with vastly superior car handling, a tweaked combat system and a range of textures that mean you almost never see the same thing twice. This doesn't mean that *Grand Theft Auto IV* lacks craziness – you can still jack any car you see and drive off piers, or crash a helicopter into the Statue of Liberty.

➔ Or you can – for the first time – play with a friend. *Grand Theft Auto IV* comes with a wide range of multiplayer modes but by far the most compelling option is simply being in a world like this with someone you know, their avatar sitting next to yours, and chatting over headsets. It is a quite surreal experience to go for a drive with your mate through a virtual city, and certainly makes car chases more exciting. And there's nothing quite like taking them up to the top of the world in a helicopter – and then jumping out of the pilot's seat.

➔ *Grand Theft Auto IV* was such a leap for the series that *Grand Theft Auto V* (2013) almost felt retrograde, simply for being more of the same. It is a brilliant game, particularly if it's your first *Grand Theft Auto* experience, and received the usual rapturous critical reception – but for the first time it felt like Rockstar North was going through the motions and didn't know how to improve on or change the basic design. The use of three protagonists, between whom you can switch on-the-fly, is a nice touch, there are still sights in this world that cannot be seen elsewhere and the production values are among the best in gaming – the only major disappointment is a botched multiplayer mode.

➔ The *Grand Theft Auto* series has sold

Grand Theft Auto IV – 'Burning Chroma' by Dead End Thrills. The PC version of *Grand Theft Auto IV* benefits enormously from the modding community, which has kept it looking better than many games released today. (Courtesy of Dead End Thrills)

Grand Theft Auto IV – 'Elevation' by Dead End Thrills. Rockstar North understands better than any other developer that cities are not built in straight lines or on flat surfaces. (Courtesy of Dead End Thrills)

more than 150 million games, a number that increases every month (and will get another boost when *Grand Theft Auto V* is re-released on PS4 and Xbox One). The games have evolved while keeping a core of freeform exploration that simply isn't matched in any other medium. A cynic could pick faults with many of its less important mechanics, but ultimately it doesn't matter that the shooting's average, the melee combat's worse, the characters clichéd and the humour infantile. What matters about *Grand Theft Auto* is none of these things.

● Unlike any games before or since, the *Grand Theft Auto* series creates an illusion of freedom and understands that making an open world full of tools and then letting players loose is one of the most enjoyable and empowering forms a video game can take. Where other games structure themselves along linear paths, with the occasional fork, *Grand Theft Auto* is a gigantic road network.

Grand Theft Auto V saw a return to San Andreas and a new twist in multiple protagonists – which allows the player to switch from one to another and 'teleport' huge distances across the map without breaking immersion.

● In concert with the extraordinary depth and quality of its licensed soundtrack, driving in *Grand Theft Auto* is at its best a semi-transcendental kind of immersion, one where the player leaves their world behind and gets lost in quite another. You are behind the wheel, the road stretches onwards, the world streams into existence and – is that the cops? Perfect.

Indie-pendence

The omnipresence of the internet, and as a result the number of PCs connected to it, has seen a flourishing of independent development. In a way this harks to the earliest days of home computers like the ZX80, when anyone who was able to program a game and get it into shops could become a developer – this is where the term 'bedroom coder' comes from. The key differences after the turn of the millennium were the tools available to make a game and the global distribution the internet allows.

In 1999 Dutch computer scientist Mark Overmars released a program called Animo, which was initially used to create 2D animations easily. But thanks to a powerful built-in scripting language, it soon became much more. Animo evolved into GameMaker, a program that through a drag-and-drop interface and its own simplified 'coding' language allowed people with no experience or knowledge of coding to create a functional video game.

GameMaker was a niche interest for a time but its growth in the early 2000s caused Overmars to seek help in expanding the program and he entered into a partnership with Dundee's YoYo Games in 2007. Since this point YoYo has transformed GameMaker into an incredibly powerful tool capable of constructing, depending on the user's expertise, nearly any type of game imaginable. Not just this, it incorporates image-editing software and most recently a marketplace where artists and programmers can sell their work directly to wannabe developers (for example, a tileset or a pack of character sprites).

There are countless GameMaker success stories. Perhaps the finest game made using the tool is *Spelunky* (2009, HD version 2012), a 2D platformer that constructs its world on roguelike principles – offering a challenge that's different every time and an endlessly

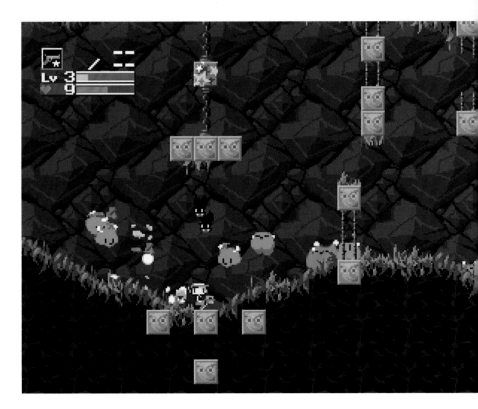

Cave Story was released
as freeware in 2004 after
five years' work by its sole
developer Daisuke 'Pixel'
Amaya. It is a homage to
games like *Metroid* and
Castlevania yet, unlike many
other games of this ilk,
rises above them by virtue
of its mysterious story and
affecting characters.

surprising world to explore. Former *PC Gamer* journalist Tom Francis developed *Gunpoint* (2013), a puzzle-platformer built around the main character's 'Crosslink' device, which allows the rewiring of elements within the environments – the game was successful enough that Francis was able to become a full-time developer. Other notables include Jonatan Söderström's *Hotline Miami* (2012), a violent top-down shooter, and Vertigo Gaming's *Cook, Serve, Delicious* (2014), a game about getting customers' food orders correct and improving your restaurant.

➲ GameMaker is the most fully featured tool available to developers, but there are others with a more narrow focus. Chris Klimas's Twine was released in 2009, an open-source tool that enables the easy creation of multiple-choice text adventures – which allows not just the creation of entire games but rapid prototyping of ideas, and has seen thousands of works. Twine's capabilities have subsequently evolved to incorporate more complex visual tricks, and its low barrier to entry surpasses even GameMaker in allowing anyone who can type a sentence to create a functional video game.

➲ There are other specialized programs, such as RPG Maker, but tools are only half the story. Regardless of what independent developers are using to create their games, and many of course are excellent programmers with no need of GameMaker, the real difference is in the ability to sell directly to players and through this create what would traditionally have been considered niche or risky titles.

➲ Lucas Pope's *Papers, Please* (2013) casts the player as a border guard in the fictional dystopia of Arstotzka – checking the papers of people who want to come through for expiration dates, fraud and false pictures. This may sound dull but it's a riveting experience that builds an affecting world

Super Meat Boy, developed by Edmund McMillen and Tommy Refenes, is a pixel-perfect precision platformer that features simply gorgeous controls and a good deal of nostalgic humour for the 8- and 16-bit era of home consoles.

World of Goo's unique visual style and gameplay mechanic, which involves connecting balls of goo to build structures and traverse the environments, saw it become one of the first high-profile indie hits.

through humanizing the player's character. This individual has a family to support and will be financially punished for failing to do his job properly so, though certain NPCs may tug at your heartstrings with pleas to be allowed through, the ever-present tension is how much you can get away with without turning off the heating.

➜ Similarly cheery is Richard Hofmeier's *Cart Life* (2011), a narrative life simulation where the player chooses one of three characters to control. All have dead-end jobs, few prospects, and a series of personal problems that range from having to walk their daughter to and from school to a smoking habit. Although *Cart Life*'s mechanics can occasionally grate this is part of its overall effect – after all, work isn't fun – and its miniature portraits of modern living can be devastating to feel unfolding.

➜ The greatest indie success story is without a doubt *Minecraft* (2009). Swedish developer

Markus Persson, better known by the handle 'Notch', was a compulsive player of games and, like all great artists, something of a magpie. His first major production *Wurm Online* (2007), co-developed with Rolf Jansson, was a 3D MMOG where everything in the world was created by players and, despite its sometimes obtuse mechanics and time-demanding nature, offered a genuinely open way of playing – some players fought all the time, others built peaceful cabins by babbling brooks, some ran large kingdoms.

➜ *Minecraft* was inspired by several games, among them the roguelike *Dwarf Fortress* (2006) and most obviously American developer Zachary Barth's *Infiniminer* (2009) – a world constructed from large cubes that players could mine through, discovering materials and treasure from which they could construct new objects. Persson loved the game and spent hours experimenting with what it allowed, finally deciding that his next

Jason Rohrer's *The Castle Doctrine* is a home-defence simulator based around the sense of paranoia during the Reaganite era, and the creator's memory of his father buying home security equipment. The player builds a house to protect their family and a vault, but when offline or 'out' of the house other players can attempt to burgle it.

Richard Hofmeier's *Cart Life* was released in 2011 and casts the player as one of three street vendors who has to make a living while dealing with the trials of everyday life – such as a smoking addiction, family troubles and money worries.

project would be something similar.

At the time Persson had a day job with Swedish developer King.com and later jAlbum, but began working on what would become *Minecraft* in the evenings and weekends. The first prototype was built quickly, and Persson decided to charge for it as a way to keep himself motivated – with the idea that early purchasers would get the game for half-price, with all future updates free of charge. From this point it snowballed.

The core of *Minecraft* is creation. In each game the world is procedurally generated as the player explores it, and they begin with basic tools that can be used to mine blocks, gain materials and eventually construct other objects. It is a first-person experience where the highly stylized visuals occasionally verge on abstraction but allow a huge draw distance, and the two most important aspects are that it can be played cooperatively and it can be modified by users.

As sales increased Persson was able to quit his job and concentrate on the game full time, meaning it was constantly updated with new materials, new features and new modes. Word-of-mouth quickly spread that this was something special, helped no end by the images and videos of what players had constructed in their own *Minecraft* worlds – towering castles, replicas of real-world towns and phallic monuments.

Although *Minecraft* is easy to play from the start, its crafting system offers considerable depth and scales up as players become more familiar with its world. More importantly it is a universe where cooperation is not just great fun but almost mandatory in order to create truly impressive structures or embark on the toughest adventures. The aesthetic is also uncommonly beautiful when combined with the game's day/night cycle, which gradually changes the style of lighting around the world as you're playing – there's

Fez by Phil Fish is a beautifully constructed '2D' world where the player can rotate the environment to navigate. Filled with genuinely tough puzzles and enormous attention to detail, it's a masterpiece.

nothing quite like finishing a job, standing back with your friends to admire it and watching the sun rise on the horizon.

 There is much more to *Minecraft*, but the game's openness to mods is what turned it into a craze – particularly among young children, for whom this is an inexpensive one-time purchase that proves infinitely extendable. The available mods are simply too numerous to cover in any comprehensive fashion but range from simple thematic reworkings such as Tropicraft, which makes the world like a tropical island, to more complex additions like Mo' Creatures, which adds over forty new types of creatures to the world and allows players to tame and ride certain of them.

 In this sense *Minecraft* has become more of a platform than a single game. The Tekkit pack, for example, combines several popular mods that together utterly change the experience – Galacticraft adds spaceships

Minecraft's magic is in the joy of construction but this is then multiplied by the addition of friends. Building anything from a small hut to a giant temple is simply a matter of gathering the resources and putting in the hours, and many hands make light work.

and the ability to travel into space; Modular Powersuits allows the creation of configurable outfits with special powers; Buildcraft allows the creation of factories through systems like pipes and pumps; Thermal Expansion makes factories even more sophisticated with options like ore refiners and energy conduits; MineFactory Reloaded then lets you automate some of these processes; if it all gets too much, use Dimensional Doors to create your own pocket dimension and get away from it all.

➲ The obvious fact that mods are user-created also allows *Minecraft*'s young player base to create things that a more official framework would stop. The lawyers may not like it but it's hard to see what harm Pixelmon – which adds a variety of stylized Pokémon – does to Nintendo's bottom line, and it lets kids combine two of their favourite things.

➲ *Minecraft* is a cultural phenomenon, though its current status may not continue forever. In September 2014 Persson announced that he had sold Mojang, the developer established thanks to *Minecraft*'s success, to Microsoft for $2.5 billion – this certainly demonstrates the size of the game's success, but also the negative side of it. Despite being a community-focused developer, and *Minecraft* being better value than almost any other game in history, Persson found the pressures of being held individually responsible for every aspect of it intolerable.

➲ What Microsoft will do with *Minecraft* remains to be seen, although it is difficult to imagine the notoriously controlling Redmond giant keeping the game as open as it has been. Nevertheless *Minecraft* stands as a singular achievement, not just proof that one independent developer can change the world of interactive entertainment, but a testament to the creativity and passion of its young audience. If *Minecraft*'s future is as bright as its present, it will be because the players build it.

Continue?

27

The landscape of interactive entertainment is ever-shifting, and now is the most exciting time to be a gamer. Technology improves every year but has now reached a baseline where the creativity and skills of developers are more important than their ability to squeeze a game into limited amounts of memory. The future is now not so much about the representational side of video games – the look, the worlds, the sound effects – as it is about submerged qualities, particularly AI and the psychology of playing.

In the future the 'big three' console manufacturers will remain Microsoft, Nintendo and Sony, with Nintendo the odd one out in its focus on creating hardware with original interfaces. The Wii U (2012) is the successor system to Wii, so-named because Nintendo believed it had created a brand strong enough to support a consumer upgrade path (compare to the manner in which Apple names iPhones: 4, 4S, etc.). Wii U is the opposite of Wii in having a complex interface, the Gamepad, a large controller with dual analogue sticks, various buttons and a touchscreen.

Sadly the Wii brand wasn't as strong as Nintendo thought and Wii U is currently languishing with just over nine million systems sold after two years. Nintendo's software is as strong as ever, with excellent first-party games like *Super Mario 3D World* (2013) and *Mario Kart 8* (2014), continuing popular series like *Wii Sports Club* (2013) and *Wii Fit U* (2013), alongside third-party gems like *ZombiU* (2012), *Monster Hunter 3U* (2013) and the superb *Bayonetta 2* (2014).

This situation results in occasional calls for Nintendo to abandon the home-console market to focus on its bestselling handhelds and on developing games for the growing mobile market. Such perspectives greatly underestimate Nintendo's commitment to the console business (as well as its

Director Shinji Mikami returned to his survival horror roots with *The Evil Within* and used the opportunity to take stock of his career by drawing many obvious parallels with the *Resident Evil* series (not least in the title). Such unexpected reflections will only become more common as today's great creators age.

Alien: Isolation – 'The Hitcher'
by Dead End Thrills. The
Creative Assembly's take on
the *Alien* licence emphasized
the powerlessness of main
character Amanda Ripley
against the Alien, in contrast
to previous takes on the
licence, which had you
mowing down xenomorphs.
(Courtesy of Dead End Thrills)

enormous cash reserves) and the sheer quality of the software it develops – the nature of Nintendo's hardware is now to take risks, rather than confronting Microsoft and Sony head-on, so one 'failed' console is an inevitable price of this approach and extremely unlikely to discourage further attempts. Nintendo remains the single strongest developer and publisher in the entire industry, capable of supporting its own platforms almost single-handedly, and it would take multiple catastrophes over many years to seriously threaten this independence.

➲ Microsoft and Sony continue to pursue a dream of being the 'all-in-one home entertainment box'. Both the PlayStation 4 (2013) and Xbox One (2013) offer cutting-edge visuals, online subscription services and slick digital storefronts, but they also act as multimedia centres capable of streaming movies and television. The PS4's controller incorporates a touchscreen, and the console

firmware allows for screenshots to be taken easily and gameplay to be streamed to Twitch – the latter a simple but effective idea also implemented on Xbox One after launch.

➲ Xbox One's interface was initially based around a standard controller and the Kinect peripheral: a motion-tracking camera that allows the console and games to respond to gestures and voice commands. Kinect was launched near the end of the Xbox 360's life to considerable commercial success, although it then failed to deliver quality software and its popularity tailed off dramatically. Microsoft, unfortunately, screwed up the Xbox One's pre-launch hype so badly that the console is currently being outsold two to one by PS4 – in essence Xbox One's initial design 'locked' games to user's accounts in an effort to kill the second-hand market, and required constant server authentication to operate. These features and others were widely perceived as anti-consumer and a huge

Japan's Platinum Games are arguably the greatest action-game developer in the world, its most recent production being *Bayonetta 2* for Wii U. Having set a new standard with almost every game it releases, the only thing that remains to be seen is whether Platinum will branch into other genres.

backlash saw them removed – but damage was done and the first major casualty was Kinect, abandoned to allow a price cut for the console.

➡ Thanks to this change neither console offers especially innovative interfaces or, at the time of writing, software. This is no great criticism: it is impossible for hardware to make a leap comparable to the original PlayStation era's 3D shift, and boundary-pushing software often takes time to arrive. And its easy to forget that while a game like *Titanfall* (2014) is a familiar shooter with added bells and whistles, incremental improvements often make great differences to established genres.

➡ The best example of this is Bungie's *Destiny* (2014), which plays much like the studio's *Halo* games but incorporates a new style of persistent multiplayer. While exploring its huge environments and battling enemies, other players will simply 'appear' with no loading screens or break in the action, allowing you to briefly team-up on the fly. The levelling system is also designed to gradually drive players towards multiplayer, with high-level content dependent on cooperation and rewarding participants with better armour and weapons. Destiny's core mechanics are familiar but the structure demonstrates how improving and refining a genre piece can make a huge difference to the experience.

➡ Early titles have also tackled more controversial subject matter. *Metal Gear Solid: Ground Zeroes* (2014) takes as its subject prison camps like those at Guantanamo Bay and Abu Ghraib. The increasing realism of the game's visual style tallies with a more mature subject matter and certain aspects of *Ground Zeroes*'s setting, such as tapes recording the torture of prisoners, are genuinely shocking. *Metal Gear Solid* has always had a deep undercurrent of scepticism about the modern military-industrial complex, while at the

Goichi Suda and his studio Grasshopper Manufacture are one of Japan's most striking and visually inventive studios but the recent *Killer is Dead* was a disappointment. Suda has always held the promise of a truly great game but is yet to definitively deliver.

same time fetishizing aspects of it, and with upcoming title *The Phantom Pain* being set in Afghanistan this characteristic is being pushed to the fore.

⊘ Such a topic may be self-reflective. An increasingly prominent part of mainstream shooters, the biggest genre around, is their links to real-world arms manufacturers. Each entry in the *Call of Duty* series has an age rating of either 15 or 18, yet is extremely popular among young teenagers and features near-perfect recreations of guns such as the Barrett M82 sniper rifle. These are commercial arrangements undertaken to grant the games a veneer of authenticity, to familiarize the players with a particular brand of hardware and to create certain associations in the mind about that particular gun.

⊘ 'We want to know explicitly how the rifle is to be used, ensuring that we are shown in a positive light,' says Ralph Vaughn, who negotiates game deals for gun manufacturer Barrett. 'Such as the "good guys" using the rifle.' This means that ideally the weapon will only be used 'by US law enforcement or US military' and certainly not 'used by individuals, organizations, countries or companies that would be shown as enemies of the United States or its citizens'.49

⊘ This is obviously an issue particularly relevant to video games in the USA, where gun ownership is legal and players may well be able to go out and buy their favourite 'virtual' weapon. It is an intersection of fantasy violence and real hardware that many find uncomfortable, one that gives a distinctly political edge to certain shooters, and yet it also gives a virtual experience that sheen of authenticity. The simple fact is that a large number of the most popular video games are still based on the central idea of shooting lots of people. Gun licensing in and of itself is a symptom of wider cultural issues rather than a problem specific to video games, but

Remember Me – 'Food for Thoughts' by Dead End Thrills. Set in a futuristic vision of Paris, *Remember Me* ultimately flattered to deceive but had plenty of interesting ideas and took risks. (Courtesy of Dead End Thrills)

it will only become more prevalent as the audience increases and the virtual parallels to real-world hardware or scenarios become more obvious.

● One of the biggest problems faced by developers in the future is this drive towards high-definition visuals at increasing resolutions. As visuals become more detailed and production values shoot up, so the costs spiral. There is no easy solution: while games improve in a linear fashion to an outside observer, and often in small steps, the work required to make even an average title increases exponentially. Big third-party publishers like Activision and Electronic Arts are historically notorious for treating developers poorly, demanding ex-tremely long hours at certain stages (referred to as 'crunch') and sometimes shuttering large studios at the close of projects.

● Industry working conditions are obviously outside the scope of this book but the impact of spiralling costs are seen in all blockbuster games. A smart example of how one developer has dealt with this is *P.T.*, the 'Playable Trailer' for a new entry in Konami's *Silent Hill* franchise. *P.T.* uses one beautifully rendered environment repeatedly, with the player walking through a small section of a house and, at the end, walking through a door that takes them back to the corridor's beginning.

● This structure suits a horror game extremely well. The setting of *P.T.* quickly becomes familiar to the player and thus the minor and major changes that occur with each repetition have more impact – it is particularly restrained in using traditional 'jump' scares, meaning that when something does happen the player is so unprepared and comfortable in the environment that the shock is commensurately greater. Obviously *P.T.*'s strategy wouldn't work for every game, and it may well wear thin if used over a longer

Shadows of Mordor – 'Slayer' by Dead End Thrills. Licensed titles remain enormously big business for the video-games industry, and among the dross are high-quality exceptions like *Shadow of Mordor*. Its key feature is a dynamic 'nemesis' system that promotes enemies who strike you down. (Courtesy of Dead End Thrills)

duration, but it is an example of a creative solution to a problem that every major title will have to confront.

→ In a more general sense the next technical frontier for developers is AI, and this is likely to remain a focus for many years to come. There are many different varieties relevant to video games: the AI of enemy combatants, such that they fight in a 'realistic' manner and provide an enjoyable challenge; the AI of 'companion' NPCs with whom the player interacts; and the AI of NPCs that are there to give the world texture. Within this are many more subdivisions, such as the distinction between an AI that will accompany the player through a game and one that will be seen in only a brief sequence. It is not just about AI reacting to a player's actions, but the sense of immersion they create through these actions. Entire games like *The Last of Us* are built around the player forming a bond with an NPC, yet the AI of this particular NPC, Elie, fell so short of expectations that developer Naughty Dog was forced to make her 'invisible' to enemies in order to ship the game, rather shattering the illusion.

→ How AI responds to player input is the problem, because players are so unpredictable, but solutions may lie in the much greater range of feedback and hardware to which developers now have access. Particularly interesting are player-facing cameras and headsets that can be used to track expressions associated with certain emotions. Certain hardware is able to not only track physical movements (such as where the eyes are focused), but also measure a player's galvanic skin response (electrical conductance), the electrical activity on the scalp (electroencephalography), pulse rate and much more. This means, in simple terms, games will soon be able to 'read' players' emotions and, in theory, alter characters and the world to respond to this. The applications for certain genres, like RPGs or horror games, are obvious, but it is more likely that such sophisticated technology will enable styles of play yet to be conceived. Everything about such hardware, of course, depends on consumer take-up.

→ Whether players will like something, and of course buy it in droves, is always the million-dollar question. One piece of future tech that has resoundingly answered is the Oculus Rift, an upcoming virtual reality headset that incorporates head- and position-tracking to create astonishingly immersive and persuasive environments. While using one to play space shooter *EVE: Valkyrie*, I genuinely forgot about the world outside, utterly lost in the illusion, and at a point where the ship turned upside-down almost fell out of the chair at my body's slight panic.

→ There is no question that the Oculus Rift 'works' in a manner that no previous virtual reality headset has managed, and an overwhelmingly successful kickstarter campaign saw the prototype funded – after which, Facebook acquired the developer and technology in a deal totalling $2.3 billion. Facebook's goals for the Oculus Rift are likely to be much more oriented towards creating the next level of 3D social interaction, but this will still be a consumer device with huge implications for gaming's future.

→ The Oculus Rift is now one of many upcoming virtual reality headsets, and will be competing with Sony's Project Morpheus and Valve's currently unnamed hardware. Each will allow developers to create a level of visual immersion never before possible, though this goes hand-in-hand with the aforementioned spiralling costs and means that the yet-to-be-tested consumer appetite will be the key. It is not so long since 3D in cinemas, TVs and gaming was heralded as the next big thing and heavily pushed by the likes of Sony, but ultimately rejected by the mainstream, and virtual reality hardware has a history of flattering to deceive – nevertheless, it is coming in a quality and manner unlike ever before.

➤ One final note on virtual reality. It is a technology that offers new possibilities for player immersion, and certain concepts seem to simply beg to be applied – such as a Superman game where the player can soar through the skies of Metropolis. But it is also so convincing an effect, in this generation of technology, that it may have unforeseen consequences on the design of traditionally popular games. For example Valve has a series of developer guidelines for anyone making demos for their hardware, prime among which is the instruction never to decapitate the player – this effect, when a player is immersed in a convincing other world, simply freaks out and upsets people. There is also the fact that you have to wear a headset and shut out the world, which is a pretty big ask from an entertainment product. I say this not to pooh-pooh virtual reality, because it is coming and it will be big, but to warn against considering it as the dominant future of video games, when it is much more likely to be simply another (amazing) way to enjoy them.

➤ This fragmentation can be seen across the industry writ large, simply because it is getting bigger every year. My generation grew up with video games as a part of the cultural fabric and has seen them evolve from rudimentary 2D diversions into sophisticated 3D worlds. Certain themes always have and always will remain, like shooting – simply because it is a fun and understandable way of interacting with certain scenarios. But these too have evolved beyond recognition: the progression from *Doom*, where your sole interaction is shooting monsters, to games as diverse as *Fallout 3* or *Gone Home* is profound.

➤ The earliest video games may have been

Super Mario Galaxy – 'Galaxian' by Dead End Thrills. (Courtesy of Dead End Thrills)

Spec Ops: The Line – 'Trapdoors' by Dead End Thrills. This 2012 entry in a long-running military first-person shooter series remains the high watermark for narrative in the genre, which is perhaps the industry's most profitable niche. Based loosely on *Heart of Darkness*, it is anything but a gung-ho adventure. (Courtesy of Dead End Thrills)

A BRIEF HISTORY OF VIDEO GAMES

designed in the late 1940s and early 1950s, but it was decades before video games became an industry and a new medium for creative expression. Video games are young. They are the only artform in human history predicated on interaction as well as interpretation – you and I may disagree over what a painting means, but our eyes see the same physical object. If we play *Skyrim*, on the other hand, each of our journeys will be dictated by the choices made along the way – the same game's elements will offer a different experience to every one of its players.

➤ Oscar Wilde posited that, through interpretation, the critic becomes the artist – he or she, by intensifying the mysteries of a great work and embellishing upon them, created ideas and new life from their subject. This is the core of how video games work. Every single copy of a game is identical, and yet what each player will do with that data is different. To continue with our last example, *Skyrim* is hailed for being a beautiful and vast fantasy adventure, but personally I find it more fun to steal villagers' clothes, leaving them in their underwear, and use magical blasts to send cows tumbling down the sides of mountains.

➤ The greatest video games contain multitudes and allow their players to assume all roles: hero, villain, trickster, tinkerer, god and slave. It doesn't matter if a game's structure is linear or open: the simple fact of allowing play creates a freeform space in even the most tightly controlled experience. In this, video games serve as both playgrounds and mirrors, idle distractions and life-consuming alternative worlds.

➤ And this is just the start. The future of video games is impossible to predict, but it will be both surprising and deliciously fun. As ever, all we'll ever have to do is press start to continue.

Notes

1 The Prehistory of Video Games

1 'Garry Kasparov plays 1950s chess program by computing founder Alan Turing', *BBC* (25 June 2012), http://www.bbc.co.uk/news/uk-england-manchester-18584312. NB Throughout, all quotes that are not otherwise credited are from interviews, conversations and correspondence with the author.
2 Christopher Strachey would go on to develop a 'love-letter generator' for the Manchester Mark 1 computer, often considered the first piece of computational art.
3 C. S. Strachey, 'Logical or non-mathematical programmes', *Proceedings of the 1952 ACM National Meeting* (Association for Computing Machinery, 1952).
4 The Manchester Small-Scale Experimental Machine (SSEM, but nicknamed 'Baby') was truly the first stored-program computer, but was built as a proof-of-concept for an early form of computer memory, the Williams tube, and so was more prototype than finished product.
5 John Anderson, 'Tennis for Two: The Story of an Early Computer Game', *Pong-Story* (no date), http://www.pong-story.com/1958.htm.
6 The scientist Charly Adama created a program called 'Bouncing Ball' for the Massachusetts Institute of Technology's Whirlwind Computer in 1950. This also used an oscilloscope for display but was not, alas, interactive.

2 Baer's Brown Box

7 Ralph Baer, *Videogames: In the Beginning* (Rolenta Press, 2005). The following pages are indebted to Baer's account.
8 Another idea Baer had in relation to TelePrompTer was to make the team's 'Computer Quiz' software work with a broadcast quiz show, using archive footage. Although the technology worked in theory and the idea was patented, this was another idea ahead of its time.

3 Spacewar!

9 Stewart Brand, 'Fanatic Life and Symbolic Death Among the Computer Bums', *Rolling Stone* (7 December 1972).
10 'The Untold Atari Story', *Edge*, 200 (April 2009).
11 Benji Edwards, 'Computer Space and the Dawn of the Arcade Video Game', *Technologizer* (11 December 2011), http://www.technologizer.com/2011/12/11/computer-space-and-the-dawn-of-the-arcade-video-game.
12 Bill Pitts, 'The Galaxy Game', *Stanford University* (25 October 2007), http://infolab.stanford.edu/pub/voy/museum/galaxy.html.

4 Atari's Born

13 Ted Dabney felt that he didn't want to run a large business. He accepted a payoff of around $250,000, plus stock in the company and the profitable pinball route. From here on in, Bushnell glossed over Dabney's role in the formation of Atari, even pretending he had built the *Computer Space* prototype in his own daughter's bedroom, and presented himself as the sole visionary.

14 Tristan Donovan, *Replay: The History of Videogames* (Yellow Ant, 2010), p.34.
15 The Odyssey's 'Game Circuits' got here first, albeit with much more rudimentary technology, but were woefully undersold by Magnavox suppliers and never achieved any kind of presence.

5 VES vs VCS

16 Jerry Lawson's opinions on the competition. : 'The Odyssey was a joke as far as I'm concerned . . . it had no intelligence. And it had overlays, remember?' The company RCA would later release a competitor to the Video Entertainment System. 'It was a piece of junk . . . They had this game – it was in black and white. It looked horrible.' These and further quotes from Jerry Lawson: Benji Edwards, 'VC&G Interview: Jerry Lawson, Black Video Game Pioneer', *Vintage Computing & Games* (24 February 2009), http://www.vintagecomputing.com/index.php/archives/545.

6 Oregon Trail

17 Jessica Lussenhop, 'Oregon Trail: How Three Minnesotans Forged Its Path', *Citypages* (19 January 2011), http://www.citypages.com/2011-01-19/news/oregon-trail-how-three-minnesotans-forged-its-path.

7 A Tale of Two Adventures

18 Julian Dibbell, 'A Marketable Wonder', *Topic Magazine* (Autumn 2002), http://www.juliandibbell.com/texts/cavespace.html.
19 This and further William Crowther quotes: 'William Crowther Interview', *Internet Archive* (1994), https://archive.org/details/WillCrowtherInterview.
20 Julian Dibbell draws a line between Crowther and Stephen Bishop, a nineteenth-century slave who first explored, mapped and named the Mammoth cave system. 'The map documented more than Bishop's keen spatial memory, though. It also recorded the colorful names he'd given his discoveries: Fairy Grotto, Little Bat Room . . . For Bishop, clearly, it wasn't enough just to map the material structure of the cave's passages and chambers. Its shape, after all, wasn't only topographical. It was fanciful as well, a network of mythic resonances and poetic leaps that had occurred to Bishop and his occasional companions as they'd explored – and that the names helped keep alive in his mind. They made his memory of the cave more vivid, and they fixed in words and images his delight in the spaces he had found.' Dibbell, 'A Marketable Wonder'.
21 A neat footnote to such tricks was that some later hacker lingo was derived from *Adventure*, specifically the magic word 'XYZZY' and 'vadding', drawn from a rearrangement of ADV (i.e. ADVENT) used to avoid those pesky university administrators.
22 Woods obtained Crowther's permission before making changes to *Adventure*, and got in touch by the simple strategy of emailing 'crowther' at every domain name then in existence. Woods correctly banked on Crowther being an unusual enough name that such carpet-bombing would get through.

23 This and further Warren Robinett quotes: Alistair Wallis, 'Playing Catch Up: *Adventure*'s Warren Robinett', *Gamasutra* (29 March 2007), http://web.archive.org/web/2007018072813/http://gamasutra.com/php-bin/news_index.php?story=13280.

11 The Rise of Nintendo

24 This and further Shigeru Miyamoto quotes: David Sheff, *Game Over: Press Start to Continue* (Random House, 1993).

12 Simpatico

25 Kieron Gillen, 'Making of: The Sims', *RockPaperShotgun* (18 January 2008), http://www.rockpapershotgun.com/2008/01/18/making-of-the-sims.

13 Doom 101

26 Steve Colley, 'Stories from the Maze War 30-year Retrospective: Steve Colley's Story of the Original Maze', *DigiBarn Computer Museum* (no date), http://www.digibarn.com/history/04-VCF7-MazeWar/stories/colley.html.

14 The Console War

27 'Interview: Tom Kalinske', *Sega-16* (11 July 2006), http://www.sega-16.com/2006/07/interview-tom-kalinske.

15 The 'Nintendo' PlayStation

28 'Atari Corporation Form 10-K Annual Report' (1995), *United States Securities and Exchange Commission*, http://google.brand.edgar-online.com/EFX_dll/EDGARprodll?FetchFilingHTML1?ID=261582&SessionID=PwW3W68chGZucz7.
29 Reiji Asakura, *Revolutionaries at Sony* (McGraw-Hill, 2000), p.82.
30 The *Sakura Wars* series is long-running in Japan but only one title has been released in the west – *Sakura Wars: So Long, My Love* (Wii, 2010). Although its focus on relationships may sound a little odd, and is probably the reason publishers are hesitant to release the games in the west, this is a deep strategy series with a surprisingly good sense of humour.
31 After this Sonic Team developed *Burning Rangers* (1998) for the Saturn, an original take on 3D environments, casting the player as a cross between a firefighter and a Power Ranger.
32 Asakura, *Revolutionaries at Sony*.
33 The biggest compliment to the N64 pad is that, almost immediately after launch, Sony discontinued its original PlayStation pad and released the 'Dualshock', which added two analogue sticks. This design remains relatively unchanged right up to the PlayStation 4, and is far from the only 'inspiration' Sony has taken from its venerable competitor.

16 A Dream Dies

34 Douglass C. Perry, 'The Rise and Fall of the Dreamcast', *Gamasutra* (2009), http://www.gamasutra.com/view/feature/4128/the_rise_and_fall_of_the_dreamcast.php?print=1.

17 An Ugly Motherfucker

35 Ellie Gibson, 'PS2: The Insider's Story', *Eurogamer* (1 February 2013), http://www.eurogamer.net/articles/2010-11-24-ps2-the-insiders-story-article?page=2.
36 'The Making of Xbox', *Edge* (21 May 2013), http://www.edge-online.com/features/the-making-of-xbox.
37 This and further Kevin Bachus quotes: Patrick Garratt, 'The Xbox Story', VG24/7 (4 August 2011), http://www.vg247.com/2011/08/04/the-xbox-story-part-3-going-public.
38 One of Sega's first fantastic games as a third party, *Super Monkey Ball* sees you guide a monkey in a ball over platforms suspended in midair, trying not to fall off. The real highlight, though, was the mode Monkey Target, where you start off flying and then close the ball to try and land on scoring zones far below.
39 Later examples built on much more sophisticated technology, such as *Bioshock Infinite* and *The Last of Us*, abdicate responsibility by making the escorted character invulnerable and invisible to enemies in almost all situations.

18 Pocket Monsters: The History of Handhelds

40 The Wonderswan was the final piece of video-game hardware designed by Gunpei Yokoi. After the failure of the Virtual Boy he had left Nintendo and concentrated on making a Game Boy competitor. The Wonderswan was a gorgeous machine that combined a bright LCD screen with good battery life and some great software, but it never really troubled the Game Boy family of handhelds. Yokoi, one of gaming's great pioneers, died in a car accident in 1997 just before the Wonderswan's release.

19 Mobile Gaming

41 Maeve Duggan, 'Cell Phone Activities 2013', *PewResearch* (19 September 2013), http://www.pewinternet.org/2013/09/19/cell-phone-activities-2013; Lee Rainie and Aaron Smith, 'Tablet and E-reader Ownership Update', *PewResearch* (18 October 2013), http://www.pewinternet.org/2013/10/18/tablet-and-e-reader-ownership-update.

20 eSports

42 Estimate by Xfire in John Gaudiosi, 'Riot Games' League of Legends Officially Becomes Most Played PC Game in the World', *Forbes* (11 July 2012), http://www.forbes.com/sites/johngaudiosi/2012/07/11/riot-games-league-of-legends-officially-becomes-most-played-pc-game-in-the-world.

21 Metal . . . Gear?

43 Solidus is explicitly linked to George Washington throughout *Metal Gear Solid 2*, and of course both were military leaders who were also presidents. The game begins on the George Washington Bridge, the finale takes place on the anniversary of Washington's inauguration, the AI controlling Raiden is called GW, and the game's subtitle 'Sons of Liberty' is a reference to the American dissident group best known for kicking off the Boston Tea Party.
44 *Metal Gear Solid 3* also allows the player to circumvent this. Earlier in the game they catch a very brief glimpse of The End and can quickly snipe him, removing the later battle entirely, or during the battle can save and quit the game. If the player then waits a week, or moves the PS2's internal clock to reflect such, The End will have died of old age in the meantime.

22 Here Comes Everybody

45 Donovan, *Replay*.
46 For the full story of this event, see Rich Stanton, 'EVE Online and the Big Game Hunters', *RockPaperShotgun* (14 May 2014), http://www.rockpapershotgun.com/2014/05/14/eve-online-diary-titan-hunters.

23 Revolution

47 Osamu Inoue, *Nintendo Magic: Winning the Videogame Wars* (Vertical, 2010).
48 Sadly the *Zelda* series continued its slow stagnation with *Twilight Princess* (2006) and, at the end of Wii's life, *Skyward Sword* (2011). Although these titles are high-quality for what they are, the structure of *Zelda* is now not only over-familiar but has been surpassed by others in the genre – most notably the *Souls* series.

27 Continue?

49 Simon Parkin, 'Shooters: How Video Games Fund Arms Manufacturers', *Eurogamer* (31 January 2013), http://www.eurogamer.net/articles/2013-02-01-shooters-how-video-games-fund-arms-manufacturers.

Bibliography

Asakura, Reiji, *Revolutionaries at Sony* (McGraw-Hill, 2000).

Baer, Ralph, *Videogames: In the Beginning* (Rolenta Press, 2005).

Julian Dibbell, 'A Marketable Wonder', *Topic Magazine* (Autumn 2002), http://www.juliandibbell.com/texts/cavespace.html.

Donovan, Tristan, *Replay: The History of Videogames* (Yellow Ant, 2010).

Edwards, Benji, 'Computer Space and the Dawn of the Arcade Video Game', *Technologizer* (11 December 2011), http://www.technologizer.com/2011/12/11/computer-space-and-the-dawn-of-the-arcade-video-game.

––, 'VC&G Interview: Jerry Lawson, Black Video Game Pioneer', *Vintage Computing & Games* (24 February 2009), http://www.vintagecomputing.com/index.php/archives/545.

Gorges, Florent and Isao Yamazaki, *The History of Nintendo 1889–1980* (Pix'n Love, 2010)

Inoue, Osamu, *Nintendo Magic: Winning the Videogame Wars* (Vertical, 2010).

Kent, Steven L., *The Ultimate History of Videogames* (Prima Life, 2002).

Kohler, Chris, *Power-Up: How Japanese Video Games Gave the World an Extra Life* (Brady Games, 2005).

Lussenhop, Jessica, 'Oregon Trail: How Three Minnesotans Forged Its Path', *Citypages* (19 January 2011), http://www.citypages.com/2011-01-19/news/oregon-trail-how-three-minnesotans-forged-its-path.

Lyon, Michael and Katie Hafner, *When Wizards Stay Up Late: The Creation of Will Crowther's Adventure* (Simon & Schuster, 1998).

Mott, Tony (ed.), *1001 Video Games You Must Play Before You Die* (Cassell Illustrated, 2010).

Pitts, Bill, 'The Galaxy Game', *Stanford University* (25 October 2007), http://infolab.stanford.edu/pub/voy/museum/galaxy.html.

Poole, Steven, *Trigger Happy: The Inner Life of Videogames* (Fourth Estate, 2000).

Rossignol, Jim, *This Gaming Life: Travels in Three Cities* (University of Michigan Press, 2008).

Russell, Jamie, *Generation Xbox: How Video Games Invaded Hollywood* (Yellow Ant, 2012).

Sheff, David, *Game Over: Press Start to Continue* (Random House, 1993).

Wallis, Alistair, 'Playing Catch Up: *Adventure*'s Warren Robinett', *Gamasutra* (29 March 2007), http://web.archive.org/web/20071018072813/http://gamasutra.com/php-bin/news_index.php?story=13280.

Index

Entries in *italics* indicate photographs.

A

Activision 53, 54, 83, 282, 314, 318, 355
Adventure 60-9, *63*, *65*, *66*, *67*, *68*, 87, 140, 291, 361, 363
Alcorn, Al 33, 41-2, 43
Alien Isolation 350, *350-1*
Alien vs. Predator 180, *180*
Altered Beast 159, 161
Ampex 33, 36, 37, 41
Angry Birds 260, *260*, 261
Animal Crossing series 237-8, *237*, 253
Apple: App Store 260, 263-4
    Apple II 58, 71, 79-80, 81, 87
    iOS 259, 260
    iPhone 260, 349
Arakawa, Minoru 114, 116-17, 118, 246
arcades, golden age of 94-109
Assassin's Creed series 281-2, 313
Atari 40-7, *45*, 49-55, 65, 66, 67, 69, 79, 81, 86-93, 97, 98, 99, 106, 118, 119, 141, 160, 179-80, 244, 259, 267, 360-1
    400 79, 81, 87
    800 79, 81, 87
    2600 50, *51*, 53, 54, 68, 66, 88, *88*
    5200 87
    arcade games and 97-9
    birth of 40-7, 360-1
    end of 86-93
    Jaguar 179-80, *179*
    Lynx 179, 244, 247
    Video Computer System (VCS) 49-55, *50*, *51*, *52-3*, *54*, *55*, 87, 88, 90, 259

B

Baer, Ralph 23-7, *23*, 28, *28*, 29, 30, 39, 47, 92, 360
Bally 41, 43, 87, 102;
    Astrocade 87
Battlezone 97-8, *97*, 141
Bayonetta 2 349, 352, *352*
BBC Micro 54, 73
Bioshock series 263, 314-16, *316*, 362
Bioware 199, 318, 319
Blizzard 210, 263, 268, 270, 272, 274, 275, 296, 297, 298
Boom Beach 262-3, *262*
Bristow, Steve 41, 46, 51
Bubble Bobble 106-7, *107*
Bungie 221, 240, 311, 353
Bushnell, Nolan 31, 33-4, 35-6, 37, 38, 39, 41-2, 43, 44, 45, 46, 47, 50, 51, 360

C

Call of Duty series 282, 314, 354
Capcom 105, 173, 174, 193, 230, 231, 232, 235, 254, 263, 313
Carmack, John 141-2, 144, 145, 147
Castlevania series 173, 192, 254, 280, 342
Centipede 93, 99, *99*

Chuckie Egg 73, *73*
Clash of Clans 262
Comix Zone 167, *167*
Commodore International 78–85, 87, 92, 93, 131
    Commodore 64 80–5, *80*, 87, 93, 131
    Commodore 128 85
    PET series 80, 87
    VIC-20 80, 87
Computer Space 31, 36, *36*, 37–8, *38*, 39, 41, 42, 46, 360
console wars 158–203, 361
Counter-Strike series 149, 270–2, 323, 324, *325*
Crash Bandicoot 195, 197, 312
Crazy Taxi 209–10, *210*
Crowther, William 61, 62, 63–4, 66, 69, 140, 291, 361

D

Dabney, Ted 33, 35–6, 37, 38, 41, 42, 43, 44, 360
Dead End Thrills 157, 230, 231, 309, 311, 313, 317, 318, 319, 327, 328,
    337, 338, 350, 354, 355, 358
Defender 93, 98–9, *98*
Deus Ex series 155, *155*, 156–7, 157
Deus Ex Machina 75–6, *75*, 77, 83
Devil May Cry series 230, 231, 313, *313*
Donkey Kong 113, 115–17, *116*, 126
    Donkey Kong Country series 176–7, 201
    Donkey Kong Jr. 117, 126
    Donkey Kong 64 202
    handheld versions 246
Doom series 142–5, *142*, *143*, *144*, *145*, 146, 147, 149, 154, 155, 180,
    201, 358, 361
Dota 2 268, 272, 273–4, *274*, 275, *275*, 330
Dr Kawashima Brain Training 252, *252*
Dragon Quest series 129, 253–4
Dragon's Lair 103–4, *104*, 105
Dungeons and Dragons 62, 106

E

E.T.: The Extra-Terrestrial 54, 88, 89–90, *89*, 93
EA Maxis 131, 133, 134
Earthbound 173–4, *174*
Electronic Arts (EA) 160, 165, 174, 180, 219–20, 282, 310, 325
Electroplankton 253, *253*
Elite 54, 55, *55*
eSports 266–75
EVE Online 298–301, *299*, 362
EverQuest 295–6, *296*

F

F-Zero 168–9, *169*, 191
Fairchild 49, 50, 51
    Channel F II 87; F8 49
    Semiconductor 49
    VES 49, *49*, 50, *50*, 51
Fallout 3 318, *318*, 358

Famicom 117–18, *117*, *118*, 125, 126, 127, 164
    Disk System 125
Final fantasy series 173, 187, 189, 193–5, *194*
Fire Emblem 250, 256
Frogger 102–3

G

Galaxian 100, *100*, 102, 114
Galaxy Game 38, 39, *39*, 360
GameMaker 341, 343
Gears of War 310, *310*, 311
Geometry Wars series 319, 320
Ghosts 'n' Goblins 105–6, *106*
God Hand 232–3, *232*
God of War series 231–2
Golden Axe 129, 159, 187
Goldeneye 007 152–4, *152*, 201, 202, 222
Gone Home 145, 148, 358
Google Android 259, 260, 263–4, *325*
Gradius 106, 127, *127*
Gran Trak 10 45–6
Gran Turismo 191–2
Grand Theft Auto series 193, 217, 218, 225, 238–9, 254, 255, 332–9
Gridrunner 80, *80*
Guardian Heroes 187–8
Guitar Hero series 308, 317–18

H

Habitat 83, 293
Half-Life series 148–9, *149*, 150, 152, 270, 323, 324, 326–7, *327*,
    328, *328*
Half-Minute Hero 254
Halo series 146, 221, 222–3, *222*, 240, 311, 353
handhelds 242–57
Harrison, Bill 24–5, 26, 27
Hase, Ted 218–19, 223
Hearthstone 263, 275
Higinbotham, William 18, *18*, 19, 20, 21

I

Ico 225–6, *226*, 228, 230
independent game developers 340–7
Iwata, Satoru 174, 251, 303, 304, *304*
Iwatani, Toru 100, 101, 321

J

Jet Set Radio series 211, *211*
Jet Set Willy 74
Jobs, Steve 49, 52, 71, 79–80

K

Kalinske, Tom 161, 163, 361
Kamiya, Hideki 230, 240, 241
Kassar, Ray 52, 88–9, 90, 92
Kee Games 46, 47
Konami 102, 103, 127, 173, 192, 209, 260, 280, 355
Kutaragi, Ken 181, 182, 183, 217

L

Last of Us, The 313, 356, 362
Lawson, Gerald 'Jerry' 49, 49, 50, 361
League of Legends 267, 268, 272, 272, 273–5, 362
Left 4 Dead 328, 330
Legacy of Kain: Soul Reaver 195
Legend of Zelda, The (series) 69, 115, 123, 124–6, 125, 126, 170, 171–2, 199, 200–1, 200–1, 229, 236–7, 236, 241, 247, 250, 253, 257, 303, 362
Little Computer People 83, 83
LittleBigPlanet series 311–12, 312
LucasArts 83, 174, 293
Luigi's Mansion series 224, 257
Lumines series 254, 256

M

M.U.L.E. 81–2, 81
Magnavox 22–31, 39, 42, 46–7, 71, 87, 92, 112, 361
Manhunt 239, 239
Manic Miner 73–4, 74
Mass Effect trilogy 318, 319, 319
Maze War 139–41, 361
Medal of Honor 154–5
Media Molecule 256, 311
Meridian 59 293–4, 295
Metal Gear Solid series 199, 218, 225, 255, 255, 276–89, 278, 282–9, 282, 283, 284, 285, 286, 287, 289, 353–4, 362
Metroid series 129, 172–3, 192, 238, 238, 249, 250, 342
Midway 43, 100, 101, 102
Minecraft 344–7, 346
Minter, Jeff 80, 98, 180, 256
Mirror's Edge 316–17, 317
Missile Command 45, 46, 46
Miyamoto, Shigeru 69, 114–15, 115, 116, 119, 120, 121, 123, 124, 125, 126, 196, 197, 251, 252, 304, 308, 361
mobile gaming 258–65
Monster Hunter series 254, 257, 263, 263, 349
Mortal Kombat 175, 175, 176, 176
Motor Toon Grand Prix 191
Mouse in the Maze 21, 21
Ms. Pac-Man 101, 102, 247
Multi-User Dungeon (MUD) 291–3
Myst 145, 147–8, 181

N

Naka, Yuji 162, 165, 188, 189, 211, 215
Nakayama, Hayao 126, 161
Namco 100, 101, 102, 190, 191
Naughty Dog 195, 312, 313, 356
NEC: PC Engine 159, 160, 164
Neo-Geo Pocket Colour 249
Night Trap 105, 176
Nights into Dreams 189–90, 189
Nim 17–18
Nintendo 69, 93, 111, 110–29, 152, 158, 159–77, 181, 182, 184, 188, 190, 193, 195, 196, 197, 199, 201, 203, 217, 218, 220, 223, 224, 225, 235, 236, 237, 238, 243–57, 303–5, 306–7, 308, 309, 321, 347, 349, 352, 361, 362; DS 251–4, 251, 256, 257, 303
Game & Watch 113–14, 113, 117, 243–4
Game Boy 244–9, 244, 257, 362
Game Boy Advance 249, 250
Game Cube 223–5, 235–8, 241, 257, 303, 304, 307
NES 93, 118–19, 118, 125, 126, 128, 129, 158, 164, 165, 173, 176, 177, 307, 349, 352
N64 152, 154, 184, 195–202, 196, 203, 223, 224, 237, 257, 303, 361
rise of 110–29; 64 152, 154
Super Nintendo Entertainment System (SNES) 160, 161, 162, 163–4, 164, 165, 168–9, 171, 173, 175, 176, 177, 179, 181, 182, 195, 196–7, 249, 303; 3DS 256–8, 257
Wii 115, 302–10, 304, 321, 349, 361, 362
Wii U 349, 352
Nintendogs 115, 252–3
Nutting Associates 36, 37, 41, 45

O

Oculus Rift 357–8
Oddworld: Abe's Oddysee 192–3
Odyssey, The Magnavox 22–31, 28, 29, 30, 31, 39, 42, 46–7, 71, 87, 92, 112, 361
Okami 240–1, 240
Oregon Trail 56–9, 57, 58, 59, 361
Outrun 107, 108, 108, 109, 190, 211, 212, 321

P

Pac-Man series 54, 82, 88, 88, 90, 91, 100–1, 102, 103, 107, 321
Panasonic 3DO Interactive Multiplayer 180–1, 181, 183
Phantasy Star 129, 210, 211, 211
Phoenix Wright: Ace Attorney 254
Pilotwings 115, 169, 196
Ping-Pong 26, 27, 30
Pitfall 52, 53, 53
Pitts, Bill 38, 39, 360
Playstation, Sony 102, 128, 169, 181–95, 196, 203, 205, 207, 214, 215, 217–18, 223, 225, 241, 277, 279, 280, 286, 287, 307, 317, 333, 352, 353, 361
Playstation X (PSX) 182, 183–5, 183, 186–7, 188, 190–5
Playstation 2 (PS2) 182, 214, 217–18, 219, 220, 223, 224–35, 240, 241, 251, 306, 333, 337, 362
Playstation 3 (PS3) 232, 287, 306, 307, 307, 310, 311, 312–13,

318, 321, 325, 337
Playstation 4 (PS4) 128, 207, 256, 339, 352, 361
PSP (Playstation Portable) 250-2, *250*, 254-5, 256, 257
Playstation Vita 255-6, *256*, 257
Pokémon 247, 248-9, *248*, 250, 254, 303
Pong 20, 41-5, *42*, 44, 46, 47, *47*, 51, 71, 95
Popeye 115, 117
Portal series 320, 328-9
prehistory of video games 14-21
Project Gotham Racing 221, 319
Psygnosis 183, 191

Q

Quake series 144, 145-7, *145*, 148, 149, 154, 331

R

Radar Scope 114-15
Rare 152, 176, 201, 202
Rebelstar 74-5
Resident Evil series 193, *193*, 230, 232, *232*, 233-5, *233*, 349
Ridge Racer 190-1, *190*
River Raid 52, 53, *53*
Robinett, Warren 65-7, 69, 361
Rock Band 308, 318
Rockstar 238-9, 317, 334, 337, 338
Romero, John 142, 144, 146

S

Sakura Wars 187, 361
Sanders Associates 23, 24, 27, 29
Scott Warshaw, Howard 54, 88-9, 93
Sega Corporation 95, 105, 107, 108, 126-7, 128-9, 159-61, 162, 163,
    165, 166, 167-8, 174, 175, 176, 177, 179, 181, 183-4, 185, 187,
    188, 189, 190, 195, 196, 203, 205-15, 217, 218, 225, 244, 247,
    361, 362
Dreamcast 205-15, *205*, 217, 218, 221, 361
Game Gear 244, 247, *247*
Master System 127, 128-9, *128*, 159, 160, 177, 205, 244, 247
Mega CD 105, 176-7, 181, 205
Mega Drive (Genesis in U.S.) 159-64, *161*, *163*, 165, 166, 167-8,
    173, 174, 175, 176, 177, 179, 184, 195, 205, 247
Saturn 177, 183-5, *184*, 187, 188-90, 196, 203, 205, 206,
    211, 361
Sega System 16 159, 161
Sega Technical Institute (STI) 165, 166, 167, 188
SG-1000 126, 127, 129
'Sonic X-Treme' 188-9, 206
Sewer Shark 105, 176, 177
Shadow of the Colossus 226, *227*, 228-9, 230
Shenmue series 211-14, *212*, *213*
Shin Megami Tensei: Devil Summoner 188
Sims series 83, 130-7, *133*, *134*, *135*, *137*, 361
Sinclair: ZX Spectrum 71-8, *72*, 80
ZX Spectrum 128 72-8, *72*, 80
Sinclair ZX80 71, *71*, 72, 78
Sinclair ZX81 71

Sinclair, Clive 71, 72, 73, 77-8, 259
Singstar 218, 241
Skool Daze 76, *76*, 77
Skyrim 318, 359
Snake 259
Sonic the Hedgehog series 161-3, *162*, 164, 165, 166, *166*, 167, 176,
    188-9, 190, 206, *206*, 247, 361
Souls games 318-19, 320, *320*
Space Channel 5 series 207-8, *208*, 209
Space Harrier 107, 109, *109*, 129, 211, 212
Space Invaders 95-7, *96*, 100, 114
Space Station Silicon Valley 203
Spacewar! 32, 33, *34*, *35*, 36, 37, *37*, 38, 267, 360
Spelunky 256, 341, 343
Spielberg, Steven 88, 89, 154, 310, 312
Squaresoft 173, 193, 194
Stanford University 38, 39, 64, 360
Star Raiders 52, 54, 55, *55*, 93
Starcraft series 81, 268-70, *268*, 269, *269*, 270, *270*, 274, 275, 296
Starfox series 115, 169, 257
Steam 323-31
Strachey, Christopher 16-17, 360
Street Fighter series 173, *173*, 175, 191
Streets of Rage series 174-5, *175*
Super Hexagon 264, 264
Super Mario Bros 73, 115, 119, *119*, 120-3, *120*, *121*, 161, 162, 163,
    164, 165, 198-9, *198*, *199*, 253, 254, *254*
    Mario & Luigi: Superstar Saga 250
    Mario Kart 8 349
    Mario Kart 64 201
    Mario Kart: Super Circuit 249
    New Super Mario Bros. 253, 254, *254*
    Super Mario Advance 3: Yoshi's Island 249
    Super Mario Bros. 2 121, *121*
    Super Mario Bros. 3 121, *121*, 122-3, 160, 164-5
    Super Mario 64 188, 196, 197-9, *198*, *199*, 200, 201, 202, 206,
        235, 308, 309
    Super Mario Galaxy 308, 309, *309*
    Super Mario Galaxy 2 308
    Super Mario Land 246
    Super Mario Sunshine 235-6, *235*
    Super Mario 3D Land 257, *257*
    Super Mario 3D World 349
    Super Mario World 121, 164, 165, *165*, 169, 171
Super Meat Boy 321, 343, *343*
Super Monkey Ball 224, 362
Super Smash Bros 201
Suzuki, Yu 107, 109, 183, 185, 211, 213, 214
System Shock series 151, 316
Syzygy 36, 41

T

Taito 44, 95, 106
Takeda, Genyo 112, 303, 304, 305
Team Fortress series 146, 147, *147*, 149, 153, 323, 326, 328, 330-1,
    330
Tekken series 102, 190, 191
Tempest 2000 180

Tempest 98, *98*
Tennis 30, 31, *31*, 39, 42, 112
Tennis for Two 19, *19*, 20, *20*, 21
Tetris 244-6, *245*, 259
Tezuka, Takashi 121, 123, 124
Theurer, Dave 98, 180
Thief series 150-1, 152
Timesplitters series 239
Toca Band 265
Toejam & Earl series 168, *168*
Tomb Raider 185-7, *186*, 312
Tomena Sonner 260, *260*
Tramiel, Jack 78-80, 85, 92, 160, 259
Turing, Alan 15-16

U

Ubisoft 281, 309-10, 313, 325
Ultima series 241-2, 294, *295*, 296
Uncharted series 186, 187, 312-13

V

Valve 37, 146, 147, 149-50, 270, 274, 275, 322-31, *323*, 357, 358
Viewtiful Joe 230-1
Virtua Fighter 177, 183, 184, 185, *185*, 191, 211
Virtua Tennis 210
virtual reality 282, 283, 357-8

W

Wario Ware series 250
Warner Communications 50, 51, 88, 90, 92
Wave Race 224
Wii: Fit 307-8, *308*
    Music 115, 307, 308
    Play 307
    Sports 115, 305-6, *305*, 307
Wipeout 169, 191
Wolfenstein 3D 142, 180
Wonder Boy III: The Dragon's Trap 129, *129*
World Ends With You, The 254
World of Goo 343, *343*
World of Warcraft 146, 292, 296, 297-8, *297*, 300, 301
Wozniak, Steve 49, 52
Wright, Will 83, 131, *131*, 132, 133, 134, 137
Wurm Online 344

X

Xbox, Microsoft 84, 207, 211, 213, 215, 216-25, *221*, 222, 240, 241,
    303, 306, 307, 310, 311, 319, 320, 339, 352, 362
    Xbox One 207, 339, 352-3
    Xbox 360 84, 306-7, *306*, 310-12, 319, 320, 321, 352
    Xbox Live 222, 240, 319

Y

Yamauchi, Hiroshi 111-15, 116, 117, 118, 119, 120, 182, 184, 251, 303
Yars' Revenge 52, 54, *54*, 93
Yokoi, Gunpei 112, 113, 115, 117, 172, 244, 249, 362